EDUCATION IN THE NEW CHINA

Education in the New China

Shaping ideas at work

YVONNE TURNER
University of Hertfordshire, UK

AMY ACKER
University of Bristol, Graduate School of Education, UK

Ashgate

Published by
Ashgate Publishing Limited
Gower House
Croft Road
Aldershot
Hampshire GU11 3HR
England

Ashgate Publishing Company
131 Main Street
Burlington, VT 05401-5600 USA

Ashgate website: http://www.ashgate.com

British Library Cataloguing in Publication Data
Turner, Yvonne
    Education in the new China : shaping ideas at work
    1.Education, Higher - China - Beijing - Case studies
    2.College students China Beijing Case studies
    I.Title II.Acker, Amy
    378.5'1'156

Library of Congress Control Number: 2001097635

ISBN 0 7546 1914 1

Printed and bound by Athenaeum Press, Ltd.,
Gateshead, Tyne & Wear.

Contents

List of Figures and Tables

Figures

Tables

Preface

September 1996 was not my first trip to Beijing, but was my first experience of working at a private institution in the Chinese education market. I took up my responsibilities as an English teacher in this very special, multi-cultural management college with its strong association to British education and felt I had landed in a strange place indeed! Predominantly international educators living cheek-by-jowl while teaching mostly Chinese students in one of the very "foreign" neighborhoods studded with bars on every corner did not remotely resemble any of my previous teaching experiences in Beijing! Quite quickly I met Yvonne Turner who had been at the College teaching a range of courses in the business department since May 1996 and was soon infected by her interest in teaching in this unique situation. We were continuously discussing experiences from our classroom teaching, concentrating on the cultural gaps in our teaching styles and our students' understanding, and proposing new approaches and techniques to meet what we determined as the major obstacles to success.

Our mutual interests in cross-cultural teaching soon led us to make decisions to stay longer at the College, Yvonne as the head of the business department and I as the head of the English department, and we embarked on an exciting period of educational exchange. Together we developed a staff training program and established weekly administrative meetings to ease out the difficulties of communication across the many cultures represented: Asian head of college, Chinese assistant head, Chinese marketing director and finance directors, British head of business and American head of English. We worked together to rewrite course curricula and Yvonne embarked in an evening a week of action learning with volunteer students. I tried to recruit more widely for teachers and succeeded in bringing in teachers from New Zealand and South Africa to add to the complement of British, Australian, Canadian and American English teachers. It proved to be an extremely busy but inordinately rewarding period of our lives.

At the end of our second year at the College, we decided we wanted to research some of our emerging questions into the teaching and learning taking place within this cross-cultural educational setting. We devised a semi-structured interview for students at all levels of study within the College, some had graduated over a year prior to the study, and asked selected students for informal chats away from the College. We were interested in eliciting their stories without dictating the content. The interviews were carried out between September 1998 and June 1999. I finished my contract with the College in May 1999 and Yvonne completed hers in June 1999.

The material from these interviews have been transcribed from the tapes and mulled over by both of us for almost two years now. Both Yvonne and I have embarked in study on Doctorate of Education degrees at the University of Bristol's Graduate School of Education where we have taken several courses together and have continued our incessant discussions on cross-cultural teaching/learning and about the data from our interviews. We feel these personal stories from students in Beijing reveal valuable insights into the educational situation in China as the private sector continues to grow. We are continuing annual interviews with a number of the participants in this study to enable us to follow the process of their educations and their lives, but have not included any information from follow-up interviews in this text.

Throughout the text we have changed names of participants, institutions and places referred to in the interviews in order to protect the privacy of all involved. We have tried to remain as true to the information as possible, but have had ethical considerations always in mind as we have written the chapters of this text.

Our thanks go to all the participants in the study including the administration at the College for allowing us to carry it out. Also thanks to the professors at University of Bristol for encouraging us with ideas, and especially to Dr. Marilyn Osborn for her support. Both Yvonne and I also want to express thanks for having had the opportunity to experience such a uniquely interesting environment for teaching and learning that we found at this management college in Beijing - it has invigorated our lives!

Amy Acker
Britain
May 2001

1 An Introduction to the Project

This book documents the results of a project that collected the educational life stories of a group of people who studied for a British business degree at a private college in Beijing between 1996 and 1999. It also presents some introduction to and analysis of the contemporary educational scene in China. In Chapter 8, we have included a discussion about some of the issues that Chinese students might face when coming to study in universities in Britain, as they are doing in increasing numbers.

The project was small-scale and not intended to produce widely generalizable results. It represents an intimate picture of the thoughts and perceptions of a very small group of people who have participated in a very particular higher education environment in China. However, their very "specialness" in this respect is what makes them interesting as a group. Part of the impulse to undertake the project was to discover whether there were any connections between their backgrounds, experiences and attitudes and some of the wider contemporary social and cultural shifts that seem to be taking place in China. At the same time, the study participants have all taken part in the state education system throughout their elementary and secondary careers. Not only can their stories illuminate existing studies of Chinese education and provide insight into the attitudes and motivations that people involved feel, but they also provide a useful social commentary on the changes in Chinese education and society that have already taken place since reforms began in 1978.

The Context

The Chinese government has explicitly and repeatedly underlined the connection between education and economic development. It is, however, also important to explore whether the reforms in education, and especially the recent opening-up of the private sector to international education providers, are also bringing about changes in cultural attitudes and behaviour. In this context, there is an essential contradiction in the Chinese government's position on education, perhaps. On the one hand, throughout its history the Chinese Communist Party (CCP) has vigorously adopted education as a mechanism for political and social orientation and reorientation, and continues to promote the moral, social and political value-based aspects of education within the state system. On the other hand, the government is faced with an acute shortage of educational provision and a scarcity of the market-based skills which it believes underscore the achievement of the economic development targets it has set itself. As a result, it has opened up education to the private sector and to international providers at the same time as largely releasing them from the obligation to incorporate the political and social educational elements into the curriculum. This is especially the case in the higher education in applied and vocational subjects, such as business studies. A condemnation of the cultural "corruption" that accompanies consumer-led capitalism continues to appear in the state-controlled media. And yet at the same time, the government is actively courting business educators to come to China from around the world, especially Europe and the USA, to create an entrepreneurial class among China's citizens. This practice seems a far remove from the original exchange of scientific and technical personnel and skills envisioned in the early educational reforms of the Four Modernizations initiative of the late 1970's, and its implications go, perhaps, far deeper.

It is impossible to know at present what this apparent contradiction will bring and what it means. It does underscore the paradox of the "one country two systems" policy adopted by Deng Xiaoping in his reform programmes. Some argue that the opening up of education implies the tacit and complete abandonment of socialist principles on the part of the CCP. Others, however, believe that it may be possible to see this change as an acknowledged part of the wider aims of reform. "We must accept 100 years of capitalism with all the increase in corruption that it will bring" Deng Xiaoping is reputed to have said, "before real cultural revolution and a return to true socialism can take place." Either way, Chinese society is increasingly riven by the divisions that exist between the emerging entrepreneurial class of citizens who are realizing the country's global economic vision and the majority who are encultured with the values of socialism throughout their educational careers.

Whatever the long-term consequences of China's opening its doors, it is interesting to explore the ways in which these changes are working at a practical level among its people. The underlying belief that informs the current study is that education is not merely technical or instrumental but possesses personal, cultural and social artefacts inherent to its content, context and process. More than trade or economic exchange, we feel that perhaps education is the vehicle driving the underlying processes of cultural globalization, especially international education in the medium of English and about Business. This viewpoint has been shaped, in part at least, from the perspectives expressed by the students we encountered at Harmony College. It seems perhaps that this community of people from the New China are developing differently from older generations in fundamental ways. The complexity from which their make-up is composed is a curious mixture of 20th century socialist culture, Confucian educational tradition, "western" marketized educational practices and their own consumer activities. Their aspirations appear to contrast sharply with those that have been documented of earlier generations of Chinese people. They express high levels of concern for self, and more individualism. Yet at the same time, they are bound by and live among the social traditions and expectations of earlier generations and from the inheritance of Chinese history.

Design of the Research

As we have noted above, the design of the project was small-scale, flexible and open-ended, very much within the qualitative frame. The initial impulse for gathering the research information, however, derived from the spirit of action research. As two international educators, we had both become intrigued by the teaching and learning dynamic in which we played a part at Harmony College and wanted to draw further insights from it. We wanted to approach the project in a more coherent fashion than the ad hoc gathering of anecdotal impressions that we had been making during our routine work. The aim of doing this was to inform our teaching practice and to help us develop greater understanding about the processes of educational and cultural adaptation that students had told us was an important factor in their performance at the College. Though clearly not specifically generalizable as a piece of work, we did feel that we wanted to illuminate the perceptions of the community at the College in such a way that we might carry greater understanding about Chinese education into our future work both in China and internationally.

We were also very interested in the people who came to the College. They were a very diverse group, for one thing, and departed from the stereotype of Chinese university students in many ways. They were very keen to buy, quite literally, into China's new economy. Many of them were the offspring of the very first generation of people in the People's Republic to work in the private sector and seemed to have been very influenced by their parent's experiences. As budding entrepreneurs themselves, their behaviour in the lecture and seminar rooms seemed to shout frustration with China's past and to give an open-armed welcome to its future. As educators and researchers we wondered about the social and cultural consequences of such an uncritical embrace with what the students labelled "the West", meaning the free market and an openness to everything international. We also saw the degree to which some students, and especially graduates, struggled with their identity in the complex and contradictory world in which they found themselves day to day.

The project evolved over several months. The first interview took place in the autumn of 1998 and the last in late spring 1999. Before beginning on the data collection, we decided that it would be impossible to make ourselves invisible in the organisation of the project because we had taught and enjoyed pre-existing relationships with all of those who were likely to participate. Since cultural exchange was a key theme for the project, we were also aware that it was inevitable that we would privilege certain cultural themes and values and did not want to overly prejudice the data collection methods. We opted, therefore, to undertake a series of free-ranging interviews that were only very loosely structured and provided the maximum opportunity for participants to express their own views in an individual way. Essentially, we sat down with participants in comfortable chairs, with a cup of tea and said, "tell us the story of your life and education so far". This approach has led none the less to some similarity in the style and content of the interview stories because they tend to approximate in a chronological development from participants' childhoods, through adolescence and into adulthood.

The fact that this group was an opportunity sample, dependent on relationships with us, has affected the project in a number of ways. First of all, we were only able to get access to those who had successfully completed their studies at the College, or who were currently studying there. The stories do not represent the entire range of perspectives that might be expressed by, say, people who had dropped out for whatever reason. We made some choices about who we would approach to participate, mainly based on English language skills, because the interviews would take place in English with only limited Chinese used for specific terms or clarification. We also made choices about those who would feel comfortable and confident to talk with us, though this was a lesser consideration. We tried to work with people who came from a variety of different home and personal backgrounds: younger and older students, men and women, people from Inner Mongolia and Southern China, those from wealthy backgrounds and those who had had to work or borrow money to attend the College. At the same time, however, we did not approach only those with the best academic skills. The final degree classifications for the group of participants ranged from one student who was awarded a university certificate because of lack of success in the degree to students who achieved upper seconds with honours.

The highly personalized nature of the student-teacher relationship in China caused us some concern because of the way that it might prejudice the views that people expressed in the interviews. We took great pains to ask people for an unbiased view, rather than to try and guess what we wanted them to say. In most cases, we feel that we were successful in getting that. For one thing, the interviews lasted for forty-five minutes to one and a half hours. We found that once participants warmed to their themes, they involved themselves in telling their stories and showed little hesitation in saying some very negative things about the College, about the "West" and, in some cases, about us!

Overall, however, if we had not had pre-existing relationships with the study participants, it would have been very difficult for us to achieve the frankness and openness in disclosure that we were able to achieve. Research access in China is notoriously difficult and people tend to be very frightened about giving information about themselves that they fear might have some personal consequences in the future. In addition, China is very much a closed and private society. People are encouraged to keep personal thoughts and feelings to themselves. Any kind of sharing that takes place, therefore, requires a very high degree of trust. We had to take great pains to assure many of the participants that we would respect their privacy and completely guarantee their confidentiality before they would agree to talk with us at all. If we had not established the particular relationships with those who took part, we would not have been able to hear such complete stories.

The essential difficulty that the composition of the group of participants has imposed on the study is that it may have a tendency to polarize the project's outcomes as negative towards the Chinese education system and positive towards the "West". This is at the same time both a problem and the heart of the project. We have already noted that the uncritical enthusiasm shown by students at Harmony College for everything western was one impulse for undertaking the project. In addition, coming from the UK and the USA as we do, we are aware that we carry with us as researchers the tacit values of the education systems of those two countries. At the same time, it is important to note that we have not wanted to privilege the cultural system or the educational value base underlying Harmony's pedagogy. We have included in the text some discussion of the negative aspects of the cultural exchange involved at Harmony and have tried to present a balanced picture of the views expressed by the participants in the project rather than promoting a partisan set of interests. Chapter 8 of the book attempts to raise some of the issues involved in cultural exchange for Chinese students coming to study in "the West". The aim is to add into existing discussions which are taking place about how to develop a more culturally sensitive higher education pedagogy in the face of increasingly global university communities.

Altogether we collected stories from 31 people, either graduates from the College or people still studying there. Since our interest was in the Chinese education system and the cultural exchange between the international education community and Chinese nationals, we did not include any of the 15% or so of students at the College who came from outside China. We considered for some time whether or not to include the stories from the two sisters who were born in Taiwan and received much of their elementary education in the Philippines. However, their parents are both Chinese nationals, they embarked on education within the Chinese state system at secondary levels, and we felt their accounts provided a nice counter-point to the rest of the group.

The Presentation of the Project Outcomes

The oral history tradition, of which the accounts we have collected in this book form a part, has a long heritage as a research method within the social sciences. Ideally, we would have presented the stories as an unedited collection to act as an open resource for students of Chinese culture and education and as a social document presenting accounts of a certain aspect of Chinese life at the end of the 20th century. However, we are intending the book for a wide international readership of students, researchers, academics and educators. We have, therefore, organised the material according to certain descriptive themes and selected parts from the stories to illuminate each one. We have also included chapters introducing aspects of education in China and interpreting some of the data. These sections are very personal, and reveal perhaps as much about our own ideas and preferences as they do about the participants' stories. We hope, however, that they set some of the context and establish the stories in a place that makes them accessible to those who have not made a study of Chinese education in the past, as well as offering a commentary to those who have.

Still, the stories of the participants emerge very strongly from the study. This is intentional. Though we have provided background context and offer interpretation in most areas, it is the personalities of the people involved that we hope ultimately shine through. We have attempted to avoid excessive duplication where we can, but have been keen to preserve the essence of the accounts. We have also included a short selection of complete stories in Chapter 9 of the book for those readers who wish to see the narratives develop as a whole, rather than in short parts.

We have edited the stories sparingly, confining ourselves to removing the questions we asked since they were mainly requesting clarification. We have also corrected some of the language, but have limited this to sections where a certain language usage required more than one reading for the meaning to emerge. Otherwise, we have left the language and choice of expressions unchanged, reflecting the idioms and idiosyncrasies of each of the participants.

Respecting the guarantees of confidentiality, we have removed most personal names, unless they belong to some well-known public figure, such as Deng Xiaoping, China's leader until 1997. We have also used a pseudonym for the College itself, which is one among many international colleges operating in China. The choice of "Harmony College" is not arbitrary, however, but does connect to its real name. We have not chosen it to imply that the College was particularly harmonious. In fact, its environment was pretty rumbustious from time to time!

A Brief Introduction to Harmony College

Harmony began in the early 1990's as a commercial enterprise shared between a Chinese government department and a major provider of higher education in a neighbouring Asian country. The education bureau, through the College's authorities, approached a British university to suggest it explore possibilities to franchise a degree in Business Administration within China through its pre-existing connections with the private college.

Initially students studied English language and the business programmes began in the mid-90's. Harmony grew from a student body of around 50 students in 1995 to over 400 by the end of the decade. The teaching and administrative staff grew from approximately 20 to around 55 full-time employees. A mixture of Asians from the parent company's home country and Chinese administrators and support workers managed the administration of the College. Academic management was international, represented primarily by the UK, USA and the College's home country. More than five nationalities made up the teaching faculty at any one time - the greatest numbers being from Britain, but also from the US, Canada, Australia, New Zealand, South Africa, Russia, Ghana, and various Asian countries. Teaching conditions were tough. The College experienced more than 100% staff turnover per year, as many international lecturers, as well as local administrators, did not complete the standard one-year contract. This was especially the case in the English language department of the

College, which recruited primarily from a young, migratory group of international teachers. Some found that China was more difficult to live in than they had expected, some that they could earn far more and receive better living accommodation from working for one of the international companies that operated in the city. Owing to its increasing student numbers and the difficulty of obtaining "legal" housing for its "foreign" lecturers (imposed by the Chinese government), Harmony moved its campus to different parts of the city twice in the space of three years.

Eighty five percent of the students were Chinese and represented all areas of China, while members of the diplomatic and business communities in Beijing made up the other fifteen percent of the student body. Students had the option of completing the final year of their degree study in China or at the partner university in the UK, so the student body was also quite transitory even for its small size.

The College set its own academic curriculum and standards for its English programme. The six-level Business programme was determined by the parent institution and the final year was determined by the British university. Outside of the final year, lecturers had a great deal of autonomy on their delivery of the curriculum and grading of papers. The College provided little formal training around academic issues such as grading standards, and little orientation for cultural concerns within the academic or personal lives of the lecturers, or of the administrative staff. Because the salary and housing provided by the College were very basic, many of the lecturers came to China for reasons other than financial incentive - most were seeking a "Z" visa allowing them to live and work in China as a "Foreign Expert". The administrative staff received comparatively low salaries, so also came to the College for other than financial reasons. Once a term, the College held a general meeting primarily to allow a matching of names and faces to institutional roles.

The external environment of the College has also been changing rapidly. Since 1978 when Deng Xiaoping launched his modernization program, China has been open to radical economic restructuring and foreign investment. Government controlled educational institutions have been encouraged to find new ways of funding themselves and have readily investigated the private business sector. The World Bank has funded universities within China since 1980 and the first private colleges began appearing in the early 1980s. Associations between Chinese and international universities became plentiful in the 80's while the 90's have brought international degrees awarded to Chinese students studying in China. Around 1997-98, several international MBA programs (American, and Canadian) opened in Beijing. All of these developments provided an extremely changeable environment in which Harmony was forced to compete. Harmony was initially proving itself against established Chinese universities to legitimize its educational approach, and later struggling in competition with MBA programmes for the mature students it had initially enrolled.

Outside the academic arena, Beijing was also changing dramatically. Physically, the traditional, one-story, courtyard houses with alleys connecting them were being destroyed and high-rise apartment buildings rising up to replace them. Financially, entrepreneurs were making fortunes and government officials were funding new enterprises - first this new found wealth bought housing, then it bought the respected, age-old commodity, education. The external environment around the College changed so fast that it was almost impossible for a lecturer even to establish a favourite restaurant or acquire a lasting address for a friend.

Both the internal and external environments of the College, therefore, demanded an acceptance of change as basic to the survival of an individual within its system. Many factors within the internal and external environments created a constantly changing collective within the College, and the external environment demanded continuous change from the College itself.

2 The Context of Contemporary Chinese Education

Introduction

As we have noted in the introduction to the project, this text does not aim to present a comprehensive account of contemporary education in China or its social context. Its scope is far less ambitious than that. In seeking to present some stories about education and contemporary life in China, however, it seems necessary to establish the historical and social environment in which the stories take place. This process of setting the context will act as a means of both grounding the information we are presenting and assisting the reader's understanding of the themes and issues we have chosen to draw out in our account. This introductory chapter, therefore, aims to summarize and comment on those aspects of China's education system and practice which are most pertinent as background to our research project. The way in which we develop the context outlines those influences that have governed our overall approach to the research. Primarily these are the historical interplay of indigenous and international influences in educational development, the dynamics and shaping of the contemporary classroom, and issues confronting equality and access for women to education.

Educational Development in China: the interplay of domestic and international

Globalization and Educational Development in Practice

Non-indigenous educational practice within China has become a common phenomenon since the reforms of the 1970's. We will discuss aspects of the privatization of education in China later in this chapter, but it is important first to consider the interplay between Chinese and international educational influences at a fundamental level in order to establish some of the broader context of the study.

The influence of education in the shaping of the geopolitical dynamic is well rehearsed. Educational research, international aid, and international policy agendas are powerfully enmeshed with individual nation states, especially in newly emerging economies or developing nations, as they respond to the ongoing pressures of economic and cultural globalism. China is no exception to this. Though accepted as a clear characteristic of the changing face of world environments, however, little consensus exists as to the efficacy or desirability of the ongoing process of globalization and the role of education within it (Green 1997; Arnowitz & De Fazio, 1997; Reich, 1997). More and more, commentators are questioning the prevailing assumptions of the supra-national sponsors of educational development initiatives and aid institutions. A key preoccupation appears to lie in concern about the degree to which apparent globalization, nominally a force for the evolution of a new transnational culture, represents, in fact, the progress of political and cultural hegemony driven by the powers of "the West".

In this questioning, many see education as culpable. Contrary to traditional western philosophical assumptions about the emancipatory and socially energizing power of education, there are those whose analysis presents an emergent "global" paradigm of education which is highly enculturated and politicized - a paradigm which is oppressive and destructive in its lack of acknowledgement for alternative cultural expressions of learning and development. This educational debate becomes pivotally important when considering the cultural implications of different teaching practices for education professionals working abroad, because they are the conduits of the cultural transfer that is taking place. By making examples of the dynamic interplay of the forces of global, international, and local cultures transparent, it may be possible to develop a more complex understanding of some of the factors at play; as a result the potential for positive cultural understanding and synthesis in educational exchange is released, whether through research, policy development or the design and delivery of teaching interventions.

The debate about education and globalization, therefore, provides the backdrop to this book. It case-studies wider issues through discussion about the interplay of political power and influence in the history of China's educational development. It also assesses the mutual influences of international, latterly global, forces and indigenous educational culture and practice. Certainly, power and politics have been inextricably linked with the development of education throughout China's history (Hayhoe 1984a, 1989, 1996; Pepper 1997; Zhaowu 1998; Goldman 1981; Holmes 1984). Arguably to a greater extent than in many other social contexts, education has been explicitly linked to the accession of political power, influence and social mobility in China. Educational reform has, therefore, been subject to sometimes extreme political forces and can be regarded as a barometer for determining wider aspects of the socio-political character of Chinese thinking at any one time. This may make the study of Chinese education in the context of discussions about the interplay between global and local, political and social developments particularly fruitful. It may also be possible to trace insights into the state of China's external relations through the medium of educational policy and provision. Certainly in the 20th century, the century of incipient globalization, China's relationships with other nations have been interpreted and inculcated into its education system by its educated classes. It has undergone significant educational change and reform, most frequently prompted by the political entente, and, therefore, yields many examples for discussion.

Chinese Education: organization and philosophy

Traditionally, education has been highly prized in Chinese society. A system of government and social organization was designed around the tenets of Confucian ethics and adopted by the emperor as a State code during the Han dynasty in the 1st century CE. Confucianism holds at its centre the value for learning and for the ideals of social mobility, which are achieved by intellectual progression and development. Education and intellectual life, therefore, was at the heart of the social and organizational infrastructure of China for many hundreds of years.

In terms of practice, China developed and maintained a highly centralized indigenous educational tradition that carried with it heavy prescriptions for pedagogy and practice (Hayhoe 1996; Thomas 1983; Hawkins 1983). A series of draconian policies severely limited exchange between the Middle Kingdom and the "outside world", through mechanisms such as the use of the death penalty for emigrants who attempted to return to China and the social isolation of traders who had any exchange with non-indigenous nationals (Fuerwerker 1998). In the same way, imperial decree carefully controlled the examination system that was the main expression of formal education in China for several hundred years and excluded the possibility of any externally-generated change or reform.

Education and social mobility   In spite of this emphasis on control at the centre of education in the country, the main focus for the delivery of education in imperial China was informal relying on an adhocracy of tutors hired by the rich or by communities to work with students of promise for the imperial examinations.   Though theoretically a meritocratic system of open access to men, the education system became the province for the wealthy and the sons of intellectuals who were able to gain access to learning through family inheritance and connections.

Indeed, it is important to note the extent to which education was utilized as the exclusive route for social mobility and the acquisition of personal power in the Imperial era (Thomas 1983).   The Confucian scholar-gentleman became the apotheosis of social success in the Imperial age. Moreover, learning was enshrined not only through the material artefacts of the examination system itself.   The study of learning formed part of the curriculum for the examinations, through the Confucian text, *The Great Learning*, one of the Five Classics and Four Books that formed the basis of the exam content. It may be possible to develop an argument about the way in which Buddhism, arriving in China from India in the 1st to 6th centuries (Shen 1996), influenced the evolution of the State Confucian ethic in China.   However, for all practical purposes, notions about education in China remained exclusively indigenous in philosophy, management and content for several hundred years.

Style   As noted above, the main mechanism for educational practice in Imperial China was informal, with elementary education remaining the responsibility of individual communities or those who could afford to hire a personal tutor for their children (Hayhoe 1984a). Education, then, became mainly the province of the wealthier classes and to a large degree, the central idea of social mobility evolved as more theoretical than actual (Pepper 1991).   Women were entirely forbidden education, in keeping with Confucian strictures explicitly opposed to their development.   More formal provision of education in China until the 19th century was limited to the *shuyuan* - the academies - whose prime purpose was to act as crammers for students aspiring to participate in the examination system. The organization of these institutions was still relatively informal, gathering around individual "masters", either retired officials or scholars, whose success in the examination system inspired a following as teachers. In the latter part of the imperial era, unofficial philosophical "institutes" also developed (Wu 1992). These were the subject of occasional imperial oppression and were frequently associated with the secret societies which were a feature of life in the later imperial period, especially in the South of China. Though providing education of a sort, their primary function, in effect, was focused on political agitation rather than participation in the legitimate examination system. Their numbers as a consequence were small and their influence severely limited.

Education, intellectualism and political decline   The dominant philosophical attitude that characterized approaches to education in China, as in other areas of Chinese politics and philosophy, lay in the conviction of the moral and intellectual superiority of the Middle kingdom and its people. Indeed, until the early 19th century, China was for several centuries, one of the largest and most powerful countries in the world, unchallenged and unthreatened either militarily or economically. The fundamentally inward-looking nature of scholasticism in the Confucian education system, however, contained inherent rigidities that came together to confound China's ability to participate in the 19th century's international industrial and economic developments. Inflexibility in curriculum, for example, was linked with a meditative approach to achieving deeper learning that frequently emerged as rote repetition and memorization (various in Biggs and Watkins 1996). The marginalization of science and mathematics contributed to the nation's lack of industrial and economic development. Within a few decades, China was swept from its position as an economic and political super-power, to become a colonized, fractured dependency.

The involvement of education in this change is significant. The prevailing values of the indigenous education system prevented the self-reform in the early 19th century that may have enabled China to develop in a way more open to international trends. In addition, the extremity of the swings in political and economic events in the Chinese environment of the late 19th and early 20th centuries placed attitudes towards education in a pivotal position in China's developmental history because of the way in which education was culturally privileged in Chinese tradition. In 1842 at the end of the first Opium war, when British gunboats achieved an easy defeat over Chinese armies that brought with it a treaty forcing China to cede territories and provide territorial access to the "great powers", China's culturally-uninfluenced indigenous education system effectively came to an end.

The 19th Century, the West, and Reform

The defeat in the Opium wars and the subsequent treaties, allowing, among other things, the development of the foreign treaty ports on the mainland, followed by the Taiping Rebellion and culminating in the defeat in the Sino-Japanese war of 1894, generated two main changes in the Chinese education system.

Tiyong: Chinese essence in foreign bottles First, the perceived humiliation of the defeat prompted Imperial officials - the custodians of the traditional examination system as well as its success stories - to look at the prevailing approaches to education in a new light and to attempt a process of internal reform of the Confucian system. During the latter years of the 19th century, a governing notion for an incipient "modern-yet-Confucian" Chinese educational philosophy began to take shape. *"Tiyong"*, as it was called, is a complex construct deriving from the thinking of scholar officials such as Guo Songtao, Feng Guifen and ultimately Kang Youwei, who actively led the short-lived modernization movement in the late 1890's. The concept in translation means: "Let Chinese learning be the essence and Western learning be the incidental" (He 1998; Sang 1998). It represented an attempt to incorporate Western studies of science and technology, especially in military technology in the 19th century, with the governing system of Chinese philosophy and ethical education.

In spite of its failure to prompt reform, culminating in the abandonment of the imperial examination system in 1905 and the collapse of the empire itself in 1911, the underlying concept of *tiyong* has remained influential in China since its inception. Importantly, this philosophy represents a governing Chinese view about the essentially symbiotic rather than assimilative relationship between domestic and international perspectives on education and learning that has coloured both policy and practice throughout the 20th century. It has appeared at key moments in the educational and political debate, through the painful struggles that have taken place to preserve untouched something distinctly "Chinese" in the face of increasing international integration.

The Confucian influence in the 19th century, which the reform movement needed to overcome, was indeed, considerable. The bureaucracy gained its primary power from its success in the Confucian system.   Chinese society had developed along the moral and ethical precepts of Confucianism to such an extent that it is almost impossible to discuss Chinese culture without reference to Confucius' teachings. Finally, as noted above, Chinese education was entirely the product of the prescriptive Confucian epistemology.   These factors joined together to demonstrate the extent of the barriers to reform that China perceived necessary if it was to regain its position in the world order.   In essence, there existed a "*maodun*" - an irresolvable conflict.   Officials recognized that the resolution to China's dilemma of modernization lay in education. At the same time, the existing education system was entirely enculturated in the traditional values and practices of a now-outdated and increasingly discredited and corrupt indigenous philosophical paradigm.   The abandonment of the ethical aspects of feudal Confucianism, embedded in China for hundreds of years, was perceived to threaten the onslaught of political and social chaos that might bring about the complete destruction of national identity, the harbinger of which had been felt in the Taiping Rebellion of 1850-1864.   The theme of the *tiyong* approach in education, then, was to unite in fine balance the needs for the preservation of indigenous cultural continuity and identity with the driving economic and political necessity of engaging with the international community.

The missionary schools   The second change brought about by the successive Opium war defeats of the 1840's and 1860's, was that they allowed the entry of foreign missionaries to China, who brought with them the missionary schools.   This was the most significant educational exchange with the West that Chinese people had to date experienced. Initially, because of their explicit proselytizing, the missionary schools were marginalized by the Chinese (Pepper 1991).   As the pressing need for reform and interchange with the West became clearer, however, the missionary schools emerged as an obvious source for foreign educational and ideological input.   One of the prime ways in which the missionary schools became important in China was through the provision of organized, open-access, basic education for men and some women, where the elitist and ad hoc education system had previously dominated.   Importantly, missionary schools also provided language training for the increasing number of people who wished to take the unprecedented step of going abroad to study.

The Triumph of the Internationalists

By the end of the Imperial era in the early 20th century, the relative state of these two educational forces presents an inter-linked picture of the wider balance of influence that existed between China and the rest of the world. After several centuries, the Confucian examination system was completely abandoned, together with the basic educational mechanisms that had supported it. This effectively disenfranchised the upper echelons of the Chinese national social hierarchy who had depended on the Confucian education system for their existence. In the face of the Boxer rebellion of 1900, which attempted to reject all foreign influences in Chinese life, the *tiyong* philosophy had failed almost completely to introduce balance between indigenous and international education systems. On the other hand, the missionary schools and the "western" style universities in China, beginning with Beiyang Gongxue in Tianjin in 1895 (Hayhoe 1996), were ascendant.

During the early years of the 20th century, various educational experiments developed in China, all modelled on one Western construct of education or another (Altbach 1996; Cheng, Jin and Gu 1999). Numbers of university students going abroad to study also grew at a phenomenal rate. Dr Sun Yat-Sen, Deng Xiaoping and other national revolutionary leaders benefited from education in the USA, Japan, France or the UK (Hayhoe 1996, He et al 1998, Sang 1998). During the early part of the 20th century, Japan was adopted as a model for emulation in the educational environment. This was partly a response to Japan's victory in the Sino-Japanese war. This victory was in part the result of Japan's utilization of Western military technology. It led Chinese people to perceive Japan as an Asian nation, which had successfully integrated the opposing philosophies of Western and Eastern through its education system (Pepper 1991). However, by the 1920s, the US model became more fashionable, with isolated experiments adopting the British, French, German and other European systems in various parts of the country (for an example, see chapter on John Dewey in Shen 1996).

Triumph Short-Lived

An important issue to consider in this discussion is that, once the indigenous system was abandoned, no alternative philosophy of education was able to embed itself successfully until the beginning of the People's

Republic of China in 1949. There are perhaps a number of reasons for this. The extent of the spiritual void which Confucian education left was inestimable. It left in its wake an era of social, political and economic chaos in China. There was no continuity of policy or practice in any area of life that would have allowed viable educational alternatives to the traditional system to develop. Economic collapse removed any possibility of investment that would have supported the development of a new public system of formal education along international lines. At the same time, the private means that had funded the traditional informal education system disappeared along with the officials who were the custodians of Imperial rule. In addition, there was an inevitable intellectual and academic skills vacuum as the pillars of the traditional system became pilloried and the new generation of young scholars, policy-makers and teachers travelled abroad in order to develop the skills that they perceived important in the process of modernizing China. Finally, in an era of social disintegration, sense of the wider collective good tended to break down, as individuals sought to secure their own and their families wealth and security by the most effective short-term means. The more long-term benefits of investment in education were very far away from the vast majority of people in such a tattered, colonized and conflict-ridden nation.

The Vestiges of Tiyong: a patchwork society

Beneath the obvious, however, the essence of the paradox presented by attempts at *tiyong* reforms remained. For various reasons, once the Confucian hegemony was broken, there was left little room for the simple integration of indigenous and international educational cultures (Altbach 1996, Hayhoe 1996, Pepper 1991, 1996). Just as Chinese people perceived themselves to be politically dominated by the whim of the world powers, so Chinese education was swept away by the dominance of internationalism. In other, more formally colonized systems, indigenous educational practice and culture tends to be destroyed as a result of its saturation by the colonizing system. It's only expression for indigenous culture in such circumstances, therefore, is subversive and underground. However, in China the total number of different colonizers was large and no one system emerged as controlling. Even the missionary schools had limited penetration across the whole country and remained predominately in the treaty ports and surrounding areas. In a country dominated by a strong tradition to associate education with social mobility, it is perhaps unsurprising that Chinese people themselves appeared to abandon their educational traditions and to openly embrace everything that was "foreign". This abandonment began with a desire to understand and use the technology that had been responsible for China's military defeat. This had been the starting point of *tiyong*, but within a few short decades, the entire structure of the Imperial system was left in decay. Socially, the morality of Confucianism remained embedded, perpetuated by the family unit in China and the way in which it dominated small-scale economic life (Chan 1998). This was linked with the increasing social divide that existed for the urban wealthy who embraced the west and the rural poor who clung to Confucian tradition. However, as an integrated empowering force, State Confucianism was destroyed after the Opium wars and replaced by a patchwork of westernizing, modernizing, industrializing, colonized successors. Historically, at least, it seems that the attempts made in China to link the indigenous education system with international or global perspectives through the *tiyong* philosophy were almost inevitably doomed to failure as the military power of the early industrializing nations forced their own cultural and educational values onto other societies through severe colonial repression.

Colonization and "Modernization"

In comparison to China, Japan was more successful in the first part of the 20th century in managing the integration of global and local - one of the reasons that China sought to emulate Japan's educational system at this time. Not only was this social and political integration relatively short-lived, however, but the Japanese political and governmental context was very different from that of China. In the former, government and policy-making systems not only remained intact but also exerted a very powerful influence over details of educational philosophy and practice. This facilitated the development of a structure in which cultural integration might successfully take place to some degree within the education system. In the latter, the collapse of China's political, economic and bureaucratic institutions and the aggressive presence of a large number of competing would-be colonizing powers effectively prevented any synthesis of local and international perspectives of knowledge or education systems from taking hold.

It is also important to recognize the connections that existed between Christian religious values and education in the industrial imperial societies of the 19th century.   Proselytization in all areas of life - ontological, political, social, religious - was extremely active if implicit in the sweeping educational colonization that took place in China.   What emerges quite strongly from the Chinese case is a sense of the overwhelming speed of dispersal and dominance of the international model in shaping early 20th century education and the virtual obliteration - both forced and through voluntary abandonment - of local contexts and diversity at this time.   The age of political imperialism, it seems, carried with it an acutely enculturated vision of the power and desirability of education both to bring about positive economic change and to develop the colonized along lines that replicated the colonizers own intellectual and social norms.

This impulse to consciously disperse the "modern" cultural value system should not be interpreted as entirely negative, however. For one thing, it is important to remember that ideas of the "modern" were generally viewed by the colonizing powers as culturally neutral at the time (Pennycook 1994). In addition, a level of contemporary debate took place in international educational circles in the late 19th and early 20th centuries about the desirability of leaving local societies and systems "untouched" or "uncivilized" as opposed to developing along "modern" lines. Indeed, some educators genuinely questioned the desirability of implanting external ideas into local contexts. Yet more, including many who came to China as missionaries and educators, acted out of a desire to tangibly enhance the quality of life of people around the world.   They brought about the collapse of indigenous education from the most apparently positive of motivations.

Retrospectively, the heart of the global-local dynamic lies in the extreme enculturation of contemporary notions of "modernity" and "quality" or "civilization".   This may be particularly important in the Chinese context since the adoption of "modern" was at the heart of China's social, political and educational objectives from the late 19th and throughout the 20th century.   This derives both from early 20th century liberalism and the precepts of proletarian modernity from Marxism.   In essence, this emphasis has inevitably brought policymakers and educators together to privilege non-indigenous approaches to education, because the very notion of modernity itself derives from non-Chinese beliefs and values.   Ideas about scientific modernity have at their heart a uniform pedagogy as a key mechanism for their transfer.   Modern education, then, has provided a catalyst for not only intellectual but also social and political convergence in China in the 20th century.

The Mid-20th Century Onwards: the People's Republic

The chaotic shifting of Chinese politics, economics and education continued through the twentieth century during the war with Japan and the struggles between the Guomindang and the Communists, culminating in the Civil war of 1945-1949. In 1949, at the institution of the People's Republic of China (PRC), Mao Zedong's primary aim was the economic reconstruction of China, and its modernization along socialist lines. In the early PRC era, education was a key factor in the revitalization and reconstruction of national identity and economy. As such, it was a major priority for the Chinese government. During the early years, a new model of education was embedded in China, though still a model adopted from outside, from the Soviet Union. In Mao's view, the USSR had moved a long way along the path of industrial modernization and, therefore, had much to offer China, especially in terms of expertise and support. The USSR was also prepared to assist with financial aid and technical expertise.

The education system was formalized. Universal primary education was set as a key national target, though the time-scales identified for achievement were unrealistic, aiming for universal education in less than a generation (Pepper 1991, Ross 1991, Rosen 1984, Kobayashi 1976). The tertiary sector was reformed to develop technocentric vocational education to support the rapid economic growth of the PRC. All of this was directly modelled on Soviet lines. In spite of the extensive borrowing that took place, however, it is still possible to trace some remnants of the indigenous system in the preoccupations, which dominated the debate about education policy and practice.

International policy vs. indigenous practice First, the policy thrust of educational reform took place at the macro level and little attention was paid to pedagogical practice (Leung 1991; Chen 1999). For lack of alternative models, therefore, many of the educators in the Chinese system remained the Confucian-educated, conservative, urban, intellectual elite who had been in place before the revolution. The methods of teaching remained firmly didactic, working out the master-disciple relationships which had characterized the Confucian approach. The inherent traditionalist conservatism of the intellectual classes in China resulted in frequently voiced criticism of Maoist policies, especially during national campaigns such as the Hundred Flowers Movement 1956-57 (Hayhoe 1996). This resulted in education and educators becoming politically suspect in China -

a far cry from their position as the political establishment only 50 years before. Here, again, an interesting characteristic of Chinese intellectual life seems to emerge as intellectual debate and theoretical divisions erupted expressly into political action, thus reasserting the intimate connections between education, the learned classes and politics in China.

Inequality of provision vs. equality of mass education   Second, provisions for tertiary education in particular, remained laid out along the traditional Chinese urban-rural divide (roughly South-East/North-West). Inherited from the Imperial age, formal education, such as it existed, mainly took place in the coastal cities, now the remnants of the treaty ports. Rural education remained largely informal and often non-existent. Investment in education during the early PRC period was primarily geared towards the so-called key schools in the urban South and East, while the North and West of the country was left to develop largely self-funding education projects, lacking both central investment and skilled education personnel to run schools. In addition, overall access to tertiary education was extremely limited. The net effect of this was to compound the indigenous divisions that existed around education in China before the PRC era and to place education in a political anti-revolutionary nexus that culminated in the Cultural Revolution of 1966-1976.

The red vs. expert debate   The historical Soviet educational model presented to China a context where political developments in Russia had integrated the intellectuals and the technocrats at a period of time predating the design of the education system. It was a system, therefore, where education provision was comparatively uncontentious and was overwhelmed by the driving need for economic development and industrialization (Pepper 1991). In China, however, issues of class and access linked with the symbolic power and role of education in wider social and political life remained unresolved. This meant that the direct adoption of the Russian model was more fractured and incomplete than Mao and others had anticipated. These external factors in this case acted as a force for integration towards the achievement of a viable socialist model of education for a worker state. The internal factors working on education acted out divisions and conflicts within indigenous culture, which did not blend with the Marxist-socialist model Mao was trying to instil. This tension was epitomized in the so-called "red-versus-expert" polarization (Hawkins 1983; Acker 1991).

When the Great Proletarian Cultural Revolution began in 1966, it was viewed, among other things, as a social and educational mechanism for purging the bourgeois "expert" elements from intellectual and educational life in order to facilitate the educational integration that would allow the implementation of the "red" Maoist-socialist educational model. In effect, it presented a more extreme attempt to engage with the conflict that the *tiyong* philosophy had tried to address 70 years before. It attempted to combine the essence of Chinese social values with Marxism, at the same time as addressing the problems posed by a reactionary intellectual elite in a revolutionary socialist frame. In this case, the archetype of the PRC Chinese intellectual was to be both Red and Expert: to possess the highest level of technical and academic skills in conjunction with excellent socialist political credentials. Failing this, the clear emphasis in People's Republican China was on political credentials - "Red-ness". The nexus of the conflict between the two was that the expertise that was perceived as necessary to enable economic modernization in China would inevitably draw heavily on models from the international community who were further along the path of industrialization than China. However, in the internally focussed isolationist political environment that characterized China at that time (and had historically), such contact with the outside world would inevitably make one politically suspect. Once again, it seems that the uneasy integration of international and indigenous culture presented problems in China's education development.

Tiyong-style integration fails again To a large degree, the early years of the PRC represent a further unsuccessful attempt to graft an external education system onto the indigenous cultural tradition. The Cultural Revolution attempted to achieve two things at the same time. First, it sought to address the problems of history by rooting out the dual vestiges of the residues of Confucian conservatism and the pre-PRC flirtation with Western education in which many of the intellectuals in China had engaged, both labelled "rightist" in Maoist propaganda. Second, it aimed to encourage the development of an indigenous version of socialist education, which emphasized the work-study elements of Marxism and China's traditional heritage. In doing so, the aim of the policy-makers was to embrace equality by removing the privileges of urban intellectual life that were also associated with the capitalist West. The literal and metaphorical purging of the Cultural Revolution era demonstrates the extremity of the struggle. During its course, the education system collapsed entirely for several years. After its reconstitution along new lines, political credentials replaced intellectual qualifications for entry to all secondary and tertiary education. Perhaps for the first time since the collapse of the empire, glimmers of a new indigenous education system began to emerge. However, the thrust of this new development was soon lost after Mao's death in 1976, when the entire educational reform process initiated in the later stages of the Cultural Revolution was reversed and those purged from the education establishment were rehabilitated. With Deng's "open door", China's unquestioning love affair of international culture recommenced.

Deng Xiaoping and the Open Door

In the immediate upheavals that followed Mao's death in 1976, it is impossible to isolate a single reason for the hasty dismantling of the socialist reconstruction of education that had begun in the early 70's. However, there are some obvious contributors to the change. First, the country was almost on the point of economic collapse and needed to reconstruct and reskill itself quickly to avoid a major catastrophe. The demand for vocational education and training, therefore, was immediate and very high. Second, the reforms that took place epitomized the victory of the more liberal factions in the very divided Communist party in China, which took power after the purging of the Gang of Four in 1976/77. In this way, the direction of the educational reforms in China can be viewed as a symbol of an internal political struggle, in keeping with the traditional relationship between education and politics in China. Third, many of the leaders who had been restored to power had been themselves educated in Europe in the 1920's and 30's, and were attracted to the potential for "modernization" that foreign ideas about education seemed to possess. This was especially true of Deng Xiaoping who took control of the Party in 1977/8 and had been educated in France. Certainly, it is clear that the last vestiges of the Cultural Revolution and early PRC education were destroyed by about 1980 when the wider reform movement and the Open Door policy had really taken hold. Entry to tertiary education on the basis of class background and political credentials was abandoned after 1978. Work-study programmes were terminated by 1980. Examinations and formal assessment were reintroduced, and systematized rustication was abandoned at about the same time (though it was reintroduced as a form of political punishment for students in targeted universities after June 4, 1989). Ph.D. degrees were introduced into China in 1981/2, where previously the research tradition had not existed in a recognizable international form, except in a very limited way in Government scientific research institutes (New Star 1996).

Re-entry of foreign education experts   In the vacuum of indigenous educational innovations that ensued after 1976, numerous foreign experts were invited to China in technical and educational arenas. Educators and researchers from Europe and the USA entered Chinese universities in a steady stream; overseas students began to study in China; and students from China began to travel overseas for the first time in 40 years. The departure of Chinese students continued with increasing ease as the 1980's and 90's progressed, though the Government has continued to express concern about problems with "brain-drain", as bright students have been attracted to the USA and elsewhere as permanent emigrants (Yan 1998).   Whilst it is possible to trace a continuous native tradition in educational practice in elementary and secondary levels, that continued mainly because of a lack of investment in practical education reform during the years after 1976. For example, the *minban,* which we discuss further below, re-emerged energetically from the beginning of the reform period and were legitimized by the government in the 1980's. Tertiary education certainly underwent significant change resultant from foreign investment and academic exchange. In terms of policy development, the tenor of intellectual life in universities, and the breadth of the curriculum and its design, clearly China has adopted wholesale the dominant themes from a wide-ranging contemporary international education agenda.

The Role of the Private Education Sector

An important factor to remember in the historical and social context of Chinese education is that though technically education was egalitarian for men in the country, the reality was always that education was an elite system, and educational opportunity was determined by those who had sufficient wealth and status to purchase its benefits. Money has always played a part, therefore, in China's education system. The idea of a right to universal or free education is something that has been largely absent within the Chinese tradition. Private educators, individually and in institutions in the 20th century, have taken much of the responsibility for the delivery of education and for the development of intellectual life in China. Even after 1949 and the establishment of the PRC, the majority of rural communities continued to be responsible for the establishment and funding of local primary schools, the *minban*, and have functioned to a great extent with the sanction but outside the direct control of the State Education Commission or provincial education bureaus.   Mainstream secondary education and urban and industrial education was funded in the first 30 years of the PRC by government organizations of one kind or another.   In 1980, however, private education re-emerged as a national force in the PRC.   Initial legislation allowed the limited development of vocational and educational training centres run by retired professionals and educators but precluded those who were currently employed to undertake such initiatives as profit-making ventures (Henze 1984).   The official aim of such opening-up was that the expertise of such professionals would supplement state education provision and enable more speedy national development.   These institutions worked in addition to the *minban*.   In reality, many ventures of varying quality developed during the 1980s and it became increasingly easy for Chinese nationals, overseas Chinese and others to found education institutions for vocational, elementary and secondary education in the years that followed.

These institutions - many of them focusing on language training for students aspired to travel abroad to study - facilitated the dispersal of non-indigenous educational practices more readily than the university sector, to which access was still extremely limited.   In the late 1980's, overseas education institutions and education initiatives entered China in increasing numbers, especially in relatively new disciplines, such as Business and Economics and Science and Technology.   For example, the first overseas-sponsored Management Development initiative began in Harbin in the north of China in 1980 and developed into an MBA programme in 1982 (Borgonjon & Vanhonacker 1994; Chan 1996).   Though these initiatives temporarily decreased in number after the June 4th incident in 1989, they continued to grow steadily during the 1990's.   In the late 1990's, China formally allowed foreign educational institutions to embark on education joint-ventures and to organize franchise operations on Chinese soil. At the macro level, therefore, the subsuming of Chinese education into a model of international practice seemed complete by the end of the 20th century.   In terms of micro practice, however, indigenous traditions still appear to hold sway.

The Vestiges of Indigenous Education

The reality of universal education is still aspirational in China, given the difficulties of attracting and retaining teachers into what is a badly paid and lowly profession to which cling the memories of political persecution. In universities, fewer than 30% of academics have more than a bachelor degree and some remain with no recognized academic qualifications (*China Statistical Yearbook 1999* and *Educational Yearbooks 1992-1997*). These seem the indisputable vestiges of the closure of the education system during the Cultural Revolution and Mao's attempts to eradicate the qualified educational elite as an influence in Chinese life. The consequences are, therefore, that for many educators teaching practice adheres to the traditional didactic methods, rooted in pre-20th century Confucianism. In the main, educators are falling back on practices which they experienced in their own primary and secondary schooling. This is compounded by the fact that teacher-training programmes in China contain little in terms of teaching practice or pedagogic education (Sharpe and Ning 1998), and focus primarily on developing intellectual expertise in subject disciplines. The traditional tension between academic freedom, intellectual enquiry and political activism remains uneasy. This limits the extent to which skills such as critical thinking, creativity and innovation, which are embedded into many international education traditions, can enter into Chinese practice. Finally, the traditional rural-urban divide in educational provision still remains, in spite of the abolition of the key schools and universities system after the Cultural Revolution. It is interesting to note, that those aspects of education thinking and practice which retain elements of distinctive national practice are those elements that have not yet been subject to significant reform, owing to lack of investment or to a lack of policy-makers attention. Overall, the thrust of reform and with it internationalization seems to be haphazardly eradicating the last remains of both formal Confucianism and Maoism in the eagerness to embrace economic development and co-operate with the international aid agenda.

The Power of English in China

A powerful artefact of the internationalization process in educational intellectual life in contemporary China is the pervasiveness of English language in education. Indeed, English has had many incarnations in China, but has always remained a second language linked to either advancing trade or study opportunities. In 1664, the British established their first trading post in China and a pidgin English quickly developed. The Chinese, however, were not interested in learning the full form of English as they had little desire to develop relations with the "foreign devils" who sullied themselves as merchants, a very lowly trade indeed from the Confucian gentleman's point of view (Cheng 1992).

After their defeat at the hands of the British during the Opium Wars, some Chinese became more interested in learning English as they saw it a prerequisite to acquiring Western knowledge. English was considered a tool to use as part of China's modernization program in the late 19th century, which was linked mainly to developing its military, therefore part of the attempt at developing *tiyong* integration. Later as China came into contact with more foreign countries in the early 20th century, more students studied English in the newly-opened universities, institutions set up with a British or American structure and in which students studied mostly English literature and had little chance to learn spoken English. Those Chinese who studied English were an elite minority and English made little impact on the Chinese language or Chinese thinking at this time (Cheng 1992).

After the founding of the People's Republic of China in 1949, Russian became the widely-used second language linked to development of the country. English was vilified because of China's position as a communist country in the Cold War and as enemy of the U.S. and other "western" countries in the Korean War. During the years of internal political upheaval from 1966-1976, Chinese people studying or reading English could be labelled as *chong yang mei wai*, "worship and have blind faith in things foreign" (Cheng 1992), so interest in English went underground only to reemerge after Deng Xiaoping jailed the Gang of Four and brought reforms to China in 1977. With these reforms, China set English as one of the subjects on the college entrance exam, so English became the main second language which the increasing numbers of Chinese students were required to study in secondary school. Without a history of teaching English in its schools, China was faced with a lack of teachers for this subject, so even in "key schools" Russian teachers were instantly converted to English teachers by the 1979 school year. Teachers taught English using Chinese language and the textbooks were often based in the political rhetoric of earlier times. Students studied English to pass exams and gained little facility in using the language. English was still a second language in China although linked to the Four Modernizations of the 1980's.

The 1990's saw English remain as a subject of the college entrance exam after its reform and the textbooks for secondary and primary school English were changed to reflect more of an interest in the language of scientific and technological development. Students today begin their study of English in the third or fourth grades of primary school and continue to study throughout secondary school with up to six hours a week of their study devoted to English. Along with this increased study in school has come a rapid increase in private classes for revision and further study of English for conversation or for passing standardized tests. The revision classes offer systems for studying English, often pneumatic systems such as "thank you" rendered into "*san ke you*" with corresponding Chinese characters which the students can then memorize. Chinese students master this memorization technique in the exam-driven educational atmosphere. They are able to pass standardized tests such as the TOEFL and to a lesser extent IELTS without necessarily being able to use English in speech or for writing prose. Alan Maley points out that this memorizing of language has "grammatical form (usually devoid of contextual meaning) [taking] precedence over meaningful communication" (Maley 1986).

English in the People's Republic of China today remains the most studied second language with the largest number of learners of English as a Foreign Language (EFL) in the world, a number estimated between 200-300 million (Crystal, 1985). English is not, however, an institutionalized language in China as it has not developed as the primary language spoken by any segment of the population and has not been adopted as an official language of the country. Kachru (1992) has established the development of new world Englishes as the language has spread to become an internationally accepted lingua franca. He promotes a model for understanding development of the English language with flexible three-group classification: the inner circle consisting of countries that use English as their primary language, such as the UK or the USA; the outer circle consisting of countries where English has become commonly used as an official language, such as India and Singapore; and the expanding circle consisting of countries where English is studied as a foreign language for communication, such as China and Nepal (Kachru, 1992). While useful in helping to change attitudes toward understanding how English exists in the world today, this model may not fully explain the use of English within a country. Zhao and Campbell promote the idea that English in China is not learned primarily as a foreign language for international communication, but rather it is studied as a means of social and economic mobility (Zhao and Campbell 1995). They attempt to determine a profile of users of English in China today and identified that study of English is most often "not an instrument for international communication or any communication at all. English is the fabled Aladdin's lamp, to use Kachru's metaphor (1986), which is perceived to be able to provide them with much needed social and economic mobility." Secondary school students study English to enable them to pass their exams and go to college; college students study English to gain a high score on the English Proficiency Test (EPT); and part-time adult students want training for the TOEFL or IELTS. Zhao and Campbell (1995) emphasize that the Chinese learner of English wants to show that he or she possesses English through attaining a tested standard, but that they do not necessarily want the ability to communicate in English.

To a large extent, therefore, it seems that the English language medium can act as reinforcement for the idea of symbolic rather than functional education in China. The subjects of learning themselves do not possess inherent value but act as empty vessels, which provide access into high status social or professional circles. In the contemporary private educational environment, offered by international institutions such as Harmony College, however, this notion is challenged somewhat. English language proficiency lends speakers the ability to participate in the international business community in China in a way that other languages are less able to do. It can also open up opportunities for the gaining of overseas experience. However, given the historical dominance of English as the language of trade, fluency with *spoken* English confers as much functional as instrumental value to the entrepreneurial classes. And in China today, unlike in its past, the entrepreneurial classes form not only the financial but the social elite. More and more, the passing of a standard test on its own may not confer as much cachet as possession of practical language skills.

The difference between symbolic English used as a passport and practical English for use in professional life is encapsulated in the diverse language teaching approach adopted in the domestic and private educational sectors in China. In state schools and colleges, the dominant pedagogy is to instruct students in an understanding of grammatical rules and linguistics. As noted above, this does not always allow students to develop any real facility with the living language. Indeed, the phonetic renditions used in revision classes for standard tests act as an obvious obstacle to use of English in a practical context. The approach to teaching in the international private sector, however, adopts the interactive principles of British/American TEFL practice and emphasizes language use for interpersonal communication. In this model, grammar plays a far less significant role and the learning outcomes lend themselves very poorly to rote memorization for exam purposes.

It is important, therefore, to consider English language education in contemporary China from a number of different perspectives at the same time as recognizing the generally pervasive and powerful way in which it is shaping the educational climate. As pressure builds up from the student community and the private sector for functional language teaching, so pressure is building on the state sector to reconsider its pedagogical emphasis in a more general sense. If English language is one of the vehicles progressing the achievement of China's international economic ambitions, so equally it may be one of the vehicles promoting change in education practice. As part of this process, the private sector in China, is acting as a dynamic force in providing educational diversity as well as chipping away at the philosophical foundations of Chinese pedagogy.

Education, Global and Local in the PRC Period

The latest developments in Chinese education open up a number of issues when considering tensions between global and local in education. The continuing struggle in Chinese education at various times throughout the 20th century to assert locally constructed models of education show the large extent to which they exist. In the most part, these local initiatives have failed - most noticeably in the post-Cultural Revolution reform era. Today, local educational values have given way in the face of the dominant notion of "modern" which has shaped China's education system and the acute demands for economic growth to support China's population. This reflects the wider struggle that exists in contemporary education to cope with the way that one enculturated model of education has been privileged for generations.

There are additional problems posed for education in China because of the inextricable links between education and economic development, a consonance that has increasingly converged since 1978. The global economy, developing largely along enculturated lines, insists on systems of education that produce individuals who can understand the rules of that particular cultural game and play it. Nations, like China which still struggle with rural poverty and lack economic self-sufficiency, are powerless to resist this pressure because the potential consequences for their people - continued social and economic marginalization and decline - may be too severe. Some commentators paint a more positive picture of the interchange of global and local in the contemporary scene. They depict the potential which lies in the reshaping of a nation state to a developmental form which can facilitate the integration of local cultural, moral and social values in partnership with the global epistemology of the educational curriculum. On the other hand, there are those who suggest that the weakening of nation state and central educational control in the face of globalization, may dilute local awareness of the range of educational alternatives that exist and reinforce the notional link between the dominant global paradigm and short-term gains in economic status. In addition there may be questions about the continuance of academic freedom and autonomy in the face of globalization, where the continued convergence of educational designs in order to deliver economic development effectively channel education along narrower and more prescriptive lines.

In a general sense, China acts as a case study, which reflects a number of contemporary preoccupations about the tension between global and local in education. Since the 19th century when European gunboats first appeared on Chinese shores and then moved metaphorically into the schoolyard, local Chinese educational culture has found itself philosophically and practically unable to resist. Within China itself, it would seem that the overwhelming desire to participate in economic globalization has thrust education willy-nilly into the heart of the educational mainstream. Given their historical difficulty in synthesizing and blending local and international together, Chinese policymakers, it seems, have explicitly chosen to reject their own local past in favour of the promise of a global future.

Women in Chinese Education

Though education has always held an aspirational power over Chinese people, and the Confucian system remains highly influential in many modern ethnic Chinese societies, it also holds values at its centre which completely deny access to education for women. Confucius' *Analects*, for example, note that uneducated women are to be desired as wives and daughters to ensure the safety and sanctity of household and society; that educated women should be spurned and not tolerated; and that men should desire to marry women who are their inferior in education and social status. These precepts, therefore, created a cultural female dependency and docility, which characterized Chinese society for hundreds of years.

Social Exclusion Embedded in Tradition

The traditional structures of Chinese education prevented women from attaining much in the way of learning. The Chinese language is difficult to learn, both to read and write and requires many years of intensive formal training in order to achieve proficiency. The only focus for legitimate learning in the Chinese curriculum, as noted above, were the *Five Classics* and *Four Books* - the subjects of philosophy, ethics and morality taught and examined in the Imperial systems that allowed men to access official positions in government or to qualify as teachers. Other forms of knowledge in China were variously marginalized as unimportant or forbidden and vigorously censored. China's boundaries were closed to the outside world for may hundreds of years, or opened in very limited and highly controlled fashion, such as along the silk road, to allow government controlled trade and commodity exchange. At various times during the imperial age, Chinese citizens, once emigrated from China's shores were never allowed to return. All this effectively limited any kinds of externally motivated change or exchange with foreigners, which might have opened the door of educational opportunity to Chinese women. In addition, women of higher classes in China were physically mutilated from childhood through the process of foot binding, effectively preventing them from moving to seek stimulation or learning outside the household precincts.

A further factor inhibiting the education of women was the historical, and still largely intact, system of patrilocal residence after marriage. Women, when they were married moved to their husband's home - thus depriving the woman's family of any of the material, or spiritual, benefits of education she may have received. The opportunity-cost of investment in education for a woman, then, was generally viewed by her family as excessive since there was little possibility of any kind of return. Women who could read and write were generally less desirable as wives, and their future work lives would accrue benefit to their husband's family and not to the woman's own relations.

Missionary Schools and Reform

With the breakdown of Imperial rule from the 19th century after the Opium wars and the Sino-Japanese war of 1894, the formal ending of the Imperial examination system in 1905 and the establishment of the first Republic in 1911, the educational picture for women improved somewhat. The entry of foreign missionaries and the development of the missionary schools in the later 19th century provided educational access to women for the first time in Chinese history. Women received teaching in basic education, literacy, numeracy and so on and at a higher level in foreign languages. Access to higher education was still the province of men, but a few normal colleges training women as primary school teachers, and care workers, began to develop in the early Republican Era in the 20th century, especially around Shanghai and the other treaty ports.

In fact, geography has always played an important part in the history of women's education in China. The development of the Treaty Ports, ceded to foreign powers by the Chinese Government during the 1840's-60's, not only introduced missionaries and educators but also set up a system of sino-international exchange in the surrounding areas. For the first time, the notion of education for women as a desirable achievement entered into Chinese society, together with other "modern", and "western" notions of equality and democracy. These influences filtered through from the south and east of China and into the main urban centres, which rapidly developed from the 19th century onwards. However, initiatives promoting education for women had limited success, as did societies formed to promote "natural feet" and the end of foot binding. The Chinese government was in disarray from the beginning of the Republic throughout the warlord era in the 1920's and 30's, a time, which may have provided the foundation for women's participation in education. By the 1930's with the beginning of the war against Japan, into the 1940's, torn by civil war and political chaos, most of the strides promoting and supporting the development of women's education had effectively disappeared.

The Communist Connection

The one area in Chinese society during the early 20th century where women achieved notional equality and some educational opportunity was through the work of the Chinese Communist Party. Throughout the civil war, fought against the Republicans, women had campaigned alongside men and had participated in decision-making and planning. Although men held all of the most powerful positions, some roles evolved for women because of the insistence of Marxist doctrine to break down the traditional subservience of women in society. The beginning of the PRC seemed to many to be the beginning of real social and educational equality for men and women in China.

Efforts to equalize educational provision and to open up education for women, however, were dogged by the burdens of the scale of the educational problems experienced by China as a whole. In 1952 over 90% of the population was illiterate, and virtually all women were unable to read and write. The costs and requirements of modernizing education and economy in China were so great that many of the policies and targets put into place became aspirational rather than real. A series of policy reversions and disastrous economic campaigns such as the Great Leap Forward effectively prevented any real progress to be made. In addition, the revolutionaries suffered from a compounding of the problems of China's educational inheritance. Essentially a peasant movement, the People's Republic held at its core an anti-intellectualism that ran very deep. These views impacted seriously on the development of real educational opportunity for women. In the early years of the PRC, many strides were made, as work-study programmes embraced women both in the countryside and the city. But then realization grew of the extent to which the Chinese intellectual class - a class on which the country depended for its educational reform and development - were a force for anti-revolutionary conservatism. So educated women began to suffer from a "double-whammy": the traditional prejudice about educated women and the more general anti-intellectual prejudice labelled as rightist or anti-revolutionary.

Beginning in the late 1960's, the Cultural Revolution, attempted to address many of these issues and to re-draw education along both more egalitarian and revolutionary lines. However, it evolved more as a political bloodbath than an effective reform movement and was characterized with infighting and power struggles which resulted in the complete breakdown of any kind of education for several years. When reconstituted in the later years of the Cultural Revolution, education did emphasize real equality of opportunity for women, and included targets for affirmative action for women, the integration of work and study and a selection system that emphasized political activism rather than intellectual credentials. Numbers of women participants increased during this period. The negative effects and the political turbulence that accompanied the process of the Cultural

Revolution, however, were so disturbing to Chinese society that on the death of Mao Zedong in 1976 and the downfall of the Gang of Four in 1976/7, the main reforms of the Cultural Revolution era were reversed. By 1980, the education system in China had reverted back almost completely to its pre-Cultural Revolution form. With China's door opening to the rest of the world, it began perceptibly to swing shut for women in Chinese society.

China's Open Door

From 1978/9 onwards, Deng Xiaoping introduced a whole series of reforms into China, aiming to complete modernization of industry and economy and to restore China to its position as a world power as it had been in the mid-19th century. He developed the notion of the Socialist Market Economy, began to reform the machinery of government and the way in which work, education and output were connected. A massive reform of the education system began at this time, within the introduction of universal nine years of education and a huge expansion of the vocational and tertiary sectors. All positive action for women, in terms of actual targets for admission to secondary and tertiary education, disappeared, however, in the rush to upskill and modernize the workforce as fast as possible. The government still emphasized the value of women in the workforce and the importance of educational opportunity, but there was little in terms of effective policy instruments, investment in rural education, or recruitment and promotion of women into influential positions in the Party or the bureaucracy which would have cemented the rhetoric with action. Numerous commentators have noted the way in which educational opportunity for women eroded during the first 15 years of the reform process.

Participation

Women's participation in education remains at a low level in China. In spite of the development of nine years of universal education in China, actual participation for women, especially in rural areas, is far below the expected figures. The UNDP Report of 1999 notes that illiteracy remains a major issue for women in China. Many commentators have discussed the disadvantages that women in rural environments in China or from minority groups suffer in terms of educational and social opportunity.

One of the key problems for women in education in China is the strong prejudice that attaches to vocational education. China's key educational gaps lie in the area of vocational skills. However, the mainstream education system remains firmly geared up to university entrance examinations - where opportunity exists for only 7% of the eligible school population - or 2.5% of the total 18 to 22 year old age group (*UNDP Report 1999*). The traditional rural/urban educational divide impacts significantly on Chinese women. The greatest participation of women in education in China takes place in the southern and eastern parts of the country (excluding Beijing, traditionally the country's education capital).

Access

A further issue lies in the area of access to education. Admissions requirements vary according to gender and it appears that this tendency is developing, as the gender imbalance in the country grows wider. Henze (1984) noted that women needed to attain higher scores in a variety of subjects to obtain university admission compared to their male colleagues during the 1980's, and there is little evidence to show that this trend has changed. While such a divide exists, clearly discriminating against women, it is difficult to imagine that basic issues of educational equality can be address within the state system.

A ceiling of toughened glass Given that higher levels of education in China are an urban phenomenon and underlying prejudices against the employment of women are most evident in rural areas, it seems almost inevitable that the polarization for social and educational reform in gender relations will continue. Girls from rural families are still considered less important by their families because they will move to their husband's home when they marry. If they do get the chance for education, they cannot find jobs locally because of employers' prejudices against them. Therefore, the only course would be to break away entirely from family ties and move to the city. The result of these emigrations is a continuing absence of positive role models for future generations of women and little evidence in the countryside of the positive community or family returns from educated women to add to the gender debate.

With an increasing imbalance in the gender make-up of the Chinese population - owing to the abiding rural preference for sons over daughters in the face of the one-child policy - and with reform of state-owned industry, male unemployment is on the increase (UNDP 1999). This is a powerful force acting against women's education in the countryside. Indications are that women are being increasingly encouraged back to the home both as wives for the growing numbers of single men unable to find partners and to relieve the employment system and provide opportunities for male workers.

Curriculum issues   As part of China's economic modernization programme, the government placed great emphasis on natural sciences and technology subjects, especially at secondary and tertiary education. However, there are a number of issues here that affect the statues of women particularly and maintain the existing inequality of opportunity. At age 16/17 students in high school are streamed into either *like* (sciences and mathematics) or *wenke* (humanities and languages) for preparation for the university entrance examinations. Final streaming depends on a number of factors: educational achievements to date and student preferences are taken into account. However, in general about 75% of students are streamed into *like* and 25% into *wenke*. In spite of this, a disproportionate number of women are streamed into the humanities area. This builds on a discriminatory set of admissions requirements for men and women where women are required to achieve higher marks than men to gain access to science subjects than men. It is also because humanities are viewed by male students and teachers as less desirable subjects for study. From the beginning of the PRC and especially during the Cultural Revolution in the 1960's, significant stigma attached to intellectuals who were pursuing humanities subjects. Still to those non-vocational humanities disciplines cling the taint of political suspicion and the possibility of future persecution. At the same time, more women are guided into these areas by teachers, thus effectively ghettoizing women intellectually and increasing the tendency for suspicion and prejudice to attach to both students and areas of study. Humanities departments in colleges and universities have tended to be less well funded from the State; there are fewer opportunities for further study and fewer exchanges with international academics. Deprived of these opportunities, students in *wenke* may be substantially disadvantaged compared to their peers in science-related disciplines.

Education and the Economy

The post-reform education system places strong connections between education and national economic development. The idea for many is that a higher level of education is highly congruent to a better job in the future. In the case of many women, however, the development of the market system is working to their disadvantage. For example, the introduction of the agricultural responsibility system has increased perceptions of the opportunity cost for women's education, as girls productive labour is lost when they are in school and the persistence of the patrilocal residence tradition after marriage persists in most areas of the country. In addition, the urban-rural divide has limited the amount of funding available for investment in women's education. What money is available tends to be streamed to the advantage of male students and scientific subjects, subjects to which women find it more difficult to gain entry.

China's Door Swinging Open to the World and Shut to Chinese Women

The picture of education and work for women in China appears to be a divided one. It can make very depressing reading. Few women in China today have the opportunity to participate in education beyond the most basic level. For those women lucky enough to live in the city or to come from a wealthier family, however, access to "modern" education and its emancipatory opportunities is a real possibility. For women in the rural environment or whose family lacks the funds to provide education, the chances of making a change to their situation remain remote.

What is clear is that while the government's reforms from the late 1970's have opened the door of opportunity for many foreign investors and entrepreneurs, it has slammed shut against increased educational opportunity and social mobility for most women. As we have noted above, the reform period brought about the abandonment of quotas, targets and formal measures promoting equality of access to education for women instituted in the latter years of the Cultural Revolution. Representation of female students in secondary and higher education remain low, especially in the sciences and technical subjects. At the same time, social sciences and humanities, which sees a higher proportion of women, remain more politically suspect than science subjects and effectively taint female intellectuals with a further shadow over their status in China. In work, few women function in senior positions and most are sidelined into "traditional" roles in the caring and service professions. Women note active gender discrimination in favour of men in recruitment and promotion in all kinds of professional areas. The re-entry of the Chinese diaspora as a factor in both business and education provision is also an ambivalent force when it comes to emancipation and equality for women. The stronger thrust of the Confucian traditional attitude to women that is evident in Hong Kong and Taiwanese societies, for example, may be contributing to the re-emergence of discrimination against women in work and schools. This difficult environment makes it especially challenging for ambitious women interested in professional development to thrive.

Private education Within the overall picture, then, it may be interesting to explore the role of the newly-emerging private education sector. Money is one of the variables, which may be a force for developing gender equality in women's education. Acker (1991) noted that money might be the key factor to break down the intellectual elitism of education in Beijing's high schools in her study of the late 1980's and early 1990's. Certainly the private sector has significantly changed the face of education in China since 1980 when it was first formally recognized. Now, across the country, there are more than a thousand institutions in all sectors, drawing on a multitude of disciplines and areas of teaching. Since the majority of these institutions lie outside of the entry systems of the state sector, it is possible for women to participate in private education more freely and fully than in the mainstream.

Minban Though the rural pattern of education is one that precludes entry to women in most cases, the existence of the *minban*, the privately-funded schools which have always formed the mainstay of rural education in China, do provide some limited opportunities for women. It is also important to note that women frequently staff these schools, especially in outlying areas, since they are so unpopular with male teachers as they are relatively poorly paid and lacking in opportunities for professional advancement. In areas where the local community is becoming increasingly wealthy, through the town and village enterprise system for example, it is possible for some women in rural communities to gain access to at least basic education and to have opportunities for further educational development. Opportunities within this system remain haphazard, however, and depend largely on the goodwill of the girl's family and the progressiveness of local custom.

Private and foreign-invested colleges The number of private educational institutions in China is growing rapidly. Women are playing a significant part in the development of this sector. Though they may be less able than men to take advantage of the limited opportunities within the state sector, more women are beginning to seek vocational or professional education in China when they reach adulthood. The growing private sector, with its emphasis on vocational and applied or technical education is an obvious place for them to find it. The state system, indeed, places significant limitations on entry to undergraduate programmes. A student must be unmarried (with no children), be under the age of 27 and physically fit if they are to enter into a state university. This also applies to most *zifei* or "self-pay" programmes as well as to programmes for competitive entry. Though China has been relatively successful in developing its adult and television education programmes, the availability of quality programmes of higher-level study on a part-time or distance-learning basis is still relatively scarce. Virtually no state-provided part-time postgraduate programmes exist in the country. The main emphasis for part-time programming undertaken by state universities has been revenue generation and is frequently aimed at overseas students rather than the domestic market. However, since the late 1990's an increasing number of state universities have begun to offer private MBA and equivalent programmes - of a variety of qualities - as an attempt to close the gap opening up between the state and private sectors in this area. The majority of these programmes, however, are offered in conjunction with a private sector partner and are, in effect, joint-ventures in the private sector themselves. For this reason, that cannot be considered part of the state sector provision of postgraduate education.

The relative ease of access into private institutions is attractive to a range of mature students and especially to women. A huge variety of programmes of study are available through the private sector, at a variety of levels. This is the sector in which international education providers are also most active. The government is attempting to regulate quality and has major concerns about the numbers of potentially poor quality programmes that are on offer. In an environment where many women lack more legitimate opportunities to study through the state system, however, these programmes are increasingly attractive. They are especially attractive since they offer a variety of modes of study: distance learning, formal full-time courses and part-time options, all of which fit into the realities of their professional and personal lives. It is in this vibrant and varied context of private higher education provision that Harmony College, the institution from which came the participants in the research project, exists.

A force for equality?   It seems clear that the ability to buy a place, especially, in a private sector school or college, is one way to circumvent the uneven admission requirements that remain in the state sector.   In addition, the vocational nature of much of the education in the private tertiary sector gives women who go there an opportunity to develop skills much in demand in the workplace.   For many women, exposure to the experience of international education and the progression to work in a foreign-invested company, effectively moving out of the Chinese environment altogether, may be the only way to legitimately participate in work other than in a subordinate or manual work role.   The social implications for these women may be serious, however.   In a society which places an extraordinarily high value on family life and where strong class and gender prejudices still cause men to prefer to marry women of lower educational and/or social status than themselves, it is very difficult for educated, professional women to find husbands and, therefore, to continue in the accepted mainstream of Chinese society.   It is even more difficult for them to continue working at a high level after the birth of a child.   In effect, therefore, single professional women are emerging as a new social class in modern China, but one that is potentially marginalized from the mainstream and does not necessarily have the capacity to act as a positive role model for future generations of girls as they grow older.   They also receive the burden of family criticism and pressure to conform to traditional expectations.   It is unsurprising, therefore, that a significant number of students and professional emigrants from China are women.

Women, private sector education and diversity   The picture for women in education in China may seem bleak but is very dynamic.   On the one hand, the situation within primary and secondary education, especially for women in rural areas or from ethnic minority backgrounds, remains largely unchanged from its traditional roots by the more than fifty years of the PRC.   In fact, it seems clear that the past 25 years of economic reform have gone a long way to undo the increased level of opportunity that began to emerge at the end of the Cultural Revolution.   Certainly the already-over-burdened state education system does not seem to be able to cope with the extra demands for improved workforce skills that economic development is placing upon it.   The response that seems to be developing from women in the face of this continued absence of opportunity is to support the development of the independent sector and to seek out whatever chances may present themselves. The social consequences of this decision-making, however, may be shaping Chinese society into patterns of further division and stratification, where educational opportunity remains the province of the intellectual of economic elite and women in deprived areas of China remain both socially and intellectually disenfranchised.

Themes and Issues Influencing the Context of the Study

Macro-policy and Social Construct of Higher Education

As noted at the outset, this chapter aims to provide an overview of the key aspects in the social and political development of education in China as background to the stories from the participants in the study. To further draw together the themes and issue which we feel are most relevant, we have outlined and summarized aspects of the development of Chinese education in a thematic map, shown in Figure 2.1. Tracing the sequence of developments shown in Figure 2.1 reveals a number of interesting cultural aspects of China's educational development, which we have developed below.

Policy Dominates Practice in Reform

First, it seems that the extent of rapid political change and economic modernization that took place in China in the 20th century led to a government focus only at the highest levels of action in determining its educational approach. The major thrust seems to have been towards developing educational structures and working with broad policy objectives around provision, institutional development, programming and curriculum. Considerations of the intangibles of a philosophy of education and teaching methodology during the 20th century have remained less affected by developments in the period and have tended to play a minor role in government policy and action. This implies that many of the pre-revolutionary assumptions about how to teach and how to learn may have been less challenged than other aspects of the educational paradigm and have undergone fewer changes as a result.

	Imperial Model	Early 20th Century Model (1895-1949)	Maoist/Socialist Model (1949-1978)	Reform Model (1978-present)
Dominant Institutional Form	Range of academies - county/provincial/ national/Imperial levels	Introduction of the university (1895); rapid development of HE along "Western" lines	Range of universities; rapid development of vocational training colleges, etc.	Expansion of provision at all levels; reemergence of the international model
Role of HE in Society	A mechanism for maintenance of moral and social order	A mechanism for moral and social order - introducing "the modern"	A mechanism for Maoist political, social and economic modernization	A mechanism for market social, political and economic reform
Educational Politicization	Intimate connections between intellectuals And political power	Traditional connections weakened connections to "foreign powers"	Co-identification of politics and education; external influence confined to USSR	Formal connections between intellectuals and political power weakened
Intellectual Autonomy	Heavy social control over education; periodic persecution of intellectuals	Social controls significantly weakened	Social control very tight; intellectuals under suspicion and subject to persecution	Heavy social control over education; periodic perse-cution of intellectuals
Intellectual Orientation	Scholasticism dominant - absence of free creative or critical thought	Scholasticism dominant - sporadic experimentation with scientific, creative and free thought	Maoism/Marxism dominant - absence of free creative or critical thought	Scholasticism dominant - attempts to develop scientific innovation and creativity
Access to Education	Elitist - HE available to social class elite	Elitist - social class elite - money and guanxi Important factors	Wide access to vocational education; widening access to formal HE, subject to political credentials	Provision limited; partial development of access via competitive merit system; formal State HE elitist

Figure 2.1: Historical Trends in China's Educational Provision

	Imperial Model	Early 20th Century Model (1895-1949)	Maoist/Socialist Model (1949-1978)	Reform Model (1978-present)
Organization and Ownership	Higher education colleges - public; vocational institutions - private	Universities - foreign/public; vocational institutions - private	State-controlled education	State controlled mainstream HE; private sector provision on the the periphery
Institutional Structure	Hierarchy of institutions, periodic political persecution of lower level/private institutions	Old hierarchy breaks down; conceptual hierarchy in place - political turbulence distorts planned development of HE	Notional equality; real inverted hierarchy of institutions, owing to politically suspect nature of education	Hierarchy of institutions along traditional lines
Formal/ Non-formal Mix	Formal institutions dominant - non-formal have little status	Formal and non-formal institutions; HE shifts to new pattern	Expansion of non-formal education provision; no formal education from 1966-70	Formal dominates planning; non-formal dominates provision
Social Use of Graduates	Study leads to work as government official	Career destinations diverse	Central State appointment and career management system	Introduction of student free choice
Breadth of Curriculum	Narrow - empahsis on interpretation of the Confucian "Classics"	Narrow - foreign influence introduces sciences and foreign languages	Narrow - focus on vocational/industrial, scientific skills and political re-education	Introduction of new disciplines, e.g. business

Figure 2.1 (continued): Historical Trends in China's Educational Provision

	Imperial Model	Early 20th Century Model (1895-1949)	Maoist/Socialist Model (1949-1978)	Reform Model (1978-present)
Level of Subject Specialism	Generalism - focus on the humanities; little research tradition	Generalism - developing specialism and research	Generalism - political studies; limited scientific research	Generalism - intro. Of research degress in the 1980's
Orientation to Knowledge	Unitary - knowledge viewed as "truth"/ "fact"	Unitarism gives way to limited development of Plural perspectives	Maoist/Marxist unitarism - absolute "truth" is given out Party	Unitary - knowledge viewed as "truth"
Pedagogic Orientation	Emphasis on "pure" intellectualism - no application of learning or teaching of skills	Formal emphasis on "pure" intellectualism; interest in "the modern" at the margins	Co-identification of physical work and intellectual thought; re-education through labour frequent	"Pure" intellectualism emphasized; limited experiments with alternative pedagogies
Teaching and Assessments	Didactic - master and disciple; Imperial examination system	Mixed - introduction of applied and experiential approaches	Polarized - education via labour vs. didactic formal teaching and assessment	Didactic - teacher-centred; centralized examination systems
International Orientation	Absence of international contact or context	International structures and systems adopted wholesale	Virtual absence of international contact or context	Massive expansion of international exchange

Figure 2.1 (continued): Historical Trends in China's Educational Provision

During periods of extreme political turbulence, such as the Cultural Revolution, this trend of the smooth development in traditions and constructs of teaching and learning was severely challenged. The strength of the mainstream tradition, however, retained its force during the reconstruction period partly because of a tendency for rejection of the political elements of that era to sweep up some of the practical changes and departures from earlier traditions of practice that accompanied it (Tsui 1998). This also reflects the closeness between active politics and education, especially higher education, that is a distinctive long-term feature in China. A rejection of the political extremism of the 1966-76 period, therefore, necessarily involved the eradication of much of the style of educational provision that went with it.

The Intellectual Tradition

A second aspect to consider here is that of the overall orientation to education and to intellectuals in China. Throughout the period from pre-revolution onwards, attitude towards education seem to characterize it as a generic tool for social engineering of one kind or another. In this construct the aim of education is to achieve some kind of single purpose or set of purposes closely related to government or social objectives. The practical consequence of this view becomes a narrow range of action for the educational curriculum, geared to defined policy aspirations. Consequently, a close expectation develops about the achievement of particular behavioural or intellectual outcomes from graduates of the system. This suggests a high level of conformity of expectation perhaps both from students and from policy makers about what a university education could be expected to "do" for individuals and the country. It also reflects inconsistencies, which are traceable in the policy approach taken in China. On the one hand, few policy instruments governing practice have been developed. On the other, where policy exists, it tends to be prescriptive in nature and draconian in the expectation that it will be able to deliver certain outcomes. Such a contradictory "tight-loose" framework seems to determine education development throughout the twentieth century.

Absence of Intellectual Autonomy

In intellectual orientation, it is clear that the liberal tradition of intellectual criticism and autonomy is absent in Chinese educational constructs

(Goldman 1981, Hayhoe 1996; Pepper 1997, Allinson 1989). Not only the closeness of the connection between education and politics/government, but also the predominant approach of scholasticism reinforces this view. The relatively low levels of research undertaken by academics in China, notably outside of science disciplines, develops this aspect further as does the remaining strength of the elitism, both in the hierarchy of institutions and in the student body that seems to be present. In some part, this may represent the relatively recent development away from a feudal social order, since scholasticism tends to be an intellectual feature of that social model. The practical implications for teaching and learning practice, however, seem clear and are demonstrated through the predominant didacticism of the Chinese system. The contexts for the development of critical thinking and innovation through new research are mainly absent within such an approach to higher education.

Scholasticism and the Influence of Confucianism

The scholastic attitude to intellectual thought which has carried across from Chinese historical tradition and was reinforced by the political totalitarianism of the Chinese state for the large part of the 20th century leads inevitably into a unitary view of knowledge and learning in teaching provision. High levels of state control and an absence of intellectual freedom and autonomy, generate an environment where the translation of specific policy aims for education are targeted through teaching style and programme content. Even where teaching methodology may not be represented directly in policy instruments, the policy-generated narrowness of the curriculum, prescription of materials available and prescriptive specification of desired student outcomes, lead to a model in which highly standardized and conforming teaching practice is almost inevitable. This is especially the case in a system where the socialist environment of the second half of the 20th century linked educators' professional compliance and performance directly with their continued professional well being. At times, such as during the Cultural Revolution period, this link developed so far that teachers' personal safety was directly connected to their conformity, though there are, indications that a longer-term Chinese attitude may also be reflected here. For example, the Confucianist tendency to emphasize the "master" as expert leads to an expectation that student performance ultimately mirrors the direct competence of the educator (Chen 1994). The purpose of the education process in this compounded environment, then, is to develop individuals who are models of certain kinds of behaviour or who develop professional or intellectual knowledge with specific uses in society. This reflects a preoccupation with the social and moral elements of educational programming and a notion of "right" behaviour, both deriving from the pre-revolutionary Confucian inheritance and from Marxist ideology (Partington 1988). The impact on teaching and learning that results from this, is the desire to learn in order to find the "right" answer and to develop into the "right" kind of person along clear and definable lines. Key areas of cultural emphasis emerge, therefore, when considering Chinese education in attitudes to the nature of knowledge, innovation and creative thinking and perceptions about its basic purposes. The processes of skills development, where critical thought and opportunities to develop across a self-determined and independently articulated path, are also largely absent in the policy preoccupations and educational traditions in China. Autonomy in programming and determination of curricula also seems to be absent within the Chinese system, focusing on a narrow range of high conformity in expectation of the role and capability of education within the system (State Education Commission 1996, Li 1994).

Attitudes of Chinese Students to What They Want from Education

As already noted, from the implications of the dominant social and political constructs of education that exists in China, it may be possible to infer a read-across from policy objectives to student perceptions about the educational process. In this way, we may be able to identify some aspects of student motivation and performance, which can inform our understanding of the study participants' stories. For example, the strong policy aims which emphasize social and civic education in the curriculum might generate students who desire to achieve certain specific aims in their lives though their educational participation and that those aims would have some direct input into society. They might have a notion of a standard educational experience, reflecting the educational process in which they had previously studied, based on learning "truths" or about morally "correct" behaviour that fits them to become useful members of society. They might expect to undergo training in interpretation of information, led by an expert educator, that enables them to make sense of contradictory or unclear issues and derive clarification through the processes of reductionism which will help them to fit their experiences into the "right" model. The main aim of the learning process in this model would be to refine non-conforming attitudes and to develop capability of understanding the precepts of an absolute model of knowledge, which can assist in resolving life's problems. A "successful" scholar, in this context, would be one who could bring the examples of the model of knowledge they have developed in order to simplify and make sense of confusion and, therefore, make a productive contribution to the continued stability and harmony of society.

Such a projection deriving from the wider context does in fact resonate with much of the literature about Chinese students attitudes to the educational experience from the pre-20th century era and into the development of modern education in China (Cheng et al 1999; Chan and Drover 1996; Ho 1986; Gallagher 1998; Little 1992; Lin 1993; World Bank 1997). It may be helpful, therefore, to examine the degree to which the study participants exhibit similar attitudes and motivations as those drawn out from the historical context and the degree to which they differ. These are themes, which we will discuss, in the following chapters of the book.

Some Themes and Questions

As China moves into the 21st century, it appears to be on the cusp of a great many social, political and educational changes. It is clear that education remains pivotal to the future direction upon which the country will embark. The tensions and difficulties of that path are clear. The upheavals of 1989 when student and academic protests about corruption led to wider debate about the modernization of education in China and the development of democracy, was swiftly followed by government clampdown and temporary restraint in the educational reform agenda. It seems clear that the problems of integration between indigenous philosophy and educational traditions and international practices, first articulated in the 19th century through *tiyong*, are still unresolved. In considering opportunities for the future, it is possible to draw some themes from the past however.

First, in China clear tension exists between the desire for intellectual debate and diversity with a political agenda that demands consistency. This results at least in part from the inherited tradition of central control and the connections between education and political influence and power. Inherently, this will add challenge into the integration of international, especially, European and US, intellectual traditions, where greater separation exists between political and educational arenas and where intellectual autonomy and debate is viewed as an inherent quality of education practice.

Second, in the 20th century particularly, China's international educational influences have been catholic rather than eclectic. Little time has been afforded for either international or national influences to take root. This has left a system adrift, caught between a mixture of change inertia and a clinging on to outdated practices in the face of multiple and uncertain reforms.

Third, the PRC has broken much of the traditional social respect in which both teachers and education have been held. In spite of a continuing culture of high regard for the participation in education, education as a profession is at the same time full of the potential for personal political risk as well as being poorly paid and valued. It is also the nexus for international exchange, enabling educators to be at the vanguard of reform and development or persecuted for their capitalist influence. This leaves the education system potentially vulnerable, given the importance that the government places on it for economic development.

Fourth, little attention in education is given over to issues of teaching and learning, either at policy levels or within the design of teacher training programmes. Little incentive exists for educational innovation coming from ground level. At one and the same time, this may prevent the emergence of a viable indigenous education system as well as creating difficulties for the successful embedding of international practice or the incorporation of transferable critical skills into learning programmes at all levels in China. In essence, the lack of penetration of education initiatives in terms of day-to-day classroom practice, still following the Confucian principles of the pre-revolutionary age, excites questions about the real extent of any notional reform that has taken place.

On the face of it, these themes that emerge present a picture of a disintegrated and unfocused education system which may not be able to meet the demands that the government is placing upon it in its role in economic and national development. The key official response to this dilemma, as noted above, appears to lie in a continued increase in international education exchange and in the numbers of foreign institutions operating in China. The government hopes that diversity in provision will absolve it from more specific policy guidance, perhaps. However, given the coalescence of the themes emerging from the "love-hate" relationship that seems to exist between Chinese and international politics and education, this may not provide a satisfactory long-term solution. To a large extent, the 21st century management colleges and language schools that are setting up all over China, institutions run by foreign interest groups, may simply be the equivalent of the early 20th century missionary schools. They may be a vehicle for the abandonment of the scanty indigenous practice that remains and a catalyst for further political revolution. The young people of the 1920's rejected the prevailing mores of the corrupt gerontocracy of Confucian officials, supported by overseas capitalists. In doing so, they were swept up in a debate, which questioned the very nature of what it was to be Chinese in an increasingly global society. The outcome was years of civil war and disruption. The young people of the 1990's attempted to reject the corrupt gerontocracy of the Chinese Communist Party, also supported by overseas capitalists. As yet, the consequences of this action are unclear. The disruption may be more subtle than that of 100 years ago, more an economic turning away from the traditional precepts of both Chinese education and society than an overt political upheaval. However, the potential for more violent consequences, as the majority of Chinese people reject the extreme "westernization" of Chinese culture, still exists. The delicate balance proposed by the *tiyong* reformers of the 19th century continually appears to defy educators and social reformers in China, and the relationship between Chinese and external influences remains complex and difficult. The opportunity for education to facilitate a resolution to these tensions remains strong but unrealized. What seems clear is that the contemporary generation of people seeking educational and personal development from within the newly emerging context of private education in China will play a significant part in shaping its future. Possibly a role similar to the pivotal role the educational émigrés of the 1920's had in shaping China's present.

3 Introducing the People

We will begin this chapter by setting out some basic information about who the participants in the project were and then move on to discussing their family backgrounds and situations. Following the pattern of the rest of the book, we have intermingled short selections from stories and narrative commentary where appropriate.

The Research Population

Thirty-one people took part in the project, 18 women and 13 men. Their ages ranged from 18 to 38 years old, with the median age being 26. The average age for men was 28 years and 11 months, for women 25 years and 7 months. The age range for women was from 18 to 36 and for men 23 to 38. Only one person in the project was under 20, a woman, with 5 people aged over 30. Seventy-four percent of participants were aged between 22 and 28.

The age range reflects the overall population of students and recent graduates at Harmony College in 1999. At the time of writing, the government has just begun to waive some of the age requirements for students entering into state universities (from May 2001). The new reforms aiming at encouraging more mature students to participate in higher education but will take some time to filter through. During the time of the study, 1998-1999, state Higher Education remained open only to single people under 27 years of age. The age range for Harmony College, therefore, contained a number of people who were ineligible to participate in the state system owing to age considerations. Overwhelmingly the majority of people at the College were those who had been unsuccessful in the competition for state university places or whose ambitions had not aspired to university at high school age. The constitution of the student body at the College, then, was largely made up of late-teens or twenty-somethings. Those participants who were over thirty in particular expressed some concerns about their age when coming back to education and the possible job consequences their decision may bring. For example:

> The bad thing for me is that I have probably lost the chance to get a promotion in my company. The other is that maybe I have wasted my time here. Maybe this isn't the same as the other students, but I am old and so when I am here, I cannot work. (AC, p.8)

For them, the challenges arising from the social expectation in China that education is intended for "young" people seemed particularly difficult. They expressed a clear drive to participate in the international system rather than remain in what they perceived to be a Chinese system of education and employment based in "ageism".

Students or Graduates

Seven of the participants had already graduated from the College and were working, or in one case, seeking work. We will discuss their professional situations further in Chapter 7, which focuses on work and ideas about the future for the whole study population. Of these graduates, one had left the College 18 months prior to taking part in the project and the remainder had left Harmony between six months and one year previously. Their departure from the College was sufficiently recent, therefore, for them to recall their experiences, while at the same time reinterpreting them in the light of the current employment situation. We included this arbitrary number of recent graduates to provide us with a broader continuum of life experiences and to better embrace participants' ideas about work both before and after attending Harmony College. The remaining participants were all taking part in the business degree levels of study at the College, distributed between first-year and final-year equivalents. Again, the numbers of participants from each level are arbitrary; depending on those who would agree to take part in the study in what was an uneasy research environment. However, the vast majority (19 people or 61% of the total) were participants in one of the two final-year cohorts at the College in 1999. The remaining five participants had all taken part in at least two semesters of degree-level study (the equivalent to one year in the UK system). The resulting group presents a fairly broad mix of experiences within the College's environment, in addition to the varied age range and the other factors, which we will lay out below. It is important to reassert that we intended the study as small-scale and impressionistic from the outset, engaged in exploring perceptions and experiences through the route of autobiography rather than producing definitive conclusions. In this environment, the broad population added variety and interest to what was already a diverse group and has considerably enriched the information we were able to achieve.

Hometowns

Participants in the study came from all over China. See Figure 3.1 for a detailed locator map for individual home regions. One of the key comments that participants made about the environment at Harmony was that not only was it international in its orientation to education, but that it was very diverse in terms of the student make-up:

> My classmates from Harmony are from different situations, different places, different areas. They have different backgrounds. But in Chinese middle school, we have all the same background and have not been out into society. We all stay in the same area, we have all stayed at school - our minds are quite pure. But at Harmony, a lot of students have working experience and some of them are quite sophisticated. (C, p.6)

As we shall discuss in future chapters, this is unusual as an experience for the study group. In general in China the majority of people experience education at an extremely local level. One of the most distinctive aspects of the College situation, therefore, was the level of diversity in its community.

Overall, education is an urban phenomenon in China. The majority of participants, therefore, have spent much of their educational lives in either large towns or cities. The scattering of points of origin is distinctive, however, and impacted on the nature of the urban experience. Three participants come from the Northeast of China, where cities are relatively undeveloped outside of a few industrial hubs and education is focused in a few central areas. Five participants come from poor regions in Inner Mongolia and the Northwest of China, where average living conditions and standards are much below China's urban averages. For these participants, the experience of going to Harmony College was as much about its location in Beijing, the political and education centre of the country, as it was about being in a private international college. The comments of one participant from Inner Mongolia are pertinent:

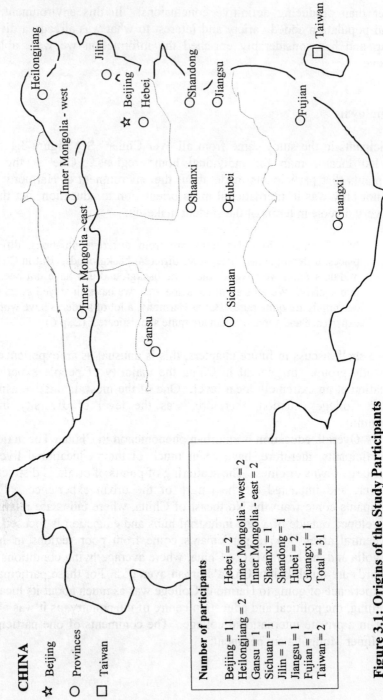

Figure 3.1: Origins of the Study Participants

CHINA
☆ Beijing
○ Provinces
□ Taiwan

Number of participants

Beijing = 11
Heilongjiang = 2
Gansu = 1
Sichuan = 1
Jilin = 1
Jiangsu = 1
Fujian = 1
Taiwan = 2

Hebei = 2
Inner Mongolia - west = 2
Inner Mongolia - east = 2
Shaanxi = 1
Shandong = 1
Hubei = 2
Guangxi = 1
Total = 31

> You know, Beijing. When I say the word "Beijing", I have a different kind of feeling. It is the capital of the whole country and it also gives you a different impression. At that time [before I came to Harmony], my world was quite narrow, so when I think of a good place to go, I think of Beijing. ... I thought it was a really good place. (Q, p.7)

In addition for these participants, the developing tug of identity between home and family in a provincial or rural situation and education and professional future in the metropolis seems significant:

> [In the future] I just want to be far from my parents. They are the reason. Also the economy is not good in [my hometown]. That's another reason but the main reason is my parents. I don't want to be controlled by them. (V, p.8)

> I feel sometimes, I really feel it is difficult to fit. You know, families are big and I have a lot of relatives or whatever and I don't like to spend too much time with them. I went home because of my parents, my sister and brother. Maybe with some other relatives, I just say some normal words, or greetings to make them happy but actually I didn't enjoy myself. (Q, p.12)

Inevitably a large number of participants (11) come from Beijing itself. Not only is the capital perceived as the centre for education, but the investment necessary for students who could still live at home was considerably less than for the "out of towners". This was an influential consideration, making Harmony a more accessible option than for the rest of the student community. Many of the Beijingers went to the College because it was quite literally "round the corner" from their homes.

In addition, a number of participants came from the economically booming south coast of the country. For them, the impulse to take part in international education supporting continued international expansion within their own regions of the country was powerful:

> I see my future in China. I think there are a lot of opportunities in China for business development, even for entrepreneurs. I believe I have this kind of sense of discovery. I see this kind of business opportunity. For example, once I had this idea of opening a shoe repair shop. It was an investment for $200,000. It had a big machine imported from Japan and there was a shop. The shoes prepared were very expensive in [the southern city where I lived], sometime forty yuan for one pair. And the business was really good. Even now, that business is really doing well. (K, p.12)

Overall, the constitution of the research population covers a very wide geographical spread. This enabled us to gauge to some degree the levels of difference and similarity in participants' educational experiences and to be able to assess the levels of change that have been taking place in different regions in recent years. It also allowed us to become more aware of the full extent of variety that is incorporated into notions such as "China" and "Chinese" as a single nation of people rather than regarding people as an homogenous civic group. One aspect of China's diversity that we were unable to explore, however, was that of ethnic diversity. 95% of the population in the country is ethnically Han Chinese, though this group in itself incorporates numerous historical and regional differences. The many ethnic groupings that make up the minorities in China experience significant disadvantage both economically and educationally. The student population of Harmony College, as a private fee-paying higher education institution, reflected that reality and we were unable to find any non-Han participants for the project.

Family, Personal Background and Class

Education in China, as well as being predominantly the province of the city dwellers, has long been associated with the intellectual classes, as we discussed in Chapter 2. To some degree private education opened up educational opportunity for those who have money but lack the connections that have traditionally been necessary to gain access. With the exception of the later Cultural Revolution period, when conventional class criteria gave way to political background as the means to educational access, the People's Republic has largely left this traditional self-selection unchallenged. When examining the social and class background of the participant group, what emerges is that they largely reflect a white-collar grouping with a minority coming from families with intellectual connections. Far more of the participants came from families with some kind of historic political advantage - as cadres, managers in state owned enterprises or well-placed administrators. This characteristic places the participant group firmly among the successful upper middle classes in Chinese society. Figure 3.2 shows the detail of the family context for participants.

A. Family Status

	Number of Participants
Both Parents Living	30
Parents Both Dead	1
Parents Married	28
Parents Divorced	2

B. Number of Siblings

	Number of Participants
Only Child	6
One	12
Two	4
More Than Two	9

C. Parent's Education Level

Highest Educational Attainment	Father	Mother
Elementary	1	1
Middle School	1	0
High School	8	16
Technical/Normal College	4	9
University Degree	10	5
No Information	7	0

D. Parent's Professional Group

Professional Group	Father	Mother
Self Employed	7	5
Government Official	4	3
SOE* Manager	3	0
SOE* Worker	3	8
Educator	4	5
Military	3	1
Administrator	4	1
Sales	2	0
Health Care Worker	0	1
Housewife	0	5
No Information	1	2

*SOE = state-owned enterprise

Figure 3.2: Participants' Family Background Information

As we have noted, there is a fair distribution across the white-collar professions, both public and private sector. Fathers tend to have higher professional status than mothers among the group. There is a relatively low number of housewives. Fourteen were still involved with the state sector for work and 12 had taken advantage of the opening up of the private sector to start their own businesses. There were few blue-collar fathers, though a much higher number of blue-collar mothers, perhaps an indication of the high costs of private higher education, which would effectively rule out participants of poorer families in the same way as it would disadvantage ethnic minorities. One of the participant's parents had taken early retirement from state enterprise work, and are gambling on the stock exchange as a source of income - participating in the most visible way in the new economy:

> Every day, they go to the stock market. ... Sometimes, they earn and sometimes they lose, but they are still interested. The market is Shanghai on one side [of the room] and Shenzhen on the other. ... There are lots of small stores, a lot of people. ... I think they do [pretty well]. They just find this interesting; they want to do something. (T, p.2)

Personal Background

Fifteen participants had worked at some time preceding their entry to the College. The remainder (16) entered the College directly from education at secondary, vocational or higher levels. Those who had worked were employed exclusively in white-collar occupations, ranging from jobs as receptionists or managers in large hotels in Beijing or Shenzhen to careers in information technology or real estate. Two thirds of those with work experience had been employed exclusively in private-sector organizations in the past, and 60% of those had worked within international businesses in China, though the only participants who had spent any time abroad were the two sisters born in Taiwan.

Work provided many participants with the initial opportunity to develop some English language skills, a prerequisite for acceptance at Harmony College. Two of the group with work experience had set up their own companies and, having made some money, opted to develop their international business skills through education before continuing with their entrepreneurial careers. One participant had worked in education, as an English language teacher, initially in the public sector and later in a domestically run private school. One had been employed as a technical translator initially by a state company and then, again, moved into the private sector. A further participant had undertaken a short career as an officer in the People's Liberation Army and received a technical training before leaving and going to work in real estate for an international company.

The main theme to emerge from those who had worked was that, diverse as their individual careers maybe, each of them had a vested interest or previous experience in the newly-opening up private employment sector in China. It was largely this that then prompted them to seek a place at Harmony College and deepen their commitment to the process of economic reform in the country.

Family Educational Background

The vast majority of participants come from homes of parents who had at least finished secondary education. Again this would place them firmly in a "middle class" bracket in Chinese society. Fathers' education levels outstripped mothers' with far more graduates from university and colleges. Only two participants had parents who had left school after completing basic elementary education. Both of these participants had made their own way through the education system as a result of precocious intellectual achievement and competitive admission to regional key schools. They had then gone on to make some money from working before beginning their studies at Harmony.

Marital Status

Twenty-six of the participants were unmarried, four married and one divorced. One of the men was married and one divorced while three women are married. The average age of single people was 25 and the average age of those who have been married was 32 years 7 months. Those who were married had been married for between 2 and 12 years, the average age at which they married was 25 and a half.

Four of the five participants who were married got married to a work colleague or someone who worked in close proximity to their place of employment. In one case, the marriage was arranged by the state company for whom the couple worked and in four cases, participants married a partner of their own choice. Two of the women who were married had a child, one aged nine and the other aged six.

Of those who were single, 55% expect to get married. However, only 32% actively expressed wanting marriage. Men were more enthusiastic than women about marriage, for example:

[Success for me is] first to have a stable family, like a good wife, a very good son or daughter, I don't care...I hope my parents will be healthy. And then I would like to run my own business some day and go somewhere travelling with my family. (S, p.8)

Forty-five percent of women were either unsure that they would marry or were ambivalent about it:

Marriage and children are not important for me...I think the most important thing is that I can do whatever I like in my career. But get married? I don't think so, probably after 30 or so, I don't know. I really don't want to even...I don't want to have a child or children, I don't like that. (M, p.15)

It is not really important for me. I mean with this kind of thing. I always think that if it comes, it comes. For sure I won't let it affect my life or what I want to do in the future. For one thing, I don't know about marriage. But children? I don't think I want children. First it takes too much time and it is a very heavy responsibility. I don't think it will be very important to me. (N, p.8)

At the same time, those women who expressed a more positive view about marriage, emphasized the central role it would play in their lives:

I think of family as a big part of, a big important part of my life. I [would] like to be a good mother or good wife...I think if my future family can have a really good atmosphere, then it will be good for my future career because I will have support. (P, p.8)

For some women, the absence of marriage has already become a factor that they feel "marks them out" among their peers:

I think marriage is quite a natural thing, but I don't want to force myself because other people say, "it is time for you to get married", so I will try to find a person to marry. I do not think that is a good way. ... You know, Chinese people always say if you don't become a wife and a mother, then your life isn't so complete, so people are always telling me. Sometimes even now I feel very bad because all my good friends have already married and I am the only one that is left. This gives me a bad feeling. It seems that no-one wants to select me. (U, p.10)

Two of the unmarried participants have a partner and expect to get married "soon". Three others were hoping to meet a partner and marry in the near future. For the majority, however, the prospect of marriage was more long-term. Nineteen percent said that they would not expect to marry until they were at least 30 years old and two others said that maybe they would marry "one day".

Three participants pointed up pressure from their families to get married:

> I'm 28. In China, that's old, an older man, right? My parents say, "You are old, why don't you marry?" Because some of their neighbours are young and they already have children … I tell them about what I'm doing now and they say, "Oh, you'll do it, you'll [get married]. (AD, p.15)

> I have an absolutely different opinion about marriage and children than my parents and my sister, so I never talk about it. If I talk with them, we will argue. My father thinks a girl should marry by 25 because after that you cannot find a good husband. I told my mother his opinion is so stupid and my mother agreed with me. My parents also think it's better to marry with a Chinese person, not a foreigner, so I don't want to get married. (H, p.10)

Historically China has been a highly conforming society which has at its foundation the idea of the family. The patriarchal system of family relationships is enshrined in Confucianism and has pervaded the social ethic of Chinese life for more than a millennium. To a large extent, this pattern of social organization and relationships has been left undisturbed by the People's Republic, except to institute a system of monogamous marital relationships in the place of the polygamy that dominated the feudal order of Imperial China. Though women have far more rights than a hundred years ago, the patriarchy remains the centre of the majority of family relationships and women are regarded as subordinate members within family circles. This is nicely illustrated by the comments of one of the participants in the study:

> In a Chinese family, it is always like this. The father decides the big things, the mother just decides what we will eat today, things like that. (H, p.5)

In modern urban China, patterns of relationships and the emergence of individualism are causing established practices to slip somewhat. The divorce rate is increasing rapidly and, in cities at least, it is relatively unsensational. Only one of the participants in this study was divorced, as much a reflection of the age group than of contemporary social custom. The vast majority of people in China, however, still marry. In practical terms, cohabitation is frowned upon and a strong popular family-based morality determines the continuation of established traditions. In most parts of the country, women still move to the homes of their husbands on marriage. Matchmakers and arranged marriages operate in abundance in both city and countryside. One of the men involved in the study, for example, commented that he was content to use the services of a matchmaker in finding a marriage partner:

> My relatives introduce many girls to me. And I recently said, "no way because I have to finish my study". ... However, [in a few years] I will use a go-between, a matchmaker. True love is quite romantic. It is maybe for people in their early twenties to teenagers. They want true love. But for me, at my age, I just want a good lady. It is enough. I do not require appearance, plain is enough. As long as she is a good lady. She can understand me. (R, p.11)

Though there is a popular preoccupation about romantic love in Chinese movies and songs, the conventional bonds of filial obedience and virtue tend to win out over self-determination and romance. It is very much the case that the institution of marriage in China is regarded as a prime mechanism for ensuring social stability and coherence.

Interestingly, those participants who wanted to marry in the long-term future tended to be seeking some kind of professional or business success first:

> [I will marry] after I get social success. Maybe for a woman, her second success will be to have a perfect family. ... Now, I have not realized my life-long dream, so I would not like to get married because if I get married, maybe I can never realize my dream. (W, p.19)

Men saw being successful as a particularly important foundation for marriage:

> I think I will be very late to [marry]. I will get married when I am much older. I will make my family become more successful. I don't want my parents to work very hard any more, so I want to support them in a happy life. (AE, p.11)

For most participants, then, there exists a separation of the idea of romantic love and the domestic obligation of marriage. Many expected to marry as a matter of social custom rather than individual choice. Fewer than 50% expressed very positive feelings about marriage. On the whole, men express more positive values to the institution of marriage than women - noting it as a mark of success or a fulfilled life. Some women also followed this pattern of thinking, but very few identified the possibility that a woman could have both a demanding career and a family. Indeed, a number of women in the study expressed that they felt marriage and children placed a significant limitation on a woman's ability to build a career in China. We will discuss this further in Chapter 7.

Children

China's difficulties with its burgeoning population are well documented, as is the government's response, which instituted a policy limiting family size to one child. This continuing policy has had a number of social and demographic impacts. The majority of participants themselves come from families of more than one child, the average being three. Six participants come from families of one child themselves, and they make up the younger group among the participants. This reflects the strong split in family planning policies in China during the 20th century. In the Maoist era, patriotic duty was almost literally expressed in the number of children that a couple produced. In the age of reform, having more than one child results in stringent financial, professional and social penalties, except for those who live and work in rural agricultural areas and still depend on large families to maintain their farm's productive capacity.

One participant, the son of two party cadres, commented on his own single child status as an unusual social phenomenon when he was young:

> I'm an only child, just me. My generation is only one. All my cousins are only one. In the past, I think I am quite unique because the policy was still open when I was in primary school. Others had brothers and sisters but I was only one, it was something a little bit unique. And I could get some money from the government, a subsidy. If your parents had only one child, they got a subsidy. I used to receive the subsidy until I was 13 or 14 years old. Then it stopped. But I thought getting some money was interesting. (AA, p.2)

Women and Children

In considering their own prospects for child-rearing, single women expressed high levels of ambivalence when talking about having a child. For the majority of the population, this builds on the somewhat remote attitudes to marriage expressed by the majority of women and the younger participants. Thirty-two percent of the total population expected to have a child at some point "in the future", while 44% of women either did not want or were uncertain about the idea of having a child. No male participants expressed any ambivalence about child rearing and all see it as a desirable inevitability in their lives.

The Power of Diversity

The overall make-up of the study population sets the scene for the degree to which the student population from Harmony College was novel in the Chinese educational context.   Not only were students at the College generally older than would be typical of university students in contemporary China, but their home backgrounds and points of origin were far more diverse. Certainly the key state universities, such as Qinghua and Peking University, competitively draw students from across the entire country. The vast majority of China's universities, however, are regional in their focus rather than national, and many vocational universities operate within an extremely local context. In addition, as we will discuss further, students at state universities have shared the highly conforming process of high school education as a single peer group, in sharp contrast to the majority of students who elect to go to Harmony. Moreover, students at the college have a huge range of personal backgrounds as well as hometowns and educational histories. A significant proportion of their families have already begun to participate in the new economy in China, as entrepreneurs, managers and administrators of private businesses and joint-ventures. One result of this diversity is that the group of participants is perhaps predisposed to be more dynamic and forward-looking than other groups of university students. They themselves and their families have taken the first step into the post-reform market world of business in China and their educational choices act both as a validation and a development of that.

The production of intellectual and political conservatives has been a key function of China's state education system, particularly at university level. The government reasserted this agenda after the June 4th incident in 1989. The aim of universities has been to train competent technicians for the state machine and not produce social innovators or critics. The homogeneity among the student body itself, owing to the training they receive during mainstream schooling, has tended to compound that pattern of educational socialization. For the vast majority of people in China, identity and enculturation remains firmly local or regional. This group at Harmony is of its own community diverse and perhaps, therefore, challenges the traditional underpinning philosophy of education in the country. We shall go on to discuss further their aspirations and the way that their education has continued to shape their identity both at school and at the college. It is important first to understand the degree to which it is still unusual in China for, say, a 36 year old mother of a nine year old child from Beijing to be sitting in the same university seminar room as a 20 year old man from Gansu (in the northwest of China). Moreover it remains novel that they would both be studying western business practices from a lecturer who comes from the USA, the UK or Australia. At the most fundamental level, therefore, the heterogeneity of the community as well as the educational options they have followed has shaped them as individuals and shaped their attitudes to society and work in very different ways than the classical *sanhao xuesheng* from one of the typical state universities. This, therefore, is the launching point for the research: a disparate group of people from China, who are already the products of the reform process in some way, came together in an alien educational environment to study a non-indigenous curriculum using a non-indigenous pedagogy. What effect would the resulting dynamic have in shaping their ideas and how would they go on to shape the world of work into which they would enter after graduation?

4 Impressions of the Chinese Educational Environment

The study participants paint a very detailed and colourful picture of the educational environment in which they received their elementary and secondary education. A number of issues emerge from the interviews that show both the remarkable uniformity of the national education system and the diversity that arises from different local practices in the regions in which the students received their early education. The wide age range of the study participants also echoes a number of the features of the social and policy environments that have accompanied educational reform in China over the past years - for example, the restructuring of the form of compulsory universal education to nine years and the impact of the 1989 June 4th incident. Linking this information with the stories that participants tell us about their families, it is possible to see the considerable progress that China has made in working towards universal education during the 20th century. It has moved from an environment where at least some family members of parent's or grandparent's generations were illiterate, had received either no education or only the scantiest elementary schooling, to an environment where all of the participants and their siblings have at least experienced secondary and/or vocational education before beginning work. This is influenced by a number of additional factors outside education itself. It does, however, seem to show the cumulative degree to which paths to social mobility utilizing education as a vehicle have progressively opened up in China over the course of the 20th century.

School Careers

Our detailed discussion of the participants' stories follows the chronological pattern of their school careers and starts with pre-school and elementary school. Participants' educational career paths are summarized in Figure 4.1.

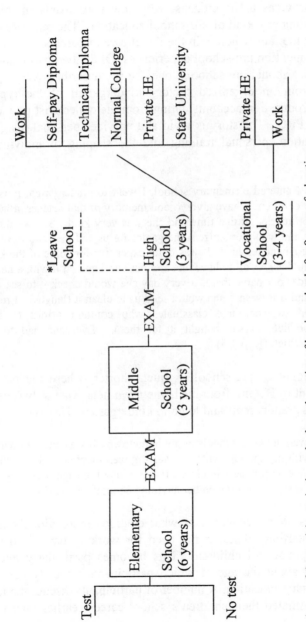

*none of the participants in the study chose the option of leaving school after 9 years of education

Figure 4.1: Paths through China's Education System for Study Participants

Early Beginnings: pre-school

In spite of the high levels of provision of formal pre-school and kindergarten care that commentators have noted that the Chinese government provides to its citizens, very few participants in this study reported attending any kind of pre-school education. The majority seem to have stayed in the family home, in the direct care of parents or relatives, or simply do not mention pre-school experiences. Of the two participants who explicitly talk about pre-school, one story describes very positive experiences from an organized factory kindergarten of the type most commonly introduced in accounts dating from the collectivist period of the history of the PRC. The story is vivid and provides personal insights into early socialization, personal training and the shaping of individual and collective:

> Before I entered elementary school, I went to kindergarten, mostly with factory children. I have a very good memory of that teacher, a lady. She was not married at that time and she was very kind. She would take us outside and would organize some games for us and then she would ask us to have a handkerchief. It was quite expensive for some of the kids, and she would ask us all to have one and put our name on it with a needle - to embroider our name there. Every day she would check it to see if it was clean and if it wasn't, she would send us to clean it (laughs). I remember we had two or three classmates who couldn't afford to buy the handkerchief, so she bought it for them. Everyone had to have a handkerchief. (K, p.4-5)

The other account of pre-school is much shorter, where the participant notes being sent to Beijing from his home town near Xian at two years old to live with his grandparents and to go to kindergarten. He says:

> There were no such schools in my hometown. It was quite a poor town. I lived with my grandparents. It was a government school. At that time, there were no private schools. ... It was a long time ago; I will try to recall it. I'm sorry, I can't remember anything about it. (S, p.2-3)

Implicit in this short account, and what emerges more directly in other stories about starting school, is the need for working parents to provide childcare for pre-school children. This becomes particularly interesting when thinking about the age at which participants typically began their formal elementary education. A number of participants discuss the fact that their parents initiated their children's school careers earlier than usual in order to resolve the problem of daytime care, especially when their parents begin to work outside the state sector:

> Since my parents needed to do their own work, nobody looked after me. They just said "OK, let's send you to school. Even if you cannot catch up, you can spend two years in the first year." (M, p.3)

For the majority of participants, however, the experiences of pre-elementary school go unnoted or unremembered. It may be that the participants do not consider their pre-school experience as part of the educational career, which is why they do not talk about it, or it may be that they feel those times too far away or unremarkable in educational or developmental terms. The limited number of references, therefore, becomes interesting because they are so isolated from the rest of the interview data.

Formal Schooling Begins: elementary school

The first and most striking factor to note when thinking about the participants' education is the wide range of ages at which they began their elementary school careers. The majority of students began their education between six and seven years old, but some began school at age eight, which seems quite late, given evolving government policy stipulating six years as school-starting age. More interesting is the number of participants who noted that their age to begin schooling was somehow atypical from their peers; most notably for those who began at age six. For example:

> When I was six years old, I went to a primary school in the small town [where we lived] and then changed to another one in Chengdu. ... I was younger [than the other students in the class]. I am used to being the youngest in my class. ... My mother graduated in education, so she thought that girls should study earlier than boys because boys are more active and like to play, so boys should go to school a little later. ... She said that girls are quieter than boys. (H, p.1)

The reasons for this variation in age for commencing formal education are diverse - some talk about their precocious interest in education, some about their parent's need to resolve childcare problems. Others talk about their parents' ambitions to give their children a head start in the education competition. However, the interesting consequence of these mixed ages for beginning educational careers is that the pattern continues throughout the following education system:

> I finished high school when I was 18. I was one year younger than my
> fellow classmates; normally it is 19. This was because I started early. My
> father let me start school when I was 7 years old. (P, p.2)

The total number of years of participation in the education system is more
important, it seems, than set ages for graduation or for progression to
university. This, linked with the comments made by participants about the
importance of educational rites of passage, such as examinations, seems to
imply a flavour of the ritualistic character of some aspects of Chinese
education. Progression through standard formal educational milestones,
either noted by minimum time spent or certificated achievements is perhaps
more important than qualitative experiential aspects of the educational
process. Given the size and diversity of the population and the variability
in both the introduction of the reforms and their implementation, some
variation in progression through the education system appear almost
inevitable.

Local School and Competition for Entry

A large majority (84%) of the participants began by attending the
neighbourhood elementary school. Three participants were sent to a "good"
school by their parents, either in a neighbouring district or by going to live
with relatives in order to be eligible to receive what was perceived to be a
better quality of education. In many ways this is unsurprising since, as we
have already noted in Chapter 3, many of the study participants come from
urban or town environments where educational standards are generally
higher than in the countryside. Not only would schools be plentiful,
therefore, but also their quality would be higher than those in rural areas
thus providing less stress on early choices. There are still perceptions
expressed about variance of school provision within the urban setting,
however, and each participant shows a high level of consciousness about
quality rankings for schools at all levels of the system, even elementary:

> I first went to school in Dongcheng District [in Beijing]... I lived in
> Chaoyang and my parents thought the quality of the teaching was not so
> good. ... They wanted me to get a better, a higher quality of teaching.
> The teaching in Dongcheng was much better than in other areas in
> Beijing. (C, p.2)

> I started school in Harbin but my parents decided to send me to Shenyang,
> because the city was bigger [than my hometown] and the education
> system, especially the teachers were better. (F, p.5)

In spite of the locally based nature of participants' first experiences of education, most of them talk of some basic skills assessment as a mechanism for entry into their elementary schools:

> There is a test, but very simple. They just asked you questions and asked you to count, "1,2,3,4,5," and to do what and what numbers. I remember every day I practiced, "1,2,3,4,5" (T, p.2)

> When I first went to school, I took an exam. I didn't really understand and the teacher showed me a picture with lots of animals and asked me to see the picture and then he kept the picture and let me say how many animals [were] in the picture and what animals I can name...Then it finished and he said, "you can go", and I got into the school. (Z, p.2)

For those who entered "good" schools, the competitive elements involved in gaining access to education seem far more explicit. For example:

> I was seven years old. I studied at the Red Bandana School in Wuhan - it was named after what the children wear round their necks. ... At that time, that school was a very excellent school in Wuhan, so that is why it was quite difficult for us to go straight into it and there was an interview. First, we just studied in another school nearby our house. Then we moved into the centre of the city and the relationship changed, so then both me and my brother went to this school. (J, p.1)

> I was six [when I started school], I was about six. ... I studied in the primary school attached to the People's University. There, it was a different system. That primary school was open to all students, even if you lived in other places, even if you lived in Xicheng District. Because, how do you say it? It's a nationally important primary school. So students of competence can apply to go there. They have a test. If you pass the test, you can go there. At that time, people could not go to primary school when they were six years old. They had to wait until they were seven. But I would have had to wait for another half a year and I did not want to do that. I was supposed to go to a primary school near my home, but it was not a key school. But because I had been accepted by that [local] school [at age six], [my parents] said to the key school, "you see, they have accepted him, although he is not the right age, so maybe you could give him the chance to take the test". And the people gave me the test and I passed. (L, p.3)

This kind of information in the stories gives an impression of the degree to which participants in the study are conscious of both the importance attached to educational opportunity and to which they identify education in some way with a direct competition with others. Certainly every one of the accounts in the study refer at some point or another to a strong sense of peer competition and the need to compete to achieve and succeed in externally-oriented activities - most commonly examinations - as part of the educational process. As the picture about elementary education begins to take shape, it seems evident that few participants ascribe characteristics such as enjoyment or personal development to their learning experiences in schools, either as a real event or as something that one could expect of schooling.

First Impressions: the school environment

Physical Space and Organization

When the participants' stories move from getting into school to being at school, they describe an environment that could be characterized as very "traditional" in style - long rows of chairs and desks, the desks being mainly fixed to the floor. Class sizes are generally large. The range reported was from 16 for one participant who came from rural Inner Mongolia where schools were few, up to a staggering 80 to 100 in each class reported by one of the over-thirty age group, coming from Hubei Province in the South of China. The average number reported, however, was somewhere between 40 and 50 students in a class (58% of the responses). For most participants, this class size remains relatively stable throughout their school careers, though for some, the numbers decrease in senior high school and in vocational colleges.

Discipline and Behaviour

Whatever the numbers, however, the environment, even in elementary school, appears very formal. The teacher stands at the front of the room and uses blackboard and chalk as the main teaching support and method for recording information. The students sit in rows, mostly with their hands behind their backs, and listen to the teacher's lessons, taking notes to learn by heart. The frequently-noted passivity of student behaviour emerges from participants' accounts not as something that arises from an internal impulse but a learned behaviour that is externally introduced by the education system and the strong discipline that characterizes relationships in the classroom. Over time, students learn to adopt increasing levels of passive behaviour in response to their environment:

[The school] was not very big, it was a small one, just beside the road. Do you know, the big road at a T-junction? So it is not very big and it had a four-storey building and a little playground. At that time, it had about 700 students. There were about 45 students in a class: it is very big. The classroom is very crowded. We have maths and Chinese and no English. At that time in primary school, [there was] no English. Then [we had] Nature and PE and Drawing and Pictures and Music. We just, in the morning, we came to school and in the middle most of the students would go home to have lunch, but some of them had lunch in school in the canteen. In the fourth and fifth years, I had lunch at school. ... The teacher just taught and the students just listened. ... Teachers just taught: they crammed things into the students' brains. (R, p.3)

You have to sit in a fixed position and maybe every two weeks, you have to change your seat. Normally, you have no right to change seats, but if you tell the teacher that you really have problems, such as poor sight, then the teacher can allow you to change. (E, p.2)

In primary school we normally have one teacher, only one teacher who can teach both mathematics and other [things]. I remember the first three years, I really didn't like [the teacher] because she was very strict and she always shouted at us and because I was not good at mathematics. She thought I was stupid and no good. ... I think nobody liked her in my class. But after grade three, she had to go to another class and we got a new teacher and then I remember everybody cried; she also cried. ... We all just cried in class, very loudly and after that we had a good relationship. I think because we were so very young, we were very, very naughty and made her very angry. At that time, I didn't understand why, but now I think we were too naughty and she was strict because of it. ... She didn't allow us to be active. ... We had to sit just like this, with our hand behind our backs. (Z, p.2)

Students couldn't talk in the class, just listen. The teacher told you what was correct and you had to remember it. You had to write down what the teacher said, and then everything depended on your notes and remembering it. You didn't have the freedom to think of things outside what the teachers said. (H, p.2)

Every child has to sit there and put his hands behind his back. [We had to] be quiet and listen to the teachers, so you cannot break the law. If you do something, make a noise or something, the teacher will blame you and sometimes they will punish you [by] sending you out of the classroom. It was very strict discipline. ...Very strict, so nobody can do anything different, just listen. (AD, p.3-4)

> In my opinion, I think Chinese education is very conservative. In the class, it is always very, very quiet. And the lecturer always talks, and there is no feedback. ... Sometimes a teacher gave you the opportunity to write on the board and all work was individual. (S, p.3)

> It was just like [the] old times: the students sitting there and the teacher writing the contents on the blackboard and they tell you how to do the mathematics and something like this. It's ordinary, I think. (Y, p.1)

> The teachers were very strict. They punished student sometimes. If a student didn't study very well, [for example if] the teacher said, you had to recite this, but you didn't, then you were punished. You had to stand and listen to the teacher or stand in the corridor, or stand in front of the class, but this never happened to me. ... When a teacher asked a question, you had to put up your hand and then when the teacher said you could answer, you had to stand up to answer. After you finished answering, you sat down. And in elementary school, you had to sit with your hands behind your back and sit straight. All the time you had to sit like this. (AE, p.2)

One or two participants further expressed a consciousness of both the formality of schooling and the importance of receiving good education in setting a foundation for possible future success. For example:

> In the primary school, the teachers were just from nearby and the education is actually not very high. The way they taught was just in the traditional Chinese way…just like something we could see in a movie or film, just desks and they write something on the blackboard. It's quite traditional. And we can ask things, but actually we learned we must listen and watch what the teachers taught us, what they say, just like that. (M, p.3)

Classroom Innovation

One of the most striking factors to emerge from the accounts of elementary school is not only the formal discipline and structure of the classroom environment but also the uniformity of teaching practice and style as experienced by all participants across a range of ages and geographical distribution. In fact, only one participant talks about a teacher adopting a different style in the classroom, so it's worthwhile to include the description:

> That teacher, Qiao Laoshi, mainly responded to us and was the main teacher in the class. He gave us 10 or 15 minutes of teaching all things in

the class and then gave us lots of papers to practice. ... If you finish, you can go to play outside. I like this very much. You know all the students concentrate their minds and their attention for the first 20 minutes, but could they concentrate for the whole class? I don't believe it. [This teacher] taught us and if we had questions, we could put up our hands and ask. But the other teachers, they just taught, taught, taught the whole class for 45 minutes. They just talked; there's no communication. ... If you have questions, just leave them until after the class. (AB, p.3)

In terms of variety in classroom practice, then, it seems that innovation was not only unusual but was also approached in an ad hoc manner that potentially left students confused and disoriented, perhaps leading them to devalue the experiences contained within the change. This pattern, as we will discuss below, continued into middle and high school.

Workload, Assessment and Competition

The reported workload at elementary level is high, and the curriculum contained mainly basic subjects, mathematics, Chinese language, natural sciences and so on. Expectations of students from the beginning of their school careers appear proportionately high. Most students reported high levels of homework, with little in the way of social or extra-curricular activities. For example:

Because, you know, in the Chinese traditional teaching system, students are usually forced to listen and forced to sit and do something required by teachers. Students are required to do a lot of things. ... Even in the first year I went to school, I had a lot of work every night. (C, p.2)

The formal assessment regime that characterizes the Chinese education system appears in a number of reports, the vehicle of assessment being mid-term and end-of-term examinations:

[Assessment] was just by examination. For big examinations, there were totally two. One is the mid-term and the other is the final examination. And maybe, usually there were some small quizzes. (W, p.4)

Again, participants expressed acute retrospective awareness of the influence of assessments as a streaming mechanism in their schooling, quite explicitly, success at examinations:

Then the teachers in the school were very strict and the scores on the examinations were very important. We had to pass 60% to pass the examination. Otherwise, you failed. ... Actually, during the six years of elementary school, if you failed an examination, you had to stay another year to see if you could pass or not. (AE, p.2)

Social, Civic and Political Education

As discussed in Chapter 2 the Chinese government stresses the importance of moral and social education in addition to intellectual development as part of the educational curriculum. An important part of the social/political side of elementary school life reported by participants in this study is the Communist Youth association or Young Pioneers, mentioned by several of the participants. However, as emerges from one account, membership of this group provided not only a social outlet but could in itself become an influence over one's future educational career:

> We had the Young Pioneers party. [This was] the ceremony for new members of the Young Pioneers when they entered. Of course, everyone was a Young Pioneer. We must be a Young Pioneer. Otherwise, it will influence entry into middle school. If you were not a Young Pioneer, they won't accept you. In the case of me and another student, we got the same marks [in the middle school exam], but I was a Young Pioneer and she was not, [so] the school will accept me. (R, p.3)

Another participant also notes that entry to this association - as to the Chinese Communist Party (CCP) in adult life - was not voluntary but by a selection process, guided by peers and teachers:

> All the students were eager to join the Young Pioneers. The first batch who joined the Young Pioneers were very admired by the other students and the teacher also said some good things about the student. ... [You could join] based on your performance. The teacher would choose based on academic performance. It really depended on your scores. ... [A young pioneer was] to give a good image to the other students to perform well, to practice good behaviour. You were a model student. We also had the *sanhao xuesheng* - the three goods student. (AE, p.2-3)

One student mentions the important organizational role that student monitors and representatives play in school life and how these representatives are selected:

> There was one tutor to look after one class. And among the students, we had, how do you say it? Five students who take charge of, like the student council. Each of them looked after different things. I think the teacher appointed [them]. The teacher always helped the students appoint, always, how do you say? Made decisions for the students. (X, p.4)

These are both examples of the application of competition and selection in defining relationship structures as part of participants' educational experiences. Additionally, they highlight the importance of cultivating personal relationships and *guanxi* as a contributor to one's success, in addition to educational merit since selection either by peers or teachers determine entry to these elite groups.

Some participants, though, talked in more positive terms about sports activities and singing contests and mention the importance that schools gave to civic activities as part of building the educational profile. For example:

> In primary school, we didn't have social activities, but we did have to, how do you say it? *Shaomu*, sweep the graves of the heroes in the war and to plan some trips on March 1ˢᵗ, this kind of thing. It was organized by the school. It was kind of more formal, not just something we participated in out of interest. It was more formal. (Y, p.2)

> [We had] quite a lot of activities, like activities between the schools, a competition-like activity. For example singing songs and doing morning exercises. A group organized the students to do morning exercises, and then all the schools would come together to see which group of students had the best performance. (AE, p.2)

Getting to Middle School

The first significant hurdle in terms of formal assessment that study participants noted in their accounts was the middle school entrance examination. This examination, taken at the end of elementary school, provides the basis for student streaming and effectively determines the pathway that will be followed throughout students' educational futures. Students have the ability to select three to six schools in advance and successful placement into the chosen school is determined by performance in the exam. While *zhongdian*, key schools, have officially been phased out at the middle school level, they still unofficially exist and are known to all as the better schools to get into, so the pressure is on the students and the exam is of paramount importance. Universally, the participants recall the examination with dread:

> You had to attend a very strict examination and also this exam is like, let me see, how to say? The exam was very horrible! (S, p.4)

One student notes the significance that placement into a poor middle school is deemed to have:

> You have to pass the exam. At that time I was very nervous, because we only took Chinese and mathematics. And [in] mathematics, everybody can get 100%. Chinese is difficult for boys, because [they] are not so good at writing papers. What I got is only, the two test together, 191.5 out of 200. The 0.5 is very important at that time. If you do not get a 0.5, maybe you will be put into some high school [which] will ruin you. (L, p.3)

At Middle School

Continuing Education in the Neighbourhood

The vast majority of students (65%) placed into the local middle school - the result for average or poor exam performance. For example:

> [I went to] a poor school. The percentage of students that could pass to go to college was very low, so it was poor because of that. But they had a junior part and a senior part. I just went to the junior middle school there, so I did not worry about that, because after the examination then you can choose. [I went there] because it was nearby. I was 13 years old, so my family didn't want me to go far. (A, p.3)

Six participants attended good or key schools, where one boarded. Six others note that their parents were able to use their *guanxi* relationships, or their wealth or move their children into relatives' homes to place them into a better quality of middle school:

> My classes were different because everybody had a different background. Everybody came into the better school by paying the money. ... There was a special class in which everybody paid money. At that time, not every home had a telephone, but in our class more than half the families owned their own telephone. My teacher said "Your parents had provided a good situation for you" ... Our grade had the best of all the classes. (H, p.3)

For the majority, however, little choice of alternative school existed.

Education and Tedium

Accounts of the dynamics of middle school life are remarkably thin. The overwhelming impression that colours stories of participants' middle school careers is of its similarity with elementary school in environment, teaching and learning style, and curriculum content:

> It was almost the same [as elementary school]. You had to finish the plan every term, every semester. (A, p.4)

> I think it was the same, all the same. The teacher was very strict, very serious and with thick glasses. Always, always, [laughter] scolding us students and telling you what to wear and how to walk. Everything, everything we do, we have to listen to them. It's quite hard for us and, you know. Actually my teacher who is in charge of my class was the teacher who taught us maths. Actually my maths is quite poor, and I was quite afraid of the maths teacher. She was very strict, even though she was quite young. At that time, she was only 24, but she was quite strict. She was always near you, always like that [leans over], and so every night I cried because I still [lived with] my auntie and I had no one to tell my feelings [to]. (C, p.3)

Forty-eight percent of participants noted specifically that middle school was a profoundly "boring" experience for them. For example:

> You cannot sit [and be] happy, you just sit here and listen, listen, listen. … It's a very boring thing. And sometimes, they choose a subject [that's] very uninteresting. …They just tell you, "You should do it because if you want to go to the high school, you must take it and take the exam in it." No choice. (AB, p.2)

Several participants in the study also noted that they actively began to dislike school at this time, for some a reaction to the personal controls they experienced on their adolescent relationships:

> [In] middle school we still had the same classes and also the [exercise] class, the same. But at that age, young people are different; they are strange. The teachers want to control students more. At that time students make friends, girlfriends, boyfriends - before at primary school there were not these things. My high school and my middle school, they were together, but I gave up. I thought it was enough to stay there for middle school; I don't want to stay there any more. I thought it was boring. It was an old school. Everything is the colour grey. Everyday you face the same colour and the same teacher. There is nothing new, nothing

exciting. So I wanted to change. ... The teachers are strict. You see they just want to control you; they don't give you freedom and the teacher and the students are just like standing on opposite sides. You know the teachers want to control you and you have to understand and have to follow them in everything. (T, p.7)

The Key School Students

Those students (19%) who were able to attend a key middle school reported a different picture to the monotony outlined above, however. It is clear that quality middle schools possess better facilities and more qualified teachers than the mainstream institutions and that the divide is even more pronounced between rural or poor provinces and city schools.

One student notes an experience with classroom innovation, similar to the elementary school account. However, he goes on to note the difficulty of adapting to the more standard pattern of teaching and learning when the new style is abandoned:

> The most important thing [about middle school] is that the mathematics teacher was the principal of the school. Our class was the special test for a new teaching method. The teacher just taught you ten minutes of the class out of the forty minutes of the class and then the students had twenty minutes to study it themselves and if you had questions, you discussed with you neighbours. It was a new kind of teaching method. ... We had six classes in the grade and they chose our class to test [whether] this new teaching method was good or not. ... We could see that it was good. We liked this kind of teaching because it made us think more, use our brains more. But in the beginning, we were not so accustomed to this style. [They taught us that way] for about two semesters. [Then] the mathematics teacher who was the principal in charge of this program was moved to another [job], a government position, so the program was cancelled at our school. ... [When we went back to the old way], it was kind of boring. You felt that the teacher can't tell you anything, can't teach you anything because you can figure it out for yourself. The ten minutes the principal spent with us was just a kind of game. It made the class interesting, so students really liked to participate. (Y, p.3)

An Emergent Pattern of Conformity and Focus

These impressions of the middle school environment come together to show the pattern of an educational dynamic that continues to be disciplined and controlled, where the curriculum is prescriptively managed, with little focus on innovation in the curriculum and with positive disincentives to active student participation. Students, having learned the behavioural lessons from elementary school, begin to develop more focused academic skills in preparation for what lies ahead:

> Teachers in that school were very strict and there are a lot of rules which limited student behaviour. Students must obey the regulations of the school. ... I think this is a disadvantage of the Chinese school. This is not a good way to lead the students to think in their own way. So in school, I just followed what the teachers say. I do not think a lot about what are my own opinions. (X, p.4)

The aim of middle school is to channel students towards success in the high school entrance examination. Many participants openly discussed the intense pressure to perform well in the exam, which they felt from both the school and family. For one student, the pressure from family emerges in a very direct way:

> [My mother] always let me read books and then prepare for my examinations. She always required me to get high marks from my school. If sometimes, I failed, not fail, [did] not get good results, my mother would hit me. ... She is very strict with me. The only requirement from her is that I should get ranked in the top three in my class. (W, p.5)

Competition and Loneliness

In this environment, where the selection of middle school can determine the course of an individual's entire educational future, it is unsurprising that parents and teachers put students under so much pressure to perform well and to attempt entry into one of the better schools. The intensity of the competitive nature of the educational experience becomes noticeably pronounced during middle school. This results in 45% of participants stating that they had few or no friends during this period of their lives and this friendlessness continues and grows into their high school careers.

Some participants do note a limited enthusiasm for middle and high school, however, based on the introduction of subjects that they could enjoy, for example:

> At middle school I thought it was better because in middle school, we had physics, right? And maths and other courses. ... That field is very interesting, especially for physics. And also I met a very good [teacher] in physics, so I liked it very much. Normally I got my test on physics and maths, always more than 90 marks, so I liked it. (AD, p.4)

Another two participants noted that asking questions became easier in middle school, as the students aged and felt more confident in the learning environment, for example:

> In middle school, the teachers began to ask students questions. This was a very fresh experience for me when the teacher asked how I felt about something or if I had any questions. At first, I didn't ask, but later I got used to that. Yeah, but not much. Still most of the time, I think still 80% of the teachers in junior middle school still didn't ask the students questions. (A, p.4)

Only two accounts, however, contain any reflective enthusiasm for middle school as a whole experience. Interestingly, they are the same participants who show confidence in asking questions in class:

> To me at that time, the teachers looked more intelligent because they know more knowledge and taught me more than before. Most of the teachers were good quality because they all had special training in an institute. I learned more at junior high school. (A, p.4)

The rest of the accounts tell of a time of adolescent angst and an increasing awareness of the importance that educational performance at this time might have for the rest of their lives.

Getting to a High School: the middle school examination

Why Continue?

What follows on from what was for most the unremitting boredom of middle school represents perhaps the most important test for Chinese students during adolescence. Though compulsory education technically ends at the completion of middle school (typically at age 13 or 14), obtaining a place in a mainstream or good high school is the only way to have any chance to get into a university, and university education is the glittering prize within the state system. It is interesting to note, therefore, that none of the study participants considered not progressing from middle school to some kind of further education. In fact, all participants who attended high school noted that they had aimed to gain entry into a mainstream high school with the specific desire of going to university. This is also the goal of their parents and reflects both their class status and aspirations.

The Examination

The mechanics of the middle school examination are straightforward. Students have a choice of six to nine potential institutions from which they may choose. These are a mix of mainstream high schools of differing qualities, and a range of technical and professional schools. For high schools, quality is formally and informally rated by their student success rate in the university entrance exam. The opportunities for school selection vary enormously in number according to the residence of the student. Students in rural or outlying areas tell of limited numbers of high schools. For students in Beijing and other large cities, the numbers of schools to choose from are much greater.

As seems to be the case with all educational and life choices, participants report that student choices are strongly influenced by teachers and parents. In some cases, participants' choices were made entirely for them.

High School Choices

Which Choices?

Of the total population of participants in the study, the majority went to a mainstream high school (71%). Given that the study focuses on individuals who have taken part in tertiary education, this is unsurprising. However, a significant majority - 19% or six individuals - went to a professional, special or technical high school and one student participated in a sport training school, as a volleyball and water polo player on a provincial team. In addition, two participants were educated outside of China for their early education and entered into the Chinese system at high school level. This group, combining mixed ages and experience over many years within the high school education system, provides an illuminating cross sample of information as the basis of a discussion about the make-up of high school education in the PRC.

Stability of Educational Careers: neighbourhood schools continue

The majority of participants remained at the same high school which was local to their homes and had some connection with their middle school (14 people, 45%). Seven participants (23%) attended a "good" local or key school, two participants were boarders at a key school and two students from rural areas effectively had no choice as there was only one high school available in their local area. Though the number of participants who attended good schools increases slightly from the middle school level over the whole sample, the constitution of that group changes significantly between middle and high school. Of the six participants who attended key middle schools, none remained in the key school for the whole of their middle and high school careers.

The Character of the High School Experience

When discussing the experiences of the group during high school years, it is important to separate out the two systems: mainstream high school and professional and technical training schools. Inevitably, where the aim and intention of the two types of institution are completely different, participants' experiences also differ significantly. The aim of the high school, as begun in middle school, is exclusively to prepare students for the university entrance examination. Vocational schools however, present an active and practical preparation for work and have, therefore, a completely different style and curriculum emphasis. We will deal with vocational schools separately and then add some generic commentary about high school as a whole.

High Schools

Size and Character

Participants present their experiences of high school as identical to elementary and middle school in style and flavour. Schools remain large - an average of the accounts of total population are from 1,000-2,000 students at each institution, 40-50 students to a class, and the teaching approach and curriculum contains the same basic elements of earlier secondary education. There is an emphasis on mathematics and scientific and technical subjects within the Chinese curriculum, together with compulsory study in Chinese language and writing and one foreign language - at present most commonly English.

All participants reported an increasing level and intensity in the pressure associated with their studies, owing to the highly competitive nature of the final assessment and examination process. This is denoted initially by the need to make important choices about disciplines of study mid-way through the high school period. Of the three years of high school, students begin their studies following a general course of study for the first year. A number of participants report that students were streamed according to high school entrance examination results at point of entry. Others report an arbitrary breakdown of class groups during the first year.

Like and Wenke

In year two, the streaming into either *like* (sciences and mathematics) or *wenke* (humanities and languages) for preparation for the university entrance examinations, as discussed in Chapter 2, takes place. The breakdown for study in either discipline within the group is even - for total numbers, ages and genders - an interesting departure away from the dominance of *wenke* as a subject for women, noted in much of the literature. The participants do note, however, that the total number of *like* classes far exceeds *wenke* in each of their high schools by an average ratio of one to four. This clearly reflects the view of the dominance of sciences over arts within the Chinese education system.

How the Decision Gets Made

The decision making process about the discipline of study and those involved in the decision varies enormously between the participants. There are those who are passionate about the sciences or the arts:

> When I was in high school, I tried to study fine arts and applied for a fine arts education in the university. ... I studied hard for one year. (AA, p.1)

In addition, however, there are those who explicitly associate some kind of practical, personal or political risk with studying *wenke*:

> Another reason is that studying *like*, you have more chance to enter university. Because *wenke* is more difficult because of the score needed and people studying *wenke* are much greater than *like*. (R, p.5)

> The reason why I entered into the *like* class is that my father suggested me to enter into the *like* class. Because my father considered that the students graduate, graduated from the *like* subjects will have a promising future in the society. For example to get a good job. The most important thing he is concerned [about] is that *like* students, in the subjects of *like*, will not be involved in political things in China. You know my father experienced the Cultural Revolution, so he feared that kind of situation. He thinks that people involved in *wenke* subjects may be more affected by political situation[s], I think. (W, p.9)

For all, *like* is the simplest choice and for those who are unconcerned about the future direction of their education, it is *like* that they choose. For example, for one student from a wealthy family who had paid for her entry to a private high school class in a government school, the choice seemed simple:

> [I chose] *like*. I liked geography but this course was not included in *wenke* so I gave it up. (H, p.3)

No participant reports making the choice entirely independently and family involvement remains high. For several participants, the decision is made for the student rather than with them, as a result of family ambition or an assessment of economic necessity:

> It's really difficult. It's really difficult to make the decision because it's, it's for your whole life, so my father helped me to make the decision. I cannot decide it by myself. (F, p.4)

One participant reports changing his mind after his initial decision, which appears to be a difficult process:

> As a student in my high school, I did not have a good time. I always had a problem with the director of the class, the head teacher of the class, the *banjuren* … That had a history. First I chose *wenke* and then later I changed. I didn't feel good studying *wenke* and felt I should go back to *like*. But the school had already arranged me in that class, so they sent me to another class. And this teacher was *banjuren* and he was really serious about the rate of students going to college. He was afraid of his plan being interrupted. He wasn't happy with me because I had missed a lot of the *like* classes. (A, p.6)

The implication seems clear, once a choice is made, the student is stuck with it. Since teacher and student performance is determined by the progression to university after the entrance examination, time lost as a result of vacillation seems irreplaceable.

Key Schools vs. the Locals

Once again, it appears that what were once key schools still receive higher levels of funding, better teachers and so on - funding decisions seem based on the high school's rate of progression. One account, where a participant moved from a key middle school to a local high school nicely illustrates the point:

[Middle school] was much more active than the primary school since the students come from different places, some of them come from big cities just like Beijing or the capitals and also the teachers are from all over the place, cities. They are different, not [like] the primary school since in the primary school, all the teachers are just from nearby. We have the same kind of style in doing things. But in the junior high school, we are different. We are different with the talking, different personality and the school is actually quite big and we can see so many students can talk to each other [and there were] all the school activities, many activities. We have more subjects and more activities. We had music and can go to the laboratory. In the different laboratories we could look at models or samples - the body, the whole body, the real thing. And we could do electronics. We could go out to the farm and look at the plants we need and use a microscope. I used the microscope and somebody else took the blood of somebody else. We could do [all this]. ...[The local high school] was different from middle school since the, the middle school was a key school in China, they are quite important. I don't know. They hire the teachers from maybe a, quite a small area, much bigger than primary school but not like middle school. The middle school can hire teachers from all over the world, all over the country. ...[It was] not as active as the middle school since the city cannot provide the funds. They cannot set up big laboratories. [The facilities] were not as good as middle school. ... The teaching was quite similar since the academic level of the teachers could not be lower than university [graduate], even if it is lower than the middle high school. [But] one [school] was the government of China and the other is one small city. (M, p.5-6)

International vs. National Schools

Within the overall picture, however, two participants - sisters who moved into the Chinese high school system from elementary education in Taiwan and preliminary secondary education in the American system in the Philippines - portray a stark contrast between Chinese education in high schools and "western" classrooms. It is worth including their accounts as a whole.

First from the elder sister a detailed comparison of her experiences in all three systems:

Well, my primary school from first grade to the fourth, I started when I was six when I was in Taipei. I attended primary school from 1st to 4th grade and it was very much. Well, I think it is not totally the same as China. I don't really know what it is like in China, but I think in Taipei it is a little more a free style and the differences are that we had a lot of extracurricular activities in school. I remember we had this, you know the Chinese thing for counting, an abacus, yeah. That thing we learned and mainly lots of things with math, I remember, and some things you calculated with your mind and there was something like a quiz bee every week. The student who gets the fastest answer or the most correct one, gets a prize or something like that. And also we had chess, sports, and lots of PE classes, everyday. Yeah, everyday in class, we took 30 minutes and everyone would stand in the gym and practice *wushu*, martial arts. Yeah, we were just little kids. There were 40-50 [students in a class]. It was a big class...Back then I was really scared of the teacher. I think most of the kids were because back then they used physical punishments, but now it is not allowed anymore. But when I was still in primary school it was allowed, and I would usually get slapped on my hands for not doing my homework or if I couldn't remember the multiplication tables, so I was pretty much terrorized by most of the teachers. Hmm...and one thing different in Taipei especially primary schools, you get ...how do you say that...counselling, yeah. In primary school, you can just go into the clinic and talk to the teacher or the nurse who is there and you say whatever your problem is at home, or at school or with other kids, stuff like that. Usually, it was very popular. Everyone goes there....

I went to the Philippines when I was ten or something, I don't remember exactly, but it was in 1989. I went to the Philippines and I started school there. I started from the first grade. The school's name is the Holy Cross High School, so it was a Catholic school. It was different and at first I was very much embarrassed because I didn't speak English at all, so people were feeling sorry for this student, I know that. I started from grade one and it was a big burden for me because I was much, much bigger than most of the kids, so I found the normal classes in school and I also had tutorials after school - during that time it was all study and no play. My family was like, yeah, you have to keep up because you are not supposed to study in grade one all the time. And you know how kids like to play, and I had to study so it was kind of hard. But then after six months or eight months I jumped to grade three. And then I studied some more, the usual tutorials every day and on the weekends, and I don't remember exactly when but I think it was in 1991 or late 90, I took a government placement test and I tested, and I actually was promoted to the first year of high school from grade three. I think I was already 13 when I took the placement test, I think. On average I was one year older than most of my classmates when I joined high school. When I joined first year, I should have been in the second year of high school. ...

Actually, the education system in the Philippines is different. They don't have junior school, but after you graduate from primary school which has six grades, you go to high school which is four years. Then after four years of high school, you graduate and take the national exam and then you are accepted to college, at 16. It was much better in my opinion compared to my primary school experiences in Taipei. It was much more relaxed and then we were all given lots of creative projects like for drama. And we wrote up plays, especially in my English class, every week we had a play, not in the class but on the stage in the school. And there were lots of really interesting activities, like dancing and …lots of stuff. I remember I was really interested in the student government in my school and I had started attending the meetings since I was in grade three. Basically, because my classmates thought oh, yeah, you are the oldest so you go. So when I started high school I got involved in the student government very heavily. In my second year, we had an election and I got elected and I was the vice president. That is the most memorable thing from my high school life. It was lots of stuff. We organized a beauty pageant for the population on the school's founding day. And everything from the coordination of the candidates to the selection of sponsors to the actually print out of the programs, we even made the sashes ourselves. Everything was really interesting. …

I had to leave in the middle of the third year. The very basic reason was that I had a lot of conflict with my cousins. Back then I was a very naughty child and you know, what do you call that? I was a very rebellious adolescent. Basically, my family in the Philippines is very conservative because it is a Chinese community, so I quarrelled a lot with my cousins and I told my father I didn't want to stay there anymore. I wanted to move somewhere else. And I think that it is time for a change because basically where we lived was a small place, a really small place. Then my father also, actually, that was the only the reason I had to get out of there, but my father would not think it was good. Now I realize that the situation back there was good for me, but then I didn't think it was nice. The other thing my father wanted was for us to pick up our Chinese again because when he came to visit, we would tell him come on speak in English because it is hard to speak in Chinese. Between me and my sister and my cousin, we had begun to speak in Filipino dialect and my father didn't like that too much because we are Chinese and he felt we should be able to speak the language. So after talking with me and the family, my father said okay now I work in China and you guys can come and study here. They have pretty good schools and everything. When the decision was first made I was very happy, like yes, yes, I'm finally getting out of here. But after you know we left in the end of August and I remember the last Founders Day that I joined in at my school, I was like, no, I don't want to leave. It was in July and it was so much fun, and I was so happy, and so I said no, I don't want to go to my father, now I want to stay, but in the end I came to China in 1994, to Beijing.

I started in what would be first year of senior high school, and that was exactly my age level. The first day of class I really hated it because I couldn't understand what my classmates were saying and I couldn't understand what the teacher was saying. It was difficult to move from a place where you are popular and everybody knows you and you know everybody to some place that you don't know anybody and don't know how to communicate with them. The lessons were totally different. It was really difficult at first and my classmates reactions didn't help at all. They were kind of like, oh, she is a Taiwanese girl so she must be like all those rich people who don't want to talk. In the first few days it seems like that because they called me by my Chinese name, but I didn't have any reaction because no one calls me by my Chinese name. When they called me by my Chinese name, I didn't realize it was me, so they are like, oh, yeah, she is snobbish and doesn't want to talk to us.

With the teaching, I didn't like it because I was used to a you know, what we had in the Philippines: it was very lively, very relaxed and you could joke with the teacher, and could join the discussion. And if you thought the teacher was wrong, you could tell them and things like this. But then in the school I went to, by the time the teacher came into the class everyone was quiet and the teacher was saying like da, da, da, da, da, and the students would just sit there and you could not talk, you could not move, you could not even go out to the toilet. You would just sit there. Because you had a break for ten minutes between classes and after that ten minutes was over, you couldn't go out of the classroom. And it was very difficult. I couldn't understand what my teachers were saying. The only class I liked was English. (laughs) The difference was that in the Philippines we had a...well, what they were studying in high school here was much more difficult than what we were studying in the Philippines. They went much, much further in all the programs. Oh, [I had a] lot of problems with that. First of all it was the language, like when you study Chemistry there are the terms, like whatever, and I couldn't understand what it was. I also had tutorials at first in Chinese, the language, and also in Math, Chemistry and Physics. My father arranged it for us because he thought it was necessary. But the tutorials were not helpful, not helpful at all. Because the teachers I had as my tutors taught pretty much the same way as the teachers I had in class. I told her that my level was not up to learning that because I didn't have the basics, but they didn't seem to get it. They just started explaining to me about probability when I hadn't even finished my algebra, so how could I understand it? So I started losing interest. I think it took about a year for me to start to like the school a little bit, in *gaoer* [the second year of high school]. By then I had blended into the class a little bit. There were some girls who liked to talk with me and ask me about things and we were kind of becoming friends. Then when I had questions in class I would ask them, so it was...in my second year in China, I started to like it. ...

I was supposed to go [to another province] to study with [my sister], but then I went for a week and said, no I want to go back to Beijing. Then I talked to my dad and had some discussions, some arguments, whatever, and in the end I came back to Beijing and continued in my old school while my sister stayed in that southern city. ... It was a lot worse [there] than the school in Beijing. The atmosphere was a lot more serious than what it was in Beijing, and the students they didn't have this thing about socializing. I mean maybe for other people it doesn't matter, but for me, you know, I talk a lot and I don't like to study all the time, so it was so difficult for me to adjust. And what really bothered me was that the teachers used a dialect in teaching in the classroom. I talked with the principal and other people and told them I didn't speak the dialect, and I knew they could all speak Mandarin, so I asked if they could speak Mandarin. But in the end it didn't make any difference. It was difficult. ...

My father wanted me to go to [university in Beijing] that is basically why I took the [university entrance] test. I was thinking to myself that after going to three years of high school in China that I really didn't want to continue to study in the Chinese education, the style, because I don't like it. It is too serious and it is so dead. I don't like that kind of ...especially in history class. There were some things that I didn't agree with what the teacher said, but I could not say anything because that is what was written in the book. No, I never tried [to disagree] because the thing is that I often had arguments with my classmates after class about things like China and other things, but they often told me that what is written in the book is the right idea because it has been proven and is written by someone with a background, so there is no way you can defy what they said. I think it is just my personal perception that if the students think in that way then they must have taken it from the teacher. So I didn't want to make it any worse than it was. (B, p.5-7)

From the younger sister, a shorter but passionate account of missing the final part of high school study in the Chinese system because of her reaction to it:

The school was a *zhongdian zhongxue*, a key school of the province. I went there for *gaoyi*, *gaoer* and a half year of *gaosan*. My father was doing business there and so I lived with him. ... I didn't join the college entrance exam, that it why I skipped the second half of the *gaosan* school year. It is mainly for revision only, so since I had my grades from taking my graduation exam, and had finished my classes, I came to [Harmony College] in 1998. ... I had spent four years in a Chinese school and I don't think I like learning in the Chinese educational system. I don't think it suits me. I wanted to have something westernized, or something different. ... I thought it was better if I changed the environment of my study...One thing is like, we were spoon-fed information from the books, from the teacher and like. Well, I'm not going to say it's bad, but all those basic things which are good, but it is something I really don't enjoy doing, just getting information from other people instead of getting it by myself. Because the teachers and the students are too serious for me. They only concentrate on one area instead of many things. I don't enjoy this way of teaching and learning. ... In the Philippines, we had two ways of teaching, one Chinese and one English and I am quite used to this way of Chinese teaching. Because I feel very pressured and locked in, so it holds me

> down. I think I can get more if I have some other kind of environment.
> (N, p.3-4)

The stories told by these two women, which they develop further based on their experiences in Harmony College, set the stage for a key discussion of the responses that the majority of the group gave in their accounts of tertiary study within a "western" educational environment. In considering the high school experiences of the whole group, they also provide a vivid illustration of the intensely competitive and disciplined nature of the exam-driven teaching and learning environment that characterizes Chinese high schools.

Loneliness: the price of competition

Concerns about the nature of competition and loneliness that began to emerge from accounts of middle school life and are clear as part of the accounts of the enculturation of the two "overseas" sisters are perhaps the major concern for students in reflecting on their high school careers. Fifty percent of participants who attended a mainstream high school noted the competitiveness and 13% commented that they had no friends at all in high school. For example, for this participant who moved to a good provincial high school:

> The classmates were not friendly. They just studied. You know they are from the countryside. Most are from the countryside. They just studied. They didn't want to make friends or help you; I wanted that, so I don't have any friends. ... (F, p.8)

Though this impression is balanced somewhat by one or two accounts talking positively about the increased level of organized social activities during the first year in high school, the overall impression of the three years of high school is that they are characterized by unremitting, lonely cramming for examinations with the remote hope of obtaining a place at university as the only sustenance:

> At that time I felt the competition in the class. For example, the good students who knew the result of the questions didn't want to tell you. ...They didn't share information, they didn't share books - everyone wanted to be best. The competition was tough. (H, p.3)

> In high school we had a lot of work to do because the university entrance exam is so important. If we cannot pass it, then we cannot go to university and it will influence your whole life maybe. So in high school

things are so simple. You just do a lot of problems, a lot of homework and memorize the information. This is the way we spent our lives, even on the weekend we have to go to school and study. And I think the teachers work so hard; they help us a lot. They don't even have time to cook for their families at home. They have group responsibilities and the school will establish their performance by results. (J, p.3)

For me, I didn't have too much happiness in that period of time because the studying, the duty of studying, was very pressured for me. And I think for most of the students it was the same because they have an objective. They must enter university, so they have to study hard. It was a burden. (R, p.5)

One student talked in detail about the public ways in which the unrelentingly competitive conditions of the high school environment were played out and her emotional reaction to it:

[High school] was just the same [as middle school]. The only thing I want to focus on is the competition to enter to university, to get high marks or good results in our entrance examination for university. [It became] even fiercer. Every week, the teacher will give us a quiz to assess us. I hate this situation very much. My teachers, each week will list our marks according to our results. Every time she or he posted the results in our classroom. I hated it very much. Sometimes when, I get high marks, I'll be happy. My name ranks [at] the top of the poster. But sometimes, when I failed, maybe when I get bad results, my name ranks at the bottom of the list, so I think it's very ... I lose face at that time. I hated it very much. I hate, I hate this kind of way. And every time, the thing I cannot agree with the teacher [about] most is that she or he will arrange our seats by our marks. For example, when I get bad results my seat is arranged at the back of the classroom. At that time I felt the stresses both from the family and the society, psychological stress. [I felt] pressured, yes, very pressured. (W, p.7-8)

Ways of Coping with the Pressure: opting out

In these circumstances, it is not surprising that the accounts are scattered with an increasing number of comments about truancy and demotivation at this time. This example, from a participant who moved to another district for her high school education, where the classroom teaching took place in a different dialect, clearly demonstrates the emotional pressure she felt from her family in spite of a waning interest in continuing with her education:

My high school was in another province [so] I was a little uncomfortable because I couldn't speak the dialect. During those years there were not many outsiders, it was 1986, and there weren't many students from other places, so I was quite alone. I had also lost interest in studying. I wanted to find a job right away. ... My mother was still teaching in a primary school, a government school. And we lived in a small apartment with two bedrooms, but shared a kitchen with two other families. Anyway, it was my mother, sister, brother and I. My mother didn't want me to quit school.   She said I had at least to finish high school; she would not change her mind. At that time, in high school we had to be separated into art or mathematics in high school. Since I was quite interested in biology, I felt mathematics was OK. I was in *like* ban. You see the math and the algebra were very difficult if you were not concentrating. If you missed some lessons, then you failed. You would find it very difficult to catch up. ... Usually it was individual study both at home and in the class. In my second year, my mathematics grade was very low, below the average. My mother was so angry with me. She said that if I dare study in this way, her heart would break because she had supported me. She really pressured me. I said okay and tried to struggle with my studies. I tried hard to manage the examination, so my grade was still above average - it was all examinations. We had homework exercise, but they were easy and the exams were difficult. The exams were what you had to concentrate on. Then in the last year, I told my mother I was not going to college. Because my situation was not so good, I didn't want to go to college. She said okay but that I should at least attend the high school graduation examination. ... At that time my grades were not so good, so I couldn't get to the top colleges, maybe enter some provincial universities but not the top ones. So I just attended the graduation examination. I didn't even enter the college entrance examination. ... I was feeling very pressured and didn't enjoy my studies. I learned some of the language and made friends but I was not really okay towards others. I didn't make many friends in class. My best friend was my younger brother, also not my mother. I couldn't tell her what I felt. At that time, my mother thought I was quite naughty. She couldn't understand me. (K, p.5-6)

Unsurprisingly given the few places available and the intensely prescriptive nature of the university entrance examination, none of the truants tell of a successful outcome in the examination at the end of their high school careers.

Vocational Schools

Compared to High Schools

The picture painted by those who attended vocational education institutions at high school level could not provide a more stark contrast with the high school stories. Those who effectively "failed" within the mainstream education system, left the highly disciplined and structured world of formal intellectual education and embarked on skills-based training for their future careers. Of the six who attended vocational schools, all except one noted their sense of relief at the differences they encountered and their enjoyment in learning their new subjects:

> I went to a specialized professional school. It was for four years. ... Like my Dad, I studied fermenting technology, for making yeast for bread and that kind of thing. I had six choices to go to high school; it was my last choice. So I have to go there. No choice. ... Because of my major, I had to do a lot of experiments in the lab, so almost half the time I spent in the classroom and the other half in the lab. ... I thought [my study] was quite interesting because it was not just simple knowledge you could get from a classroom, but also you could combine your knowledge with practice; it was quite interesting. The teachers were kind and helpful for us. Also the class in our profession was quite big, our college was quite big. They had one library building, one laboratory building and two teaching buildings. (C, p.3)

For the majority, this enjoyment is in spite of family disappointment and pressure as a result of their lack of achievement of a high school place:

> Every parent wants their children to go to university. Actually, my parents were disappointed with me because my results were lower and I could not go to college. But when I went to this specialized professional school, my study was not so bad, so they became happier. (C, p.4)

The participants noted a higher level of social activities and a strong sense of emerging into adulthood in a responsible learning environment that encourages higher levels of independence and self-managed learning:

> It's quite different from middle school and the teachers treated us like an adult and they didn't force us to do this or do that. I think it's quite different. I felt that we could have our own right to control our daily life. ... I was able to study actively, not passively. Teachers do not force you to study; instead they encourage you and support you. They encouraged us to do some other activities instead of just studying at home and in the classroom. (C, p.3-4)

This presents a strong contrast to the highly governed and prescriptive approach, which characterizes high schools.

By the time the vocational study is completed, however, the enjoyment in the novelty and variety of the curriculum is replaced for all participants with a sense of resignation and acceptance of the future of work as a technician, ungifted with the benefit of a university degree:

> I think I chose the wrong school. I went to a school, which I didn't like. ... Sometimes I think it was interesting but it was very hard. ... It was not my first choice; it was my fifth choice. ... When we make a choice, it's very important for us and so parents always make the choice for us. I want[ed] to go to another school but [my parents] said, "you shouldn't. You have to choose this one because it's better for your future career", and I couldn't persuade them, so I chose that one. The first choice was a high school because, you know, everybody in China wants to go to university. It's the very best way to get a good education. If you can go to senior high school, you can go to university. ... (Z, p.6)

For all participants who attended a vocational school, it is possible to identify an active sense of frustration owing to a strong perception that the lack of a degree places a tangible ceiling on an individual's ability to progress within the world of work. The majority of vocational students, therefore, either elected to go immediately to Harmony College to continue with their educational dreams in the private sector or did so within three or four years of completing their vocational studies:

> [I went to Harmony] because of the fierce competition in China. You need higher education otherwise I probably could not get a good job. And my parents hope for me to have a bright future. ... I had never been to college and my parents wanted me to have this kind of experience. (C, p.5)

The Sport School

One participant's experience of high school education stands out as distinct from the rest in either the high school or vocational sector. A gifted sportsman, from an influential family, he attended a provincial sports school and competed in a number of events. His story tells of the structure and organization of a very special kind of vocational training:

> When I was young, I studied in a school founded by my grandfather's father. He did business in Indonesia, so he was an overseas Chinese. When he was an old man, he and other people working in Indonesia collected some money and invested in opening a school: a primary school, a middle school. When I was young I studied in this school. At about 15 years old, my father sent me to a sports school and I trained in water polo. ... [At this school I studied] just sport. Because this is a provincial team's school, and the money was not enough for us to train, so the government

gave money to this school to train us. I studied there for about three years. Then our water polo team was broken up because the money was not enough. They needed to put more money into it. Then I entered middle school but I trained in another sport - volleyball. I hoped to go to another sports college, but my grandfather and parents decided that maybe it was not good for me because if I kept studying in this way maybe I would just become a coach and it would not be so good for me. ... In a high school, the teachers teach and the students don't speak. You cannot do anything, only answer the question if the teacher asks. ... At sports school there were no lessons, only training. If you want to win the game, you must work together to reach the goal. When I trained it was very hard. If you do not do things the way the coach expects, then they use a big stick to hit your hand and sometimes you need to stay under water to help your breathing, so sometimes he uses the stick to push you under the water and keep you there. It was very hard. ... In sports school it was hard on your physical body. (I, p.4)

After leaving the training school with effectively no academic qualifications, he ventured to Harmony College to study English, and thence to proceed via the access programme to degree study. No other option, apart from relatively unskilled work, would have been available to him in the domestic environment.

Higher Education

Diverse Options after Secondary Schooling

Participants' destinations after completing high school or vocational school education are very diverse (see Table 4.1 for a detailed breakdown) and reflect both the wide range of opportunities that exist outside of university entrance, discussed in Chapter 2, and the range of ages and situations of the participants. This spread provides us with limited opportunities to discuss the detail of higher levels of education in China. However, there are a few insights that can derive from the participants' stories.

**Table 4.1:   Participants' Destinations after High School or
Equivalent Education**

	Male	Female	Total
State University	1	2	3
Normal College	--	2	2
Private College*	--	1	1
Self-pay Diploma	--	1	1
Technical Diploma	2	2	4
Harmony College	5	5	10
Work	5	5	10
			31
Offered a place in State HE but chose Harmony College	3	2	5

*excluding Harmony College

Going to Work

Of the total population, 32% of participants left school and went on to work for a period of time before entering Harmony College as students. Unsurprisingly, these participants tended to be among the more mature students at Harmony and the majority lacked the personal funds to pay the College's fees until they had worked for some time. We will discuss their experiences in work in more detail in Chapter 7.

University Education

As a result of the fierce competition and very limited number of places available, only three participants took part in university education in the state system. One, among the oldest participants in the study, pursued a degree in Russian language, reflecting the political trends of the time during which she was an undergraduate; one studied Meteorology and one Economics (she went directly from a State university on graduation to Harmony College). Their experiences reflect a broadly similar educational experience to that of middle and high school. However, they report an easing of the competitive strains and stresses:

> In university, nobody, no teacher, is directly in charge of the class and the class is so big for one class. So when you got there, the teacher may tick your name or not. Sometimes students don't go to class because they think it is boring and are not interested in it. … [It is] not, pressured. You just want to pass your exam. But some courses are really difficult, like statistics and economics, so if you want to pass, you have to attend that class. But other subjects such as philosophy and Chinese and such, we have just a few students attending in a very large classroom. (J, p.3)

The implication here seems to be that the competition directed at obtaining a university place is regarded as so intense that getting a place is in itself enough and performance at university becomes less important, unless perhaps an undergraduate wishes to pursue an academic career. This is unsurprising, given the lack of a degree classification within the state educational awards and the historic practice of centralized job allocation within the government system, which until recently removed some of the importance of performance scores as an influence on job destination after graduation.

Professional and Vocational Training

The majority of participants who went on to some kind of post-high-school education (73%), attended professional or technical colleges in order to study a two to four-year professional diploma, including teaching diplomas. In addition, a number of participants (four) went on to study English language and associated subjects, which led them on to the advanced English language training programme at Harmony College, and most participated in some kind of English language training during their ongoing studies.

Two participants elected to move out of the state system altogether at this stage. One went to a self-pay diploma class within the university where her parents worked as academics and within which she received her education from elementary upwards. The other, from Inner Mongolia, an area not privileged in terms of state education provision, chose to move to the provincial capital to embark on studies within a domestically organized private college. Her reasoning for this choice presents an interesting reflection on her experiences within secondary education and an eagerness to join in the developing climate of change in China:

> I went to a private college in Hohhot, the capital of Inner Mongolia ... So at that time, I learned something. Because the college as a private one, we spent more money than other students, but the college invited the best teachers from other colleges or found some very experienced ones. ... [The college] was set up by a private man and my major was... [He was] just a person from Hohhot, a local person who set up a university. You know he did a good job. I enjoyed that two years. ... You now, I really wanted to go to a private university. I wanted to know what kind of system it is because I really didn't enjoy the formal system. I mean China's formal education system. ...[In the formal system] I think what I learned is not useful. It's just not useful. Like my major is science and all the students got the impression, you know, after you learned it, you just learned it for the examination. The major incentive was just to go to university, a good university or maybe a bad one. That way it looks like you are well-educat[ed] and you will maybe have the opportunity to go outside of town because the town is not very developed. They all like to go out and have a look, to work, to go to some other provinces, just have a better living standard in the future. That is the main incentive for almost all the students and their parents. Their parents always have a high expectation of their children. ... I wanted to know about the new system. At that time, I just think [that] I depended on myself whether I learned or not. I don't know. I just had the impulse to go out and have a try. (Q, p.4)

In spite of her initial enthusiasm, she goes on to discuss her difficulties with the new approach to teaching and learning she and other students encountered:

> In that college, the teaching style was totally different. ... The teachers taught us in English, not in Chinese, so at first you find it so difficult but later on you like it. Most of the [teachers] had been abroad before, so they could speak good English and were quite experienced. ... Most of the students were from the local schools or the nearby province, so their way of thinking was still not very active. Even in the class just out of 20 students in one class, only two or three, or maybe five students were very active [in responding] to the teaching style. Some of them couldn't accept it. They complained a lot. They said the teachers didn't teach them well. They would just complain. ... At that time, for the private college, the local education bureau provided the standard teaching textbook for all the teachers and for all the students. But at our college, we just used that book for two months. We finished it, because it was totally rubbish. And then we used the book that the teachers selected for us. They thought it

> was quite useful. ... They always asked questions. I mean the teachers. If you don't understand, you could ask them immediately. It was quite interactive. Sometimes, they even walked around and suddenly we had special teaching, and we talked to each other directly. (Q, p.4)

This participant's early experiences gives a small insight into the flexibility that the emerging private sector is afforded compared to the strictures of the state system and foreshadows the experiences of many of the participants at Harmony College which we will develop in following chapters.

Harmony College

Thirty-two percent of participants proceeded from secondary education directly to Harmony College, mainly because of a lack of success in the university entrance examination. All of them reported an eagerness to move out of the state education system and to participate in the new opportunities available in private higher education. An additional 16% of participants proceeded directly to Harmony College after completion of either further or higher studies in the state system. What seems clear is that the majority of participants elected to go to Harmony College as a second choice to entry to a conventional university but in preference to study at a state vocational college. This reflects the frequently reported lack of attractiveness of vocational education as a whole in China and the surge of interest in business and related subjects as opposed to more conventional vocational choices since reform. Developing this trend, a further 16% of participants were successful in gaining a place at a state higher education institution but elected to go to Harmony instead. This group consists of the two sisters who came as later entrants to the state system of China and who chose to return to an educational style which they felt would be similar to that in which they participated during their early school years. In addition, one participant embarked upon vocational training within the state system and elected to make a switch halfway through a course in machine building in order to go to Harmony. For this group, it seems, the opportunity to study within the international sector represented enhanced opportunities over state colleges in enabling participation in China's economic development. For example:

> I was enrolled in the Beijing Language Institute, Yuyan Xueyuan, to major in German. But when I stayed [with] my friend for one and a half months and travelled in Beijing, I saw an advertisement from the newspaper about this Harmony College. I found it very interesting since my father told me long ago that a man should not major in a language but should major in business. (V, p.2)

The Social Context of Higher Education

Overall, then, from the scattered information contained in the accounts, higher education presents a broadly similar set of experiences as that of the mainstream primary and secondary education systems in China.   The participants seem to represent a fairly "typical" group of citizens in China during the past twenty years. Universally, they aspire after the attainment of a university place in order to gain social status and the possibility of better job and living standards. For many, higher education is also the passport for geographical mobility, which they feel is unattainable for many in the country. Certainly, whatever their family roots, their continuation within the education system makes them become more urban over time, owing to the concentration of colleges and universities in cities. As reported in Chapter 2, education in China seems to be a firmly urban phenomenon. Lacking the opportunities to succeed in the competition for university, the participants are confronted with a series of other choices, most of which they and their families feel to be less socially valuable than a university place. It is this sense of social limitation and the educational vacuum that it draws from, therefore, that has created the demand for private international colleges like Harmony. As we will go on to discuss, the concern with the social access that education can achieve rather than its inherent functional aspects is perhaps one of the most influential factors in assessing the inter-cultural provision of private education in the contemporary Chinese environment.

5 Interpreting Themes from the Stories about Education

Introduction

The stories that we have brought out in the preceding chapter present a rich picture of the kinds of experiences that a range of people in contemporary China have gone through as part of their educational development. Inevitably, each of us will read and reflect on their stories, bringing our own perspective to what they have to say. Clearly the accounts of only 30-odd people from a country as large and diverse as China cannot be considered representative of a whole generation's experience of education. That was not the intention of the study, which was more about developing something much smaller and more intimate. However, there are some ways in which the impressions woven by the insights we have into each of the participants' lives can act as case studies for wider sets of experience and from which we can tease out some themes and issues. It is in this broadly interpretive frame that we have drawn our understanding and made the analysis included in this and following chapters.

The Character of the Educational Experience

The overall picture that emerges from participants is that education is not something that is meant to be enjoyed and social activities are neither a necessary nor desirable part of the educational experience. Many participants report acute feelings of loneliness and isolation; some note a complete absence of friends during their childhood. None of the participants in reflecting on this side of their educational lives, however, consider their lonely emotions to be unusual, but consider them more a routine part of growing up and going to school. Participants report working very hard and expecting to do so, as their teachers and families expect of them. Several participants, however, also note how these expectations can lead to feelings of intimidation in their school environment. This is vividly captured by one person's story of her first day in school:

> I still remember the first day I went to school. I was very nervous and I remember the classroom was very quiet, nobody was saying anything. You could just hear the teacher's voice. I think she asked me to do some work. ... Everybody kept silent and did some work. Suddenly I wanted to go to the toilet. I didn't know how to do it. I just looked at her and she was just doing something else. I didn't know whether to shout, call her or put my hand up, so I put my hand up but she doesn't attend to it. So I just walked up next to her and said, "Can I go to the toilet?" and she said, "Why didn't you put your hand up before you walked up? Who told you you can walk next to me?" very strictly. Anyway, she allowed me to go to the toilet. ... So I think that primary school, I don't know, they just want to control students. They used discipline. [If] they asked, "Don't move; don't talk," [You] just did what they asked you, just followed them. Sometimes you felt very excited and sometimes very nervous, especially when the teacher asks you a question. But just in the class, it is different. When I study, I feel it is boring. (T, p.3)

Mobility

In considering the mobility of the group, the picture is one of remarkable stability. Only 35% of the total number of students report moving schools or homes at all in their childhood or adolescence. Of these, the majority (63%) moved only once with the remainder moving three or four times. Only one student reports a pattern of continuous migration - moving an astonishing ten times during her educational career - and that is the result of belonging to a military family where migration once every year or two to another posting was the norm.

This pattern of residential stability and homogeneity reflects the social systems of the Chinese environment where for many, especially older participants, relocation was not an option for citizens but determined and managed by the government via the *hukou* or residency permit system. It also seems to reflect a typical educational experience for average students in China throughout the 20th century. Ties to locality, to family and community are strong - especially in the absence of other kinds of friendship - and the educational, political and social systems have always reflected that. A number of participants at various times note that the schools they attended are those which formally belong to their parent's place of work. The old state system in China guaranteed not only job and home to the workers but also education and support for their entire families.

The purpose of the state-owned factories was that they became self-perpetuating communities and were able to supply their own future labour needs as well as developing their current stock of skills. It is only in the recent post-reform era that any kind of personal or educational mobility has been a reality for the majority of Chinese citizens. It is interesting to note that all of those who report a family relocation identify the cause as an economic one, where a parent changed their job, received promotion or chose to leave the state sector for self employment. Such a move typically involves being separated from the connections to extended family within the childhood community. As a result, with the exception of the lone military migrant, the participants who have moved during childhood are predominantly from the younger groups of the age ranges of the total population - when migration became possible for a larger number of people in China. Therefore, of the total group, 84% begin their education at the most local school in their original hometown and this figure drops only to 65% at the end of secondary education.

A National Curriculum

An interesting factor in considering the classroom dynamics outlined in all of the accounts is the remarkable uniformity of teaching method and behaviour, especially when one considers that teaching methods are not included as a significant part of teacher training programmes, and that many other policy and institutional factors are subject to wide variation across the study population and the country. Not only is the curriculum centrally organized and uniform in its content, it seems, but the style of delivery is uniform as well, as each generation of teachers emulate the kinds of practices which they themselves experienced as students in their own educational careers. This theme strongly resonates with the concerns expressed by Li Peng at the National Education Conference in 1994 and in numerous State Education Commission reports. The government is attempting to address the issue of reform in teaching practice to some degree but the retrospective accounts of the study participants clearly show the extent of obstacles that remain to be overcome if these attempts are to be successful.

Discipline

What emerges quite clearly from the stories is an environment where teachers demand high levels of concentration and conformity from the student body and where a variety of disciplines and humiliating pitfalls could open up to the incautious, overly curious or non-conforming student, though none of the students mention any form of corporal punishment as a practice in the classroom. The emphasis seems to be punishment in the form of shaming students in front of peers or families. In some cases, this has left a lasting impression:

> Actually, I was a smart kid when I was in primary school. I would actually just listen to what the teacher said and if there was something you should do, a question that the teacher gave, you would just do it. ... I should tell you more. When I was in primary school one of the most impressive things that I remember was once when we took a test. The teacher just wrote the question on the board - we didn't have handouts at that time. The teacher then just told us what to write just like this. The style was set. But I didn't follow it. Actually, I should have got full marks, but the teacher just gave me zero, and she told me I was one of the students [like] she had never seen before. "You are made of special material." It really made me think. Oh, it hurt me actually. You had to write [the answer] in a special style, but I wrote it just like this. Actually the answer was right. Sometimes [school] was like this. I had nothing to say because she was a teacher and it really hurt me because she said this in front of all my classmates - that I was made of a special material, that I was the monkey's tail - *houzi weiba choudatian*. It's kind of insulting words. It really made an impression on me and even now I remember this. (Y, p.1)

Direct challenges to or criticism of the teacher appear to be particularly difficult:

> I remember one teacher, when we were studying ancient poetry. We had some problems and one student said, "Oh, teacher, you are wrong," ... But the teacher was very angry with this student, "No, I'm teaching YOU, you are a student!" You know that feeling is very bad. (AB, p.3)

In retrospect, the participants do express fairly strong views about the intense nature of classroom discipline. This they present as an active contrast to their later experiences, especially in view of their higher education experience in a "western" college environment. It's difficult to be clear about why this happens. Commentators have noted the relative formality and discipline which exists in the Chinese education system, even from an early age, and the expectations of self-discipline and submissive behaviour in Chinese society. The process of childhood nostalgia at work could also influence these reflections, however. Possibly the study participants hearken back to the tough but unambiguous times of childhood, where, from an adult perspective, life was clearer and more structured.

Teachers and Mentors

The stories include a number of accounts of teachers who have been influential both in positive and negative ways, some of which are included in the previous chapter. They range from the kindergarten story of the good teacher to a variety of stories about teachers who have humiliated or hurt students' feelings. Certainly the level of personal relationships that strike up between students and teachers is interesting and many participants talk about the desirability of getting to know teachers personally or about support they or their families have received from teachers during their education. For many of the participants the personality of the classroom teacher, as well as their level of professional skill and workplace motivation, seems to be a key influence in determining the emotional response to education in later life. Indeed, there are a number of accounts, which reflect the importance of the strongly personalized, and parental role teachers take with students in China, right up to high school levels:

> In my senior high school [a key school], the teachers were the best quality I have ever met. They had all graduated from the best universit[ies], even from Beijing, and they were all good quality. They treated students like friends and would talk to you. Some older women were almost like your mother. They went to the dormitory and to class and if they met you by chance on the school grounds, they would always have a talk. Even the students whose marks were not very good, they encouraged them in every way they could. (A, p.6)

From stories like these, it is quite possible to see the continuing influence of the Confucian master-disciple construct of teacher-student relationships within the contemporary educational dynamic and the importance of the pastoral aspects of the teacher's role. The character of the student-teacher relationship also has profound implications for the style of classroom dynamic. For example, a number of participants reported that, while they felt it impossible to ask questions or to participate within the formal structure of the classroom, they felt very comfortable to approach the teacher and talk with them outside the classroom. It is important to pay regard to the social dynamic, therefore, that characterizes the educational experiences of the participants. For most, there is a strong divide between their public behaviour within the educational context and their private behaviour. As we will explore further, this has profound implications for the way in which groups of people work together in teams and their more general behaviour within society.

Emotional Reactions to Education

Though many of the participants express anger and sadness about their formal educational careers, many note that this feeling has arisen as a result of direct comparison with the "western" approach to education later in their lives and is not necessarily anything that they felt to be unexpected while they were participating in their school education.   Far more of the participants talk about their educational performance in terms of being ashamed and letting their families down, instead of externalizing their emotional feelings onto the object of the education system. A sense of shame, it seems, acts not only as the mechanism for student discipline in the classroom but drives motivation at home as well.   Several of the participants talk quite openly of the pressure that their parent's expectations places on them in their education. Here is one story about bringing home a report card:

> Every end of semester, they gave you an exam, and then they also gave you a report book for your marks. Very terrible thing (laughs). Every time they gave it to me and said, "ask your parents to sign their name on it." [They wanted to] make sure [parents] know your marks. Every end of semester you had to do the hard job. When in primary school, all of the parents are full of ..., have very high expectations. Full marks are 100. They all want their boys and girls to get above 90, so only one or two mistakes is enough. (T, p.4)

This viewpoint is consistent with the findings of other studies exploring the emotional context for Chinese learners of all ages and emphasizes both the internal and external discipline-based notions that underlie ideas of character formation in Chinese educational programmes. What is different here is, perhaps, the number of participants who did openly expressed anger to us about their earlier education and the accompanying desire to "put right" past experiences by embracing the new in their current lives.   For example:

> The way of education in the Chinese system, er, in my opinion, there is something wrong with the Chinese education system. Normally, Chinese teachers always tend to teach the students in a style, in a way of stuffing, just like a [Beijing] duck. Yes, like stuffing a duck. In the whole class, from beginning to end, the teacher always talks himself and the students

seldom speak, seldom ask questions, even when answering a question, [the only time] is when the teachers ask them. They don't take the initiative to ask questions. ... In my situation, I was very shy. If I raised my hand, I always felt that maybe my classmates would laugh at me. "Oh how did she ask such a stupid, stupid question!" I was always afraid of that. I think my character is deeply influenced by this kind of teaching way. (W, p.4)

I cannot remember [primary school] very clearly, but what I can know is that the teacher in the school is very strict and there are a lot of rules, which limited student behaviour. Students must obey the regulations of the school. ... I think this is a disadvantage of the Chinese school. This is not a good way to lead students to think their own way. So in that school, I just followed what the teachers said. I did not think a lot about what [were] my own opinions. (X, p.4)

For the majority of the study participants, then, schooling was not a happy experience:

Actually, my school life was, ermmm, it did not make me feel so excited. Actually, I think my childhood is not exciting or fantastic, just hard work. ... I have this kind of feeling. (C, p.2)

This recurring theme takes more shape when participants describe the loneliness and competition that characterized their middle school and high school experiences. Nor does it appear that those most angry about the structure and style of the Chinese education system are necessarily those who have been most negatively affected by, for example, poor performance. As this theme develops, it does seem to emerge that the participants in the study may be articulating a shift in the value system held by younger Chinese people, as they become more individualistic and more demanding of personal freedom, self-determination and free expression. Certainly for this group, in the comparison between Chinese and international education systems, the Chinese system comes out poorly when measured along a number of scales.

Teaching and Learning Style: questions and participation

Some of the most interesting information emerges from the descriptions of the interaction between teachers and students. The formality and emphasis on teacher-centred methods, outlined in the descriptions above, strongly indicate an environment of passive and conforming behaviour from students meeting teachers' expectations.   Certainly this emerges very clearly when participants begin to talk about the interaction between students and teachers around questions and behaviours adopted to clarify or develop teaching points that the teacher is making in the classroom. Questioning by the students seems to be unwelcome to the teachers and, as noted above, students take in information in a very passive way:

> Students do not usually put up their hands to ask questions.   They just follow the teachers thinking; they follow the teacher's idea.   Very few asked questions. (X, p.5)

> I would actually just listen to what the teacher said and if there is something you should do, a question that the teacher gave, you would just do it. (Y, p.1)

From time to time in some situations, the teacher may ask questions of students, usually questions of clarification or to check understanding. Alternatively, they may ask questions of bright or favoured students. Certainly, few students would volunteer to ask questions in the classroom and many express the view that only those who feel very secure or confident in both their own ability or the teacher's regard would normally venture to do so, for example:

> [If you could] do the questions, you could put up your hand.   And, you know, at that time, I was aggressive, so I always put up my hand to answer the teacher's question.   If you answer correctly, the lecturer will give you some [words of] motivation.   He would ask everybody who could answer. … Normally, if a teacher felt that the student was no good, they wouldn't ask them.   I feel this is a little like discrimination.   [For example,] if a student is not good in the examination or test, they don't talk to them much. (AD, p.4)

The other key factor suppressing a student's willingness to ask questions appears to be the risk of embarrassment or humiliation in front of the peer group, supporting the strongly differing codes that seem to exist for public and private behaviour.   Once again, the element of shame enters into the dynamic in such a way that the group implicitly acts as a governor over the behavioural expression of the individual, setting clear parameters and norms within which self-expression can be sought:

> I am very shy.   If I raise my hand, I always felt that maybe my classmates will laugh [at me].   "Oh how did she ask [such a] stupid, stupid question!" I [was] always afraid of that. (W. p.4)

> I like to ask questions, but I always considered whether it was worthy of asking or whether I should [find the answer] myself. ... Sometimes if a question was stupid, because students have many different ideas, and if you come out with an idea that people think is strange, then maybe it's not worth asking. (AE, p.4)

What seems to emerge quite strongly is that student participation in the classroom is not within the framework of the conventional educational dynamic. This arises from a number of possible causes including the "education-as-stuffing-a-duck" philosophy, social taboos about speaking out, respect for the role of teacher, the dominant ontology which respects the inviolate nature of knowledge, and the emotionally-charged atmosphere of the classroom where any challenge to authority could result in retribution. However, a number of participants focus on this aspect of participation as a key weakness of the state system in comparison to their international education, as we shall discuss in the next chapter.

Political Turbulence and Education

It is important to remember the extent to which the education system in China has been at the heart of the changing political dynamic in recent years as well as at the forefront of economic development. Information appears in several accounts about ways in which political upheavals, either during the Cultural Revolution in the 60's and 70's or latterly as a result of the June 4th incident in 1989, have exerted a profound influence on the quality, shape and continuity of education that many people in China have received. Given the strong social and civic aspects that played an important part in the policy design of education in China in the 20th century, this shaping by political events is perhaps inevitable. The practical impacts on individual lives, however, can be quite significant. For example in this account of schooling during the Cultural Revolution:

> In the Cultural Revolution, [a favourite teacher] was struggled against by the students, but I loved her because she normally takes care of me and she is very kind. ... At the beginning of my [elementary] school, we just read and recited the quotations of Chairman Mao...[we had] nearly no textbooks. And when I was studying after that, I had a book, but it was simple and we had so many meetings, many, many meetings. (G, p.5)

The age distribution of the participants means that many were only indirectly affected by the Cultural Revolution, which saw the closure of all educational institutions for two to four years at the end of the 1960's.

However, a larger number of participants directly felt the impacts of the Tian'anmen incident in 1989. Many different reasons are cited for the student protests that took place across China. A catalyst for the demonstrations was the death of Hu Yaobang, a senior cadre who was known as a supporter of education. With the far-reaching effects of this demonstration and its eventual violent ending, education at all levels was bound to be affected. Several participants in the study comment on how the June 4th incident affected their lives, either at school or university:

> I took an examination to go to middle school but actually the examination was quite easy. ... You know the events that took place in 1989? So at that time, I remember, we just could not concentrate on our studying, and our teachers had to go out to, how do you say? Support those students, and so that year the exam was quite easy for us, and I got high marks. This made it easier for me to go to the good high school, which I went to. (C, p.2-3)

> When the June 4th happened, and before that a lot of students [at the teacher's college] were trying to go on strike and things like that. ... All of us went to the railway station to try to travel to Beijing. But this news was leaked before we got to the railway station, and all the trains, which passed by Baotou and those leaving from Baotou stopped. ... People especially from the city bureau went to talk us into going back to our schools. I remember very deeply ... what one of them who was talking to a group of students said. ... Get some effectiveness. I thought for us the most important thing was to study. We could do nothing unless we got some things like knowledge or wisdom to arm ourselves with. We cannot change the situation if we are not strong enough. So after that I focused all my time on studying. (U, p.2-3)

> When I got to Beida, I distrusted it. The atmosphere was changed. ... I went to Beida in 1989. I went to military training first. ... The reason was about the June 4th. Yeah. They thought it was dangerous for students to come direct into the university and be talked to by the older students there. The training lasted about ten months in Shijiazhuang. ... We changed our mind[s]. Washed my brain. ... The main class was politics, about the history of our revolution and something like that. ... When I arrived at the Beida campus, I thought the education system was changed from before. The government had changed the principal. They gave us a severe mark system to leave no time for us to think, or to read. ... And because the military training - it still changed some people's minds, especially from small places. ... From my observation, I believe their thought would be shaped. If they had come to Beida first, they would have been shaped as a human rights fighter or a freedom fighter. If they came to the military training first, they became a good party member. On

Beida campus they tried to keep some military system. But I was not changed from the military training. I was still the same. Sometimes I think my going to Beida, some part is my parent's fault. They wanted me to do that even if it meant military training. (L, p.4-5)

No matter at what age or at what level of education, all across China students felt the influence of this pivotal demonstration as the reforms of the new China came into question. At this time it seems that some of the set roles of student, teacher and political cadre were beginning to undergo questioning, followed by a swift reinforcement of the government's doctrine in the general tightening-up that took place in the aftermath of June 4th.

Money, Opportunity, and Class

A particularly interesting theme emerging from the context of private education in China, is the new role that money seems to be playing in ensuring that educational opportunity is attained. No longer do political or class credentials, such as those of intellectual classes, provide the only opportunity to gain educational advantage. Money has clearly played a part in the accounts of many of the participants. Not only do they all have money to pay for expensive private higher education, but also in the past a number of them have attended *zifei*, self-pay, classes in state schools and colleges. In addition, parents have utilized relationship networks to open up improved chances for their children. They have done this either by sending their children to live with relatives to ensure that they received education in a "better" school or district, or by cultivating relationships with those who could open up educational chances that would otherwise be absent. These reflect, perhaps, more traditional patterns of securing educational opportunity and respond to similar practices that have taken place in China from the imperial age onwards. The explicit way in which money is openly acknowledged in this connection, however, seems to be something of a departure in the mechanisms for the operation of *guanxi* in Chinese education.

Variability within Uniformity

In spite of the overwhelming uniformity in descriptions of environment and pedagogy, the students' reported experiences of education still contain differences. Most notably this is the case in two areas. First, it is important to distinguish between those who attended schools in the countryside from those who attended in the cities. Second, we must note the gaps in experiences between the children of intellectuals, government officials, or whose parents are wealthy, and those whose families are working class in state factories or self-employed artisans and workers in the private sector. It is quite clear that the achievements of the Chinese government in terms of contemporary educational reforms reflect the general historical trends. These have worked at the macro level and have yet to touch more detailed and sensitive issues of classroom practice and teaching and learning strategies. It also shows the degree to which access to education and the social opportunities it brings may be open to luck and opportunity or to the personal drive of children and their parents. In a number of cases, participants talk extensively about the very active roles that parents took to ensure their children received adequate education. This factor has previously been noted in a variety of studies investigating Chinese education in mainland China, Hong Kong and elsewhere. It seems from the accounts in this study, however, that in the case of the Chinese mainland, parental drive and pressure for children to obtain education may not just demonstrate a focal point for parent's social aspiration or ambition for their children. Instead it represents the realization of a bald necessity, especially in the countryside. If parents are not active in negotiating educational opportunities, their children may well go without and without all the opportunities in life that education may bring. There is more than an implicit sense in the participants' accounts that reveals the patchy coverage of educational reform across the country and reinforces the role of *guanxi* connections in securing educational advantage in China.

Education, Personality and *Guanxi*

As we have introduced above, a clear factor to emerge from the participants' stories is the degree to which their experiences, especially during the early years of education, are touched by the personalities of the people involved in education. The degree to which personal politics is an accepted part of classroom dynamics in Chinese classrooms also becomes obvious through the participants' stories. In the accounts of the two participants whose parents are teachers, this emerges most strongly and yields powerful insights into the micro-political atmosphere of their schools. Here is one such account:

> You see in China because of the politics, all of the teachers are educated
> by the central government, they use the same system to educate the

children. So it is the same system…lots of politics, talking about "we don't like him" and "we don't like him" and they quarrelled sometimes, that kind of stuff. This group was unhappy or that group was unhappy and two or three would always be together and the others would be outside. They often found something to fight with each other about and tried to get rid of each other. It was very strange. In the class they sometimes showed this kind of emotion. But the children had no idea. I heard from my mother at dinner and other teachers would come to my home and talk to my mother and I just heard them discussing. … I didn't feel it was strange [to be in the same school as my mother]. If the teacher were a friend of my mother, she or he would treat me well, better than the other teachers. If they weren't friends, they would treat me… I remember in one mathematics examination, I got a perfect score, 100%, no fault, but because the lecturer was not a friend of my mother, she tried hard to take off four points. You could see the four points were just taken off; it was not because the maths was not right. (A, p.2-3)

The *guanxi* system or system of personal connections dominates life in Chinese society. In its most negative expression, it can emerge as corruption; for the most part, however, the networks of particularistic relationships reflect the localized community focus of life in Chinese society. This applies to life in the education community as much as anywhere. Participants report becoming actively involved in cultivating influential relationships and avoiding the giving of offence to others from an early age as students. Such behaviours introduce and hone interpersonal skills that become vital in later life and are an important factor in the informal socialization processes of school and college life.

Adolescent Rites of Passage: punctuated by examinations

Participants in the study when talking about their mainstream educational experience, mostly discuss examinations as the milestones and rites of passage that marked their adolescent years. There is a scarcity of references to friendship, or social activities and the frequency of references to drudgery or the burden imposed by education. When taken together, the omissions reveal adolescence as a difficult and dull period of time for the study participants, irrespective of their age. When this view is added to the accounts from those who were mature students at Harmony College, it is evident that the participants do not collectively believe that life is meant to be *enjoyable* in any real sense until independence and adulthood is achieved. Irrespective of the age and length of participation, that period does not begin until after the end of formal education. As we will discuss further below, one of the starkest contrasts with the "western" education in which they took part and their previous education experience within the Chinese system, is the incorporation of "fun" into both the formal curriculum and the community life surrounding the College. This is the case even for those who have undertaken degree-level studies in the state system.

Conclusion

Overall, the value of the accounts about early educational experiences as related by the participants have in their presentation a vivid, if impressionistic, picture of the cultural sounds and sights of Chinese schools from a student's viewpoint. These impressions have actively helped us as practitioners to contextualize the attitudes and behaviours that we have seen students from China adopt in many educational settings. They have also helped us to direct our energies towards the development of more culturally sympathetic teaching strategies across a range of areas. We will discuss some of the implications for cross-cultural teaching in Chapter 8. As much as anything, the stories reinforce the sense of the extent of change and turbulence that has swept education in China in recent years. There is direct tension to the underlying educational and social assumptions that the participants express - of stability, continuity and harmony for both life and education.

From the initial picture painted by the stories, it would appear that the Chinese educational environment is very formal and intimidating to the students. At the same time, it displays a strong sub-plot of informal contact between students and teachers with teachers engaging in active pastoral care for students and developing personal relationships with the children in their care. At elementary level, participants reported a number of organized social activities, sports and cultural elements in the curriculum, which enabled them to form good peer relationships with classmates and to develop friendly contacts with the teaching staff at their schools, but these activities definitely varied from school to school and were very much determined by location. Given the strong thread of educational continuity in terms of locality, it is possible to understand why the notion of *tongxue*, or "classmate", emerges so strongly within the educational tradition in China. At one and the same time intensely individually competitive and group-governed, the classroom dynamic appears to take on a special importance in a system where education is so highly prized.

6 The Teaching and Learning Dynamics of Harmony College

The participants' accounts of their early educational careers set the stage for their reflections about their educational lives at Harmony College, where for the most part, they first came into substantial contact with a new educational culture. The stories about the context from which participants came helped us enormously as educators in understanding their behaviour in the learning environment when we met them at Harmony College. Comparing the participants' views about their interactions within the two educational environments seems both necessary and inevitable. This chapter, therefore, sets out the main facets of the participants' views about the education they received in Harmony College and the impacts it has had on their lives and the way they are thinking about their futures. We begin with a brief discussion about why participants' chose to go to the College, and then move on to consider the teaching and learning dynamics and the impacts that the educational experience has had on participants' thoughts and feelings.

Why Study at Harmony?

A Big Investment

In thinking about why individuals made the decision to go to a private language and business university like Harmony College, it is important to take into account the financial magnitude of that decision in the first place. This is one dimension which reveals the significance of the undertaking and underlines the importance of the decision-making processes involved. As we have noted in the introductory chapters, education is very much a privileged urban phenomenon in contemporary China. Moreover, in spite of dramatically increasing wealth in Chinese coastal cities, the fees for studying in Harmony College were extremely high for the domestic educational scene and the College operated, therefore, within an elite market.   Though not the most expensive international business college operating in China, the fees for a year's study at the College equal the sterling costs for a postgraduate home student in a British university, in an economic context where the national average wage was over 50 times lower than in Britain. The fees for one semester of English language study (of a three-semester year) were the equivalent of one and a half-year's income for the average family in China. When living expenses and the opportunity cost of loss of earning potential during the study period are also taken into account, the total cost of the financial commitment to go to the College is huge.   Clearly in such an environment, only the very rich and privileged, or, as was the case for many students at Harmony, those who had worked and saved for many years were able to take up the opportunity. For example, one of the participants noted that she had saved for over ten years to be able to undertake further study but had only finally been able to realize her ambition when she had made more money through successfully investing in the new Shenzhen stock exchange. Even in a country like China that has traditionally valued education and the social opportunities it can bring, the commitment involved in studying at Harmony is significant. Fully comprehending the enormity of this undertaking sets an appropriate frame for understanding participants' expectations of the return that might derive from their studies. For all of the participants, going to Harmony College is such a big investment that they expect to see strong and immediate benefits in professional, financial and personal terms.

An International Experience and the Attraction of International Business

Within this context of wanting to see tangible benefits from their investment, the reasons participants disclose for going to Harmony College vary a little but essentially cluster around a coherent group of themes. The international orientation of the College was the primary draw because of the social value that participants ascribe to contact with foreigners:

> [I wanted] to learn something new in a foreign system. … After that, maybe I could take a place in a foreign company. … I thought at that time that people would see a diploma or degree from a foreign country as important. (L, p.8)

Though only 23% of participants entered directly to the business programmes offered by the College, this was a function of the College's entry requirements more than student motivation.   For example, four participants explicitly mentioned the advantages that they felt the study of international business practice would give them in later life. Interestingly all of these participants either had previous work experience or had already taken part in a domestic higher education programme and were actively seeking careers as entrepreneurs. For school leavers, the motivations tend to be more diffuse and connected to their family's ambitions for them rather than personal goal achievement. The underlying motivation for all participants, however, remains the desire to take an active part in the entrepreneurial revolution they saw as sweeping China's economic development ahead. In this context, participants' regarded the West as a model from which to learn, which is what prompts their entry to Harmony:

> The interesting thing is that the Chinese have imported economics from the western countries. ... We all think the western people do so well in financial things, like economics. You can compare. (J, p.6)

The English Connection

Unsurprisingly, since the majority of the participants entered into the English programme before progressing into the business degree programmes, most people initially came to Harmony seeking to improve their English language skills through contact with teachers who were native speakers of English. The root reason for this was the high correlation in participants' minds between facility with English language and the ability to find high status, highly paid work in China:

> When you are finding a job, you say, "Yeah, I studied at Harmony and our lecturers were foreigners and I studied courses in English." I think it's helpful and very competitive. (F, p.11)

> The competition in China is so strong. You need higher education otherwise I probably cannot get a good job. (C, p.5)

> I want to be an educational administrator, so the reason I came to Harmony is, to improve my English, especially my spoken English because I heard the classes are conducted in the British way of teaching and provide a complete English language environment. (W, p.14)

In motivational terms for the participants, it seems that the combination of the study of "western" business in an English language medium taught by foreign teachers was a potent mixture. Several people expressed the view that extensive contact with foreigners alone, outside of the educational exchange, had the power to convey competitive advantage in the Chinese job market. For most, therefore, there is a palpable sense that this educational experience is exotic. Excitement and anticipation at the chance to play a part in China's increasing prosperity seem played out through working in the private sector and in particular in the international business community.

A Passport Overseas

More than mere contact with foreigners in China, for four participants the ultimate objective in going to Harmony College was to exploit the links between the College and the British university to go abroad to study. Three participants had previously been rejected for visas to a variety of countries on more the one occasion. This seems highly influential in the initial decision to go to the College. For example:

> I came here because I did not get a visa for XXX. ... And if I spend one year here, I can go to the UK to study. (AA, p.7)

The visa question remains important for may Chinese students who still find it problematic both to obtain a passport from the domestic authorities and then to get through the stringent vetting involved in applying for a visa from the host country. Recent changes instituted in the UK's system for admissions for overseas students from countries such as China have reduced the number of obstacles to international study somewhat. However, since a period of overseas study remains socially unparalleled in China and confers a distinct competitive advantage in the domestic labour market to those who can afford to get it, it is unsurprising that there are those who have no ambition other than gaining international experience in mind when they apply to the College.

Motivation and Gender

Male participants frequently expressed more concrete motivations attached to their study with the aim of achieving some definite objective. Most frequently, they discuss the desire to obtain a foreign degree, a qualification which they feel will lend them a direct competitive advantage in the search for jobs. For some, the aim of going to the College is to obtain a certificate, and they seem unconcerned about the learning process. Two male participants wanted the quickest route to a degree – it takes four years in the domestic Chinese system and only two and a half in Harmony's intensive study system - and two wanted to spend the minimum amount of time in the College in China before progressing directly to study in the UK:

I want to get the degree as quickly as possible and I saw the advertisement about Harmony. They can provide university graduation in two years. So I came. (AD, p.11)

If I want to go abroad to study, I have to have a degree [to study for an MBA]. I am 24 years old this year and it would take me about 3 years to finish my degree and then it would take me one and a half years to apply for a visa, so altogether four years to continue my study for an MBA. It would be a lot of time, you know. (Y, p.9)

Women on the other hand, expressed interest mainly in more process-focused and disperse objectives in coming to Harmony to study. Four expressed a simple desire to experience a teaching style different to that in Chinese schools and four wished to continue with education in order to generally improve their future without discussing a definite objective. For example:

Honestly, I didn't know much [about the College]. Even after I stayed at Harmony for one year, I didn't know it completely. ... I thought here is one college that will let me study further and I believed it can provide good quality. What I learned could be useful, in the future. That is why I studied there. (Q, p.7)

This contrast in gender orientations is significant since it reflects themes running throughout the stories in the project. In a general sense, the male participants appear goal-oriented and desirous of tangible achievements denoting social and educational success. The women are more varied in their views about self and success and present a more diffuse sense of the usefulness of goal achievement compared to going through a process or experience. At the same time, however, women express realism about the necessity of "doing well" in education in order to develop a professional career in China. We will develop this theme further in Chapter 7.

Family Support and Involvement

Families played a very important part in participants' accounts when they were making the decision to go to the College. In one third of the cases, the families on behalf of participants made the decisions without their involvement in the decision-making process:

Actually, I didn't have the chance to make the decision. My parents decided for me. My father's friend introduced the College to him. ... My father told me about it. He told me that every teacher in this College was

> a foreigner and you must speak in English. I thought, "Oh my god. I'm really nervous. Speak English! It's terrible." But my father said it was good. (H, p.5)

> My parents introduced [the College] to me. ... My parents did business at the time so they wanted me to learn business at Harmony. (O, p.4)

> I chose a university in Xinjiang. ... But my mother chose the position for me again. She told me to go to Beijing and I agreed. I wanted to very much. She thought studying in Beijing would be better for me. (AE, p.7)

In many cases, this family decision about the participants' futures was made in response to their lack of success in the university entrance examination and the parents desire to take control in response to this failure. Even where a participant had been successful in the exam but were unable to proceed to a good quality university, families made the decision to invest in private education instead. Family support of one kind or another, therefore, is a recurrent them in nearly all of the stories. In more than 60% of cases, participants' talk about families offering emotional support which was fundamental in making the decision to go to the College and often to remain there:

> My father just let me know this information [about Harmony]. He told me there was a school operated by foreigners and all the teachers were foreigners. Just give me the information and let me make the decision. And I think it's OK. ... So I made the decision to come here. (C, p.5)

For 55%, this support included financial assistance with all or part of the expenses associated with attending the College. This is particularly the case for women. Seventy-eight percent of women in the study received financial support from their families and in all but two cases, this represented the provision of the total costs and living expenses during the course of study - a significant investment in the woman's future. Only one woman, a mature student, talked about a lack of support from family, compared with four men who specifically noted either a lack of family support or open opposition from family members because they felt the male participants should have been making headway earning a living instead of investing further in their education. This may reflect the slightly older age profile of men involved in the project. It illustrates the notion prevalent in China, that education is intended for the young and not the mature student. By contrast, it may also reflect the more general belief that it is especially important for women to have a solid educational base if they are to succeed in the workplace, in the face of the widespread gender discrimination that persists in the Chinese labour market, whereas men can become successful without the benefit of higher education.

The College's Teaching and Learning Dynamic

Overwhelmingly the comparison between the system of teaching that existed at Harmony College and the Chinese system focused around the relative dynamism of the teaching and learning environment. Seventy-four percent of participants note that teaching style was key difference they experienced in the College compared to their earlier educational experiences:

> I thought the foreign style of learning would be more active than the Chinese and I wanted to try it. (A, p.8)

> When I started, I felt better because, in terms of the classroom, it's not the traditional Chinese classroom with the tables in rows, it's just a circle. In that way, we feel we have close communication with our teacher and we always have a lot of games. I think it's fantastic and [it] made me feel, when I woke up in the morning, I desire to go to school. I really desire to go to school and [when] we finish our class, we feel the time was so short. We even wanted more time to talk with the teachers and to study. That kind of feeling we never had in Chinese school. (C, p.5)

> The first thing is that you have to ask questions. It is completely different from a Chinese high school because you are not supposed to question what a teacher has taught you. In Harmony the environment is very easy and very relaxed. Well, the teaching style, I find it better because it is not only just lectures but there are practical situations where you can use what you have learned and discuss it with classmates and things like that, and that is done in class. This never happened in a Chinese high school. (N, p.4)

Other factors, which characterize the learning environment, discussed by the participants are shown in descending order of frequency in Figure 6.1.

It is interesting to note that that aspects of classroom dynamics present the main focus of attention in this list, especially in an institution where the study disciplines were also largely new to participants and yet figured rarely in their accounts. The contrasts between the data in the list and accounts about the domestic education system are stark.

Table 6.1:   Teaching and Learning Dynamics at Harmony College: the top 10 characteristics

Characteristic	*Response Rating*
1. Active Learning Style	42%
2. Independent Learning/Self Reliance	39%
3. Students Encourage to Participate and ask Questions	35%
4. Less Formal than Chinese School	29%
5. Relaxed Environment; Learning has Practical Application	26%
6. Learning is "Fun"	23%
7. Students Encouraged to be Creative	19%
8. Learning is "Not Boring"	13%
9. Coursework is Part of the Assessment	7%

Not only did participants note a wide range of differences, but the depth of feeling with which they connoted the differences in teaching and learning environment are significant. For example:

> The students can actually speak up. They actually ask questions and when they hear something they don't think is true, they actually argue. That is something that would never have happened in my high school. (B, p.8)

> [The main difference] is the teaching method. ... I feel it is very interesting that we cannot get a "correct" answer from the questions. ... I really like this method because it doesn't limit your thoughts and gives you a chance to improve your knowledge. ... When I studied international business and management [at a Chinese university], all of the teaching focused on the theories, which were not so useful when you go out to practice. In international business here at Harmony, [the lecturer] mentioned so many famous companies and there were practices in the class. All of those things I never had in my previous university with our Chinese teachers. (J, p.7)

What emerges form the participants' accounts of their reactions to Harmony is a sense of an increasing awareness of the importance of the process of education as well as its outcomes. For some, the primary motivation was to achieve certification as a passport to high paid work. Once at the College, however, this perception seems to undergo a shift to focus to the qualitative aspects of learning. All participants share in the view that it was no longer possible for them to engage with their education in an instrumental way, processing aspects of knowledge but remaining unaffected by its setting. Success from any viewpoint in this new environment required an active engagement with the subjects of study and its dynamic simultaneously. Of necessity, this imposed a burden to learn and develop new skills at the same time as extending cognitive capabilities.

Independent Learning

The strong emphasis on independent learning and informality relative to the Chinese system of didacticism and control seems quite clear. That is not to say that everyone at Harmony enjoyed the differences or thought they positively enhanced learning. Though many felt energized and enthusiastic about the teaching approach, 16% of participants noted that they felt intimidated by the need to participate in the lecture or seminar room and several discussed the painful adaptation that they felt was necessary to succeed in the new learning environment:

> I think the teaching style is different. I [had] never seen it before and it made me very nervous. (E, p.11)

> I think my personality probably limits my participation, but I feel I can overcome this. ... I am always nervous [when I must] make a decision. ... I am not very independent, so I think at Harmony, I have to make some decisions and it is hard for me. (O, p.6)

Some perceive that this process of change is connected with the long term socialization that they have undergone in the Chinese education system, while others ascribe this difficulty in adaptation to age:

> I think maybe it is quite early for using this [teaching] method in China because the educational and social background of Chinese does not prepare them to understand it. They do not have the idea of this kind of method. The education is so, ... flexible and it requires that the participants have some knowledge and skills to meet the teacher's requirements. It is not easy, for most Chinese students it is not easy to adapt to this kind of method. (R, p.10)

> When I studied in middle school, the teacher told you what you should do, but in the western style, they don't tell you at all. You should think about what you should do and how you can study well. It was completely different. So you cannot expect to know from your teacher what you should do. ... For me, I had not been learning for a long time and it was difficult to adapt to this style. (F, p.10)

Because you have been controlled for many years, the way of thinking has been controlled. You lack something like imagination. You cannot think very widely because you can never develop your imagination. (T, p.12)

At the same time, some (16%) asserted that the ethnic cultural behaviour patterns of Chinese and "westerners" were fundamentally different, in ways more profound than merely educational socialization, and which affected the success of the cross-over between the two systems:

The Chinese student, the Chinese people and the foreigners, they think in a different way. I think that is why we can learn a lot from foreigners. I don't know why Chinese people have common ideas. ... I think they get the information form the TV, the propaganda, especially their parents. You know our parents almost all think the same thing, feel the same thing, have the same argument. From the beginning our classmates' parents - not different, all the same. (D, p.8)

The way of thinking is really different. ... [Foreigners] have no strange feeling like Chinese have. They just find it general, very normal to cooperate. There is no purpose or any enmity if you are good. There is no enmity. Instead they have a really nice reflection and co-operation. They say "Oh, that is very nice." ... I found that most foreigners are very good in reflection and co-operation. [They] Just do it. That is very important. If it works, just do it. Don't waste time. But Chinese people, even if it is logical and it works, Chinese people will still feel opposite to the job. There is still no effective co-operation. It looks like they are lazy or careless about the job. It is very terrible. I really don't like this. So In China, unless you have power, [you must] just give up the job because you will have problems, and ...it will get even worse in the future. It is very terrible but that is the culture. (A, p.12)

One participant uses a concrete example of a problem-solving technique she had learned at Harmony College to illustrate the differences in logical reasoning she perceived existed between "westerners" and Chinese:

The most different thing, is the way of thinking. For example, in practical ways like brainstorming. At the very beginning, I could not understand it. First, they ask you to write everything down that is in your mind, and at first it is a big mess. Then at one point you think, "It's mad. How can you work like that? It has nothing to do with the topic". For example, you look at a car and you need to think of all the things in your mind at that moment. I cannot understand, but the lecturer told us to do it, so I do it. And then we get rid of the things not connected and then select the points and put them into different sections and then put them together to form a structure. But the Chinese way is first of all you have to have a structure. First, have a nicely, well-prepared structure. So this is, you know, quite a different way, a different procedure. At that time, when people ask me about the differences between the way of things - the Chinese and the western way - this is my feeling, my own opinion. I feel it is really a big difference. It is from different directions but you meet at the end of the project, you fulfil the same target. The way is quite different. (P, p.5)

English Study

Many of the participants contrasted the differing levels of activity and participation in the classroom through a discussion of English language teaching specifically. As we have discussed in the introductory chapter, the emphasis in English teaching in the domestic system, as with the rest of the curriculum, is formal and focuses on the abstract study of grammar rather than oral fluency. This is far removed from the interactive conversation-based style of teaching at Harmony College and illustrates the counterpoint between the two approaches:

My first impression was that this was very good English [teaching]. And my second feeling was that they taught us how to *use* English. They asked us to tell them to explain what a word meant, not to translate it into Chinese but explain it. I felt very bright that I could really improve my English. I had only studied English in the Chinese way - the teacher was Chinese and spoke only Chinese in the classroom. Now I felt, "Oh, this is the way to improve my English, to think in English and explain in English, and this would help me construct sentences." It made sense so I studied very hard. (A, p.9)

Even though English was my favourite subject in school, the teachers just taught us grammar or memorizing something to pass exams. They never let us talk. So we had no opportunities to talk English in the school at all. But Harmony's English programme offered us this opportunity to develop our oral skills very fast. (C, p.5)

When I was in the advanced [English] class, every class was just playing a game with the teacher together. This is really interesting. I think the way of learning another language should be like this. The previous time I had spent with our Chinese English teacher, we had learned so much about the grammar and after I came here, I found this is not really a good way to learn a language. ... I learned to use a word, how to use it. Before I came here, I really couldn't understand the words you were saying. ... We spent so much time in school studying English, and I find the result was not so good. (J, p.6)

The teaching of English is quite different from the English teaching in middle school. At that time, my teacher was an old man, about 60, and he just asked us to read the text, just read and then he dictated words. He just asked us to remember the words and the grammar rules. That's all. It was the traditional method of teaching English in China. But here it is very different. I think the teachers try to make us use English naturally. For example, they give you a picture and ask you to describe it using your own knowledge of English. Or they give you a sentence and let you use your head to imagine and tell a story behind a sentence. So it's quite different and makes you use English. (R, p.9)

The Advantage: relaxation facilitates learning

On balance, the majority of participants point to their experiences at the College as positive. Those expressing frustration at the prescriptions of the Chinese system in particular reported that the open and relaxed methods facilitated their learning:

The atmosphere in the classroom was very relaxed and it was easy for me to accept learning. Learning had been very boring for me, especially in classes in senior high school, so I changed many ideas. I felt it was very stupid. This relaxed atmosphere helps me learn. They give you knowledge just through talking about something. It is not pressured. The teachers teach from the book, but they transform the knowledge. ... You know most of the books are really hard to follow sometimes, the words or the sentences. To me maybe it is fresh or strange to accept or follow, so it is a little unclear. In the class, the teacher explains through his or her words or through his or her experience and this makes you connect the information you read. So, Oh! You got it! This often happens to me. When I listen to the teacher, I often experience this "Oh, I got it" and I can go back to the book and see if I can understand more. (A, p.9)

I think the most important thing the Harmony teachers gave me is to let me be my own self. ... They just guide you to do something. Give you guidance but not force you to go somewhere or to do something. (Q, p.8)

For many of the participants, the opportunity to think widely around a given topic and to explore teaching points in relation to other issues, personal experience or practical examples, rather than just "sticking to the book" was an important aspect of the learning dynamic in the College:

Besides the textbook, I can also think a lot of things, things which may not be directly related to the book. It can be related to other things, maybe things totally outside business. ... In the past, the teacher only tells [us] how to do the right thing in the textbook and we just focus on how to do this, and no time to think. (E, p.12)

Even where subjects of study stress high levels of theoretical or intellectual content, establishing a context of inter-relationships and thematic linkages into other areas was something that participants report having valued and which they contrasted to conventional practice in the domestic system.

The Disadvantage: relaxation requires self-discipline

Though the relaxed and independent setting in which learning took place is something that the majority of participants seem to have valued, at the same time it was the main disadvantage they identified in the teaching approach. The removal of clear controls and boundaries and the emphasis on student-centred rather than teacher-centred learning caused some participants to feel tempted to abandon their diligence in approaching their studies:

> Because it is so relaxed in the classroom, sometimes you don't feel like you are in class. So after going through high school that has a rigid and serious atmosphere and you are being pushed, you are kind of used to it, so when you come back to the relaxed style, you think, "Great, I don't have to study." (B, p.6)

> There are good things and bad things about [the teaching style]. [The] good thing is that students can more easily be involved in the course topics. [The] bad thing is that Chinese need to be in control. If you lose control, get into that condition, Chinese people always will go beyond. ... Then you will feel, just like kids in a family with no parents, they will do just what they like. If you feel more relaxed, they think there is no pressure. Foreigners like to be relaxed and they still have pressure so when they do the work, it is very natural, they have the responsibility to do it. In China, you have to have control, order, and they can do the job effectively. If it is more relaxed then the student or the worker will feel, "Oh, it is fine, I can do this again because it is okay." And again and again and then you will feel totally relaxed and not care at all about the job. [laughs] This is Chinese. (A, p.13)

> Sometimes it can be too relaxed. You can just go down, down, down and not do any work. No teacher is going to come running after you to get your assignment done, so you can just be totally relaxed and do nothing. It is not a disadvantage but something I don't think all students can deal with. I think Chinese students are used to the control of the teachers. (N, p.5)

Interestingly this factor also applied to the social environment at the College. One participant, who had attempted to organize a series of student events talks about his disillusionment because few people would involve themselves voluntarily in developing the social side of student life at Harmony:

> [I stopped trying] because nobody wants to help me. I do everything by myself. ... If I want to organize a party or an activity, then they think it is too hard because if they do all the work, then maybe nobody will come, or they think something will happen. ... If I encourage them to carry on because they are upset, they will do nothing. I always keep trying, but because nobody wants to help and I also feel tired, I have kind of given it up. (I, p.5)

The self-determining environment and independent learning style at Harmony, then, appears to be a two-edged sword. On the one hand it can act as a powerful force to re-energize and revitalize disillusioned students' orientation to learning. On the other, it can create a certain giddy bewilderment for students who have been unaccustomed to taking responsibility for the organization of their personal or educational lives. The implications of enforced development of self-dependence for many aspects of participants' lives seem clear. It is no surprise, therefore, that this aspect is one of the main long-term inheritances they felt that they have taken from the College.

I Can Fail?

A further underlying factor causing concern to participants in the cross over of educational traditions was the anxiety caused by the idea that they could fail to obtain their degree certificates. For students in the domestic university system, once the huge hurdle of the university entrance examinations has been overcome, the possibility of failure as an undergraduate is almost non-existent. Failure at Harmony, on the other hand, was a very real prospect in the participants' minds. Therefore, a constant anxiety appears to have influenced many participants as they grapple with the problems of developing the skills to manage work independently quickly enough in order to pass examinations and the unfamiliarly assessed coursework.

Group Work at the College

The Novelty of Group Work in Education

One particularly important set of contrasts around the teaching and learning dynamics at Harmony focuses on the unit of organization for student learning. In the state education system, student work tends to be undertaken on an exclusively individual basis. For example:

> During the whole time of my primary school and my high school, there were not any chances for me and my classmates to work in groups. (W, p.4)

> I encountered presentation and team work here which I had never done before. In the Chinese university and all the schools, they are all focused on individual work and you don't need to know how to work with others in a group. The teachers will tell you what to do and you just do it. The important thing is there is always a correct answer. When you finish your work, then you check with it. (J, p.3)

> The Chinese way is to encourage you to think for yourself rather than exchange [ideas]. Sometimes they exchange, but they encourage you to do your own thinking a lot. (P, p.5)

> If you study in a Chinese university, you never have any group meetings. They never have this kind of idea. They don't know what it is like. (S, p.7)

Even where students are involved in practical subjects such as in the sciences or have the opportunity to work collectively on a project, this activity tends to be broken into individual parts for the purposes of task execution:

> When I was studying in a laboratory, I was with a group. One group would be about 3 students. ... I worked with the same students for one subject and we just had a fixed group. We had six or seven subjects, so different groups. ... I think the difference is that in Chinese school, [when] we did our group work, we still did it individually, even though we are a group, but we don't like to work with each other. (C, p.7)

The Group Dynamic

In addition, a number of participants characterize the group dynamic within the Chinese environment as one which is very competitive:

I think group work is a little difficult. Because everyone has their own ideas and they don't want to work together. (I, p.3)

I thought group work was a waste of time. ... At university and at school, some teacher would say, "you should help". They think that group work is just where [good] student helps a [poor] student. ... But the [good] student does not want to waste their time because the entrance exam is most important. ... You know, I was taught by my parents when I was very young. "You grasp knowledge and we grasp knowledge and some people grasp us who grasp knowledge. Using knowledge is not as good as using people. And getting power." They told me some leaders in their institute did not have any good knowledge but they were in high positions, [which my parents] did not feel was good. I did not understand. But from about 25 years old, I could understand a little. The most important thing is not you yourself. Your [personal] quality. It's about the quality of how to use others. (L, p.11)

One participant sets out the social dynamic underlying group competition:

It is very complicated. A Chinese group in a Chinese situation is different. A Chinese group in a foreign situation is another thing. In Harmony, it is like a foreign environment and the Chinese students are pure Chinese students. They come from the same background. You know they know each other. They have strange ideas, strange minds because of a lot of historical reasons. We have opened the door because we seek a lot of things from foreigners and we are undeveloped. All this forms our ideas and also personality. So when we work together, we talk together, if one student is very active in talking, the other students will definitely think that this student wants to be a leader, wants to be head of something. This is the same thing in any business in China, company, factory, even in school. The other students will not cooperate with you. ...You have to be quiet but you have to participate on the topic. You cannot just be silent, but must talk about something. So you must in a very proper, appropriate way, talk to each other. You cannot show too much pride, too much, how can I explain this? Chinese people are just like that. They will not show this, they just will not cooperate with you. Just no co-operation at all. They may agree but after that they will just forget about it. So group work in China is always terrible. ... Another reason is a word we call *zibang* "look down on yourself". They think they are really no good, so they don't want to let you know how bad they are. ... Mostly the reason is that they don't want to co-operate with the head. (A, p.10)

The Origins of the Competition

This competitive dynamic seems to stem in part from individual competition inculcated within the state education system but it extends further into workplace associations in general. Some commentators have noted that competition is a generic characteristic that differentiates the nature of the collective in Chinese society from that of other Asian nations. It connects to the exclusive and family-based system of particularistic relationships that dominates social interaction in the country (Chen 1989). This is important, since a stereotypical view of Asian societies may lead us to think of the collective as something that functions through a hierarchy based on disciplined mutual support and collaboration to achieve the goals that the group has set for itself (or been set). Such a definition of the collective may indeed apply in some circumstances to other Asian groups, Japan, for example, or among ethnic Chinese groups in Taiwan, who can be classified as neo-Confucian. However, the character of the group dynamic within mainland China appears to be very different from either of those examples. Here group members are openly competitive with each other and use numerous tactics such as shaming, withdrawing co-operation and politicking to control other members' co-operation with outside authority, innovation or active participation in the task.

In a broader social environment where hierarchy remains important, however, this can create key dysfunctionalities in the operation of peer groups, since the group tends to engage in lengthy jockeying for leadership positions before work can begin. Once a leader is appointed and a command and control hierarchy is in place, subordinate group members are effectively absolved of the need to actively participate unless directed. In addition, where a leader is not formally appointed by a legitimate external authority, unresolved political problems can remain simmering in the group and can undermine its ability to function.

Group Work at Harmony

In contrast to the competitive individual assessment regimes within the Chinese education system, at Harmony College work and assessment took place both individually and in groups. In particular, at higher levels in the degree programme, the products of group work were subjected to important course assessments, which had some effect on final degree classification. This included group case-study analyses, making group research reports and oral presentations based on group marking schemes. These assessed approaches to group work applied some pressure to the group dynamic. They effectively prevented an individual abandoning the group in order to obtain better marks by working individually and underlined the general importance of group co-operation and support. Indeed, one second-year degree-level skills development course offered at the College departed from the examination format altogether and focused exclusively on continuously assessed group-work activities. This particular form of learning and assessment was far removed from anything, which the participants had previously experienced and was a specific focus of interest both for us as researchers and for the participants' in their recollections.

Factors Influencing Group Dynamics

Within the group of participants in the project, there were a number of specific reasons that seemed to underlie their responses to group work activities. In addition to the general context of a tight clan focus in Confucian-tradition societies, high levels of family involvement in participants' education appear to have encouraged participants to view their role within the groups at Harmony as a clan representative in direct competition with other group members for performance rewards. In other words, to meet parental expectations, participants need to do "better" than their peers, not perform at the same level. In comparison, ethnic or social bonds were relatively weak and undermined the spirit of positive co-operation and mutual help.

Inevitably, adapting to peer group work took some time and was an important aspect of the wider adaptation that participants needed to undergo at the College. In addition, increasing levels of personal individualism seem to have acted to mitigate against the spirit of co-operation within groups. This is because of a widespread perception held by participants of individualism as a positive and progressive opposite to what they perceived to be the manacles of socialist collectivism that existed in China pre-reform. Underlying these aspects is the specific motivation that caused many participants to come to Harmony in the first place - a sense of the increasingly competitive labour market in China. After graduation, participants believed they would be in direct work competition with each other and, therefore, some interpersonal powerplays seem to have crept into the group work activities at Harmony.

Attitudes to Group Work

The net result of these factors influencing attitudes to group work is that 39% of participants stated that they actively disliked working in groups at the College. For example:

> I don't like group work with Chinese students in Harmony. In a word, group work at Harmony cannot reach the standard you want, the teachers want. Actually, you want people to work together, communicate with each other, and share their ideas and then go to work. That doesn't happen. (A, p.10)

> Teamwork is horrible actually. I mean, sometimes the individual ability is quite different when you share. [When] doing any work or doing some brainstorming, some people are quite lazy, don't want to work, just get the marks. (V, p.6)

Conflict seems to feature in a large number of the interviews when participants are discussing group work and many noted that they found the group process very difficult to manage. They did not express surprise about its existence, however, but accepted that it routinely takes place, that it is personal and that unresolvable conflicts frequently prevent the accomplishment of group tasks unless they are broken into individual parts:

> [The main pressures in group work are] time problems and energy problems and sometimes you have to communicate with others. Sometimes you have a big problem and you're not sure what to do about it, and during that time, maybe you will be angry or something like that. And your emotion will control your thinking, and you don't have time because of a lack of ability to solve the problem, so you become very, very angry with each other. (D, p.9)

> Group working? Sometimes I feel annoyed when we have conflicts. I really want to get agreement in the group but everybody has their own character at Harmony, their own habits. We could never get agreement. We could never finish the task. (Y, p.9)

The picture presented about group work is that "face" for the participants is not so much about maintaining modesty from an internal perspective, but that it is the avoidance of ridicule, being shamed by others, and losing position in the hierarchy. Looking stupid in front of other people is a major concern because of the implications this has for power and position in the group. This susceptibility to shame and its corollary, the tendency to shame others when they show weakness, acts as a disincentive to taking the initiative. It also means that personal squabbles and perceived slights can come to dominate the group's attention however important success at the group task can be for all individual members:

> Sometimes we just spend too much time quarrelling and we cannot reach any kind of solution. It is always the person who can speak most and who

> can speak loudest that takes the leading role and we do things according to what he or she said. (U, p.9)

In comparison to the high number of people who expressed dislike, only 23% of participants said that they liked or enjoyed group work. For those who managed to find a way through to difficulties of the interpersonal power dynamic, however, group activities seem to be particularly invigorating:

> I do like group work very much. I feel I can learn something from others, even though there is always a conflict in group work, and we always waste so much time to balance our arguments and we get so tired when we work together, compared to individual work. But when we do have agreement about how to do this thing or that thing, then we get so happy about it and this is central to improvement for all of us in group work. (J, p.7)

> Group work? [It] is important. I learned from this. Not only learned knowledge, but also learned the way you get knowledge. (AE, p.8)

Even though this enthusiasm is high, it is frequently invested with a sense of frustration. As participants views about the value of group work shift from "difficult and not useful" to "challenging but useful", so their attitude towards other people in the group setting also changes. For some frustration sets in, therefore, because of the continued need to work with what is perceived as the entrenched behaviour of others in group activities:

> They just divided the questions into parts and this person is responsible for this and the person is responsible for that. I thought group work should be working together, but almost everybody tends to say, "Oh, it's faster and more convenient for everybody to do it this way". So the result is part a, part b, and part c, without any integration. (N, p.5)

Many participants felt that this effort was difficult to sustain in the long term unless they put themselves into a multi-cultural or non-Chinese environment where issues of maintaining face and group competition seem less acute. This specific view becomes, for many, key in determining where and in what kind of organizational setting they feel able to build their professional lives after graduation.

Groups and Gender

Responses to group work divide along gender lines. Three quarters of those who said that they enjoyed group working were women, while men pointed up difficulties with conflict, competition and leadership squabbles. To some degree, this may reflect the challenges posed by mixed-gender peer group working for some men in the Chinese environment, especially when the men are slightly older than the women. This aspect features in one woman's account where she describes the need to take specific action to counter her male colleague's assumption that he would take the leading role in their group:

> When I first came into contact with group work, I was confused. I got a headache. I really didn't like it. I thought it was not useful. ... I had many conflicts with [my male colleague]. We really argued. He never consulted with us. He always decided and then said, "You must follow. I am correct and you are absolutely wrong. What you think is rubbish." Like that. Someone just said to tell him his English was rubbish, and he really didn't understand. (Laughs). I did it. He was very angry with me. But I talked directly to him and it was very useful. Finally, I thought it was good, quite good, much better than at the beginning, ... [At first], I thought it was wasting my time. I must spend a lot of time talking with others and staying with others even though I didn't like them. It was terrible for me. But actually, except in a social situation, you have to be with many types of people including people you hate. So I thought it was correct. I have to do that. (H, p.8)

Some men were concerned about the usefulness of group skills applied to the professional work environment:

> I think it is necessary to learn to communicate with other people. I think it is quite useful. When I have a job, I think I will get in touch with many people, so it will be quite helpful. (O, p.5)

Overall, however, in spite of ambivalent emotional responses to the practical issues involved in group work, 48% of participants noted that they felt the skills developed through group working at Harmony would be helpful in their future careers. In addition, 23% - all women - noted that their skills in communication and co-operation had improved as a result of group work at the College, which would be useful in both social and professional situations. For example:

> I did not like [group work] but, yes, I know it's helpful for me. For example, now in my company, all kinds of people work together and they

are all from many programme and many countries. So because I have practised before, I am prepared for this difficult life, so I think it's easy to adapt. (F, p.11)

It is good because you learn how to deal with the situation, like when others don't agree with your idea, or when a group member had to write the whole project and do everything yourself. You overcome the unfairness that it was group work but the others don't pay attention. Also I understand myself better. That is the most important thing. I found that sometimes I was quite selfish and I would feel it was unfair if I did the whole job. And sometimes I would find myself very bossy. (K, p.12)

This is compared to 13% who felt that group skills learned at Harmony would not apply to their future work. In particular, those who felt that such skills were not useful were predominantly older and had worked or sought to work within the domestic or state-owned sector rather than the international business community:

I don't think [group work] is helpful you know. Because in my opinion in work, in an office, there is not group working, just individual working. And also if there is work together, there must be conflicts between group members. Even in work because everybody wants to get promoted, so they have to contribute well to a project, or maybe they go to the managers' office and say, "that person is no good," and, "that person is no good." It's not good, I think. (X, p.14)

This group of participants appear to perceive that the disciplines required to work within the Chinese sector require the kind of passivity and conformity they reported was inculcated by the domestic education system rather than the individualism and participation of Harmony's western pedagogy. For them the group working approach at Harmony seems to have been akin to opening Pandora's box, a factor that disabled them from working effectively in their chosen environment.

Group Work as a Facilitator of Change

Working in groups, therefore, has acted as a powerful symbol for the cultural cross-over represented by Harmony's teaching approach for many participants. It is something that they feel to be extremely challenging within the overall learning dynamic. For many, it brings with it a more direct focus on peer relationships than they may have encountered before in education, where the dominant relationship has been between student and teacher. The consequent need to develop management strategies to cope with the pressures of direct contact, communication and confrontation while still completing the task requires a particularly exacting set of skills. What is clear is that the form and style of group working that took place at Harmony was alien to the constructs of groups that have historically predominated in China. It throws into relief the extent to which the learning processes at the College were enculturated as much as the substance of the curriculum.

Cultural Implications of Education at Harmony

Education Changes People

Leading on from the discussion of group working and culture at Harmony, it is important to consider the wider aspects of the cultural exchange involved in the teaching and learning dynamic. It is clear from the participants' accounts that the experience of involvement in programmes at Harmony College has had a profound effect on many of them. The majority of participants expressed the view that their education at the College had not just been instrumental in nature - where they have acquired knowledge about some concepts from the western business environment. Instead, they point in particular to the skills elements of the courses as transformational vehicles for personal and cultural change:

> Concerning the theoretical things after the text or the exam, I have forgot them really. But concerning my way of thinking, I have changed a lot. That is one of the most important parts I have learned from the College. I think this is the only, I mean this is my property or my treasure. I think that what you are thinking guides what you are doing. (P, p.6)

> I think it is a good way for me. And for Chinese people because Chinese people always follow the traditional way of learning and thinking. When I came to Harmony, I learned a lot of things such as critical thinking and now I make decisions myself, not depending on other people. Before, I depend on my parents, my sister - now I have my own opinions. (X, p.13)

A fundamental shift in participants' views of themselves and of their relationship to Chinese society seems to have taken place during their process of education at the College. Major causes behind these shifts in attitude could be the College's emphasis on self-reliance and independent learning, a lack of external controls and hierarchy in the educational environment, and the development of group work which was focused more on task and problem solution through co-operation than personal competition and face-saving. Participants asserted that they had assimilated some aspects of different, "non-Chinese", cultures both from the subjects of study and the community at the College. This assimilation of culture appears to have been both the incident and the core of much of the learning that took place:

> I think mostly I have changed in style. For example, from my father's point of view a foreigner is a foreigner and a Chinese, is a Chinese. They are different. But for me, I think everybody is the same…[My parents] didn't want to see how much I have changed since I went to BIMC. They just want to know how much I have studied. (H, p.8)

Most participants, however, do not cast a deeply critical eye over the wider appropriateness of the cultural impacts of their study and their abandonment of Chinese social and cultural mores. From their perspective, the opportunity to change themselves in order to get a good job and to achieve higher social status is an unadulterated good. The self-perception of becoming more individualistic and outward looking is seen by many as instrumental in achieving that aim. For some the practical difficulties of attaching aspirations to one cultural system and living day to day in another are tense and frustrating. One participant talked at length about his concerns for the widespread neglecting of Chinese culture in favour of "westernization" that he believed is taking place and the way it is affecting his generation:

> When I first came to Beijing, I was very interested to find out how old Beijingers lived, but I couldn't find it except when I went to the *hutongs* or to see an older part of the city. But for this younger generation, people are just assimilated by discos. I mean they don't have many roots in Chinese culture. That is their problem. This is the problem for this generation. They are gradually losing our culture, our values. They are learning western [things]. I'm not saying that everything from America or the west is bad, but they don't have the same contact with Chinese culture as they have with western culture. They don't know much about our history about how the old Chinese, the old values, how this culture is, what this culture is. They don't seem to care to learn that. They listen to CDs with English songs and when you talk to them about classic Chinese music, they say they have never heard it. But they know a lot of Grammy winners and this sort of thing. They know it, probably better than people in the US or the UK. This is what is happening. (AA, p.12)

These comments come in spite of the fact that this participant eagerly anticipated studying abroad and relished the opportunity to take part in bringing the global economy to China.

Such apparent contradictions are common in the participants' accounts as they attempt to discover what the long-term significance of moving out of the mainstream of Chinese educational culture might be for them. Studying at Harmony College was very much part of a process of assimilating and reflecting on changes in an era of extraordinary dynamism in China. It may have acted as a catalyst for those included in the project but is by no means the only factor in challenging participants' views of themselves and the world around them.

A Challenge to Personal Identity

For some, this process of reflection and change appears to have far-reaching effects. Three female participants discussed the ways in which they felt they were fundamentally changed as a result of their experiences at the College, even to the point that they were no longer "Chinese":

> I remember when I just came here, it felt besides [having] a lot of activity and the English and also because we had never connected with a foreign teacher before. ... I felt I had not enough time to let me think of the way [to do things] in Chinese. [I am] less Chinese and more English! (E, p.12)

> Maybe the disadvantage is that I am changed. ... Before, I was very pure, maybe 100% [Chinese] and now I'm not. That makes it very difficult to work in the government companies or work in the traditional Chinese [company] because you are fed up with their attitude. (T, p.13)

This potential erosion of ethnic identity poses significant challenges to the participants involved, especially in a society such as China where conformity, a sense of patriotism, and national identity are viewed in the most positive terms and where the conventional purpose of education is to augment levels of civic identity and social responsibility among the intellectual classes. One implication of this seems to be that those who have studied at Harmony College may be socially marked out from their peers in ways that have important impacts on their lives but which are perhaps more subtle than those who have gone directly overseas for their education. Indeed, for most participants in the study, there is a palpable sense of something important about the continued cultural iterations and interpretations that take place on a daily level as they move between international and local cultures in their thinking, learning and routine lives. These continued processes of interpretation, re-interpretation and sense-making seem to have wrought some powerful effects over those who have chosen to see them.

Final Words

More specific conclusions about the nature of the changes which participants have undergone are difficult to achieve from the interview data. Merely that participants felt themselves to be different some time after they had completed their studies may not be enough to sustain a strong argument about the shaping of a new generation of Chinese in response to the pressures of globalization. However, the stories remain illuminating. What emerges quite clearly from them is participants' sense of unease within their own culture and the fractures that pattern and frustrate the way in which they view themselves and their futures unfolding in the Chinese context.

7 Work, Gender, and the Future

An important aspect of our discussions with the study participants focussed on thoughts and feelings about their personal and professional futures. We have discussed some of these themes in Chapter 3, which introduces the participants' backgrounds and the personal and professional contexts from which they came. In the course of the research, however, we deepened our discussions further in this area in response to a number of issues that emerged from the stories that the participants had to tell.

First, it was quite clear from the outset that the participants saw a high correlation between their chosen educational paths and the direction of their future professional and personal lives. This is in keeping with traditional Chinese views about the general utility of education as a factor in the acquisition of professional status. Given that the subject of study for the participants was primarily business administration, it also seemed important to explore with participants the linkages that they saw existing between their studies and their future lives in the world of work. Even where this did not manifest itself as a subject-specific concern, however, it was clear in the given rationale for the choice of an international education as a means of moving into work with international companies. Second, the basic theme of the study itself was to investigate the ways in which particular forms of education, pedagogical concerns and cultural modelling of the teaching and learning dynamic influenced the beliefs, values and identity of those who participated in them. In addition, weaving into these themes, is our underlying interest in the gender dynamics that existed for the participants both in education and work. We have already noted that more than half the students at the college were women, unusual in conventional Chinese higher education. We have also introduced a number of the issues that confront women in work and in education in the country. Considering the ways in which women have experienced their education at Harmony, therefore, and the way that these experiences may have shaped their views about work is of particular interest. This chapter seeks to summarize participants' views of their environment at home and at work and to further examine the ways in which the suggestions of a shift in personal identity, which we noted at the end of the last chapter are borne out in choices about the future that the participants have made.

Prior Work Experience

Of those who had worked prior to entry to Harmony, the pattern of work was extremely varied, as we have noted in Chapter 3. The two oldest participants, at 36 and 38 years of age, had extensive experience in state-owned companies, but had also worked in the private sector. One of them had - unusually in the Chinese context - changed jobs more than ten times in the previous decade, after a chequered educational career during the Cultural Revolution. The other had followed a more conventional path, joining the Chinese Communist Party and working in a state-owned enterprise in a technical capacity before leaving to join a private sector firm. The vast majority of participants with work experience had been employed in the private sector: in hotels or international companies, which acted as the financial and environmental catalyst which brought them to Harmony. Interestingly only one participant - who had maintained his work while studying at the college - expected to work in the same organization that had employed him before going to the College. Most had either already left their employer, permanently or on a leave of absence, and expected to change not only their work organizations after graduation but also the professional sectors in which they were employed. For them, Harmony College was the specific vehicle that facilitated a step-change in their professional lives. In addition, a number of participants (19%) expressed an interest in starting up their own companies, especially among the more mature participants in the study. For the group as a whole, study at Harmony College seems to represent a potentially life-changing step towards shifting career orientation rather than maintaining professional development within an established field or area. Those trained as engineers were seeking work as marketers after study at Harmony, those who were teachers were looking to develop as human resource managers, those who had been hotel receptionists wanted to move into finance.

Aspirations for the Future: work and education

Going to Work

At the time the research interviews took place, 32% of the participants were already in work, after leaving the College. Of the total cohort, a further

23% were aiming to begin work immediately after graduation. Twenty-six percent intended to continue with their education by pursuing further degrees, universally at overseas institutions, either in the USA or the UK. The remainder had either not completed their studies at Harmony or had no fixed plans at the time of the interviews.

Of those employed, six had found permanent posts in international companies and four were working in Chinese-owned private sector organisations. No one had sought work in the state sector. Of the latter group, however, only one participant (the oldest participant in the study), having attempted to find work in international companies without success, regarded this post as a permanent work option. The rest all stated an intention to undertake further studies overseas and had engaged in short-term work until their application process was completed. The functional range of organizations in which the participants was employed was extensive: real estate, finance, hotel management, a television sales company, publishing and construction are examples. Of those who were working in the domestic sector, the job functions of all except one focused on their English language skills in capacities such as liaison with international customers or suppliers. Of those in international companies, English language was the universal working language. The job roles they fulfilled were predominantly in sales or administration (70%), with one manager, one editor and one stockbroker.

The profile of these participants, therefore, seems to bear out the functional orientation of the education offered by Harmony towards employment in the international private sector. This trend is illuminated further by the views and work aspirations of the rest of the participants. Thirty-nine percent of the total population aimed to work exclusively in the international business environment when they began their jobs. Their enthusiasm for working in this sector, irrespective of functional activity of the company is palpable. For example:

> In a foreign firm, foreigners do things actively and they are not lazy. They know how to get their job done in time and how to manage their time. Otherwise they will be fired! They have a very strong pressure on them but in Chinese companies and factories, they are always putting off doing things and ...as soon as they go into the office, the first thing they do is not working, but reading the newspaper and drinking cups of tea. They don't have much pressure, so I think it's meaningless to work. ... Just to earn money but without contributing any effort. ... I want to combine my knowledge learned here with practice. I really want to fulfil myself. (C, p.7)

> Because I am not young, I think time is important. I would like to come into the financial organization a foreign organization, which has invested in China...I think it is a much higher layer in business...I think the degree is more accepted in the foreign country and I think the Chinese banking system is changing in reform...They cannot provide the good things they used to provide, like a house. Now they do not provide houses - the most attractive thing for us. And I think about the money we'll get in a foreign company. (L, p.12)

> Of course [I will work] for a foreign invested company because I took three years and spent a lot of money studying this international business administration and I would like to use my knowledge. ... Business administration is also useful for a Chinese company, yes, but for a state-owned enterprise, it is quite difficult. First, they do not use people like me or other people who have studied abroad because they just want to use members of the party. They just use their friends and relatives all the time. (R, p.10)

Only three participants, the two oldest and one other who intended to work in his parent's company, expressed any enthusiasm for working in a domestically-owned organization. Further, 10% of the participants noted that their aim was to be able to work overseas, in spite of the practical difficulties that still attends this decision for most Chinese:

> China is a big potential market, everybody knows this. Although the present is not very good, but in the future Chinese people will understand how the world is going on. ... I have a plan. I will study for my master degree abroad and see what the world is like. ... Now China is in recession. I mean in a bad stage, so that the time is not good for me to come back. I'll stay abroad for longer and wait to catch some opportunity in China. (V, p.8)

Overall, therefore, irrespective of the point of origin for any of the participants, the overwhelming majority appear to be placing their job hopes in the continued opening-up and reform of the Chinese economy and business environment. The reasons given for wanting to focus on the international sector range from the functional desire to be able to put to use the language and practical skills learned at Harmony to the notion that international firms were at the vanguard of reform in China.

Further Education

The participants' international focus does not end with thoughts about work. Forty-five percent of participants in addition to the number who were moving directly to further education after leaving Harmony, said that they intended to go abroad for further study at some time in the future. Most commonly they asserted this would happen when they had worked for one or two years in order to earn sufficient money to support themselves in this venture. In total, therefore, more than 80% of participants identified some kind of strong ambition to work or study in a country other than China and to pursue long term employment outside of the domestically-owned sector. As we have noted in Chapter 6, several participants talked about specific difficulties they felt they would face in working in Chinese companies owing to the cultural shift they had undergone during their studies at Harmony. Whether implicit in their articulated future choices or explicit in the way they voice their concerns, therefore, it seems clear that this small group of participants do not expect to invest their professional futures in China itself except in the most general sense. Rather, they strongly identify themselves with non-indigenous professional and cultural forces and expect to put their energies into the construction of more global corporate concerns.

Limits on Skills Integration and Development in China

These issues suggest a series of implications for the participants and for the role of international education as a factor in Chinese society. Given the predilection of the participants to stay out of the domestic employment sector, it seems clear that opportunities for them to integrate the skills and capabilities developed during their education at Harmony into existing domestic businesses are limited. The presence of international education programmes such as that at Harmony may have the potential, therefore, to create further divisions between organizational and social systems in China than those that have already existed.

The government's focus in opening up education to international investment and support was driven primarily by a lack of capacity in the state sector and its stated need to import "advanced technical and managerial skills", by which it appears to have meant "western" management practices. The underlying reason for this policy has been the need to update China's inefficient state-owned enterprises and to instil the market-based ethic into the domestic workplace. This instrumental view of educational reform has not seemed to take into account the corollary of the opening up of education in this way. If the views expressed by the participants in the study are at all representative, this could be the complete abandonment of the very employment sectors that the government believes would most benefit from the newly imported skills and expertise. This presents something of a dilemma both to the policymakers and to the individuals involved. Indeed, the government has expressed concern about the brain drain that took place during the last years of the 20th century from China to other countries through the process of educational emigration. From the profile of the participants in this study, it is possible to extrapolate an environment of evolving internal brain-drain, where those who have gained international experience in China focus exclusively on international investors for work in preference to domestic firms. The participants are, in addition, effectively betting on a steady continuation of reform and opening up, though they express some anxieties about that, which we will discuss below. Should that prove not to be the case, it is likely that a potentially difficult professional or personal transition would confront them. There are implications for both the participants and for Chinese society more generally of the extreme preferences they express for their professionally international ambitions.

Success and the Future

In continuing to explore the ways in which going to Harmony College has catalyzed change in the students perceptions, it is helpful to consider the ways in which they describe their personal futures and their aspirations in association with their educational careers. We asked all participants about their ideas of "success" and what might constitute fulfilment in life for them. With such a broad canvas and a varied group of respondents involved, it is hardly surprising that the answers we received in this were very varied. There are, however, some very clear themes that seem to enliven all of the accounts.

First, the idea of pursuing some kind of high status professional career, as well as one in the international sector, seems to colour most accounts. For example:

> In my opinion success means to be admitted by society, by people around you...It is a complex composition. It consists of your educational background. For example, if you are university educated, maybe you are a doctor...and also your social position or your rank in the company. (W, p.18)

Certainly social position and status figures as more important than wealth. Only two participants also ascribe very positive characteristics to the acquisition of wealth while three assert that they are not at all interested in becoming particularly wealthy:

I have the kind of feeling inside that I need to do something, that I want to do something, but honestly, I still haven't found out what it is. I just feel I want to go ahead. I should say I just want to live well and enjoy life. Obviously, the financial condition should be an important part of it. You know, some people asked me before, "Do you want to be rich or not?" I said, "Yes." Why? Because in that way you can live well, you can do something you like, not just consider if you have enough money to survive. (Q, p.10)

I think money is not very important. I mean money cannot bring anything but what is necessary. Being rich is not equal to happiness, so I don't want to be very rich, just OK. I want to be happy. (H, p.10)

One participant further identified herself as a failure owing to the inequalities that she felt she had experienced as a Chinese woman working in an international firm. For her, success correlates very closely with accomplishments and positions gained at work:

When I had just graduated from university, I thought I was a success. I worked in a company and I worked hard and I got promotion quickly. Then I went to a different organization and it was better than the factory, so I was moving up. When I stopped working in the government and went to a foreign company, then I felt, how do you say it? I just felt nothing. I think it is maybe the same for Chinese in a foreign country. If I work in a foreign company, I can't get a high position. First, I am a lady, I can understand that, but second, I am Chinese. These two things kept me from getting a high position. When I worked in a foreign company, I thought I was quite good. When I was in a Chinese company, I was younger and I was in charge of a group of people and most of them had graduated with a master degree and had already worked in a foreign company as well. That was difficult and is why I am studying. When I stop studying here, I will go back to a Chinese company. (AC, p.10)

For only three participants do the traditional values of helping society or family enter into the discussion and only one expressed any sense of making a contribution to the enrichment of society:

[To be successful] you must do something useful for society and help more people be successful. ... In my mind, I hope that someday I can be like the president of Harmony College. ... I am not very satisfied with the Chinese education system. [I want to] do something for Chinese education and something in which I am interested. (I, p.6)

> I will make my family became more successful. I don't want my parents to work very hard anymore, so I want to support them in a happy life. (AE, p.11)

For most of the participants life fulfilment and success are defined by internal and personal criteria:

> I think for me, [success is] to try to do my best to achieve what I have learned. I think success is a kind of personal thing. It is not something else. It is a kind of personal feeling. You have achieved the goal you want. (Z, p.11)

> I think success is not that you have to do a very great thing or achieve anything great. You have to set your own personal objective and try to achieve it step by step, that's success. (C, p.7)

> [Success is] when I feel I am completely successful with what I've done, not something tangible, like an award or a position, but the emotional feeling. Whether the actual result is a failure or an achievement, I don't really care. I think success for me is when I know that I have done my best and cannot go any further. Then I feel successful. (B, p.11)

For some, a sense of both individualism and fulfilment in life comes from engaging in lifelong learning and the acquisition of knowledge and experience:

> Success to me is to have more knowledge, and intelligence. To gain a wider knowledge and gain more experience, and be just like a consultant. I like to give information. I like to tell you how to do [something] and tell you the principle of how it works. If I can be proficient in an area that I like, I will be very happy. I don't like money. I don't want to be very rich. I want to just feel…a very knowledgeable person, to have a lot of international experience. (A, p.13)

One participant, alone of the whole group, differentiated himself through his participation in a form of spiritual practice. He makes an account of the way that his Christian beliefs have supported him in the challenges that he confronts and he hopes will continue to sustain him:

> [When] I was not a Christian, success meant that I had a big job and an admirable job, a position and I don't have to worry about a car or things - it was all material things. … But now I'm changing. Now I don't think this is what I can call success. Now success means to me doing things I feel like. Sometimes there is a lot of competition that forces me to do

[something]. I know that it is not right, that this is wrong, but I have to do it, because of a profit maybe. Now success for me is that I can kind of keep myself doing things that I think are truly right. ... I did see a lot of corruption when I was a sales person. If you don't give a gift, don't give some money, you can't do the business. You know this is what I call competition. Because if you want to make a profit, if you want to survive, you have to do it. You have no choice...[When I became a Christian] it had a big effect on me. When I was in my hometown, my mother was a Christian. I had a friend who was a Catholic. My father is a communist, but my father supports my mother. This is freedom. ... Maybe, it can give me some help from the psychological side. In the old times, when I got a lot of setbacks like I couldn't get my money back [from a business investment], I would get really angry and it was really a hard time. But from a Christian's view, this is not really a big problem, so I just accept it. I treat it differently and am more peaceful. (Y, p.12)

Taken together, these factors perhaps suggest a much broader sense of individualism and egocentrism among the participants than commentators would conventionally ascribe to Chinese people. Certainly their aspirations seem distant from the citizenship values that the Chinese government seeks to develop through the state education system. In this context, the number of participants who expressed the strong desire for personal freedom and self-determination is interesting, since they come from a social context where the collective, usually the family or the state, takes a very active part in shaping individual lives. Indeed, several participants were actively seeking the opportunity to move away from family and close connections as part of their quest for personal freedom and for greater personal fulfillment in their lives. In particular, few who travelled to Beijing from outside the city to study at the College expected to return to their home province, both drawn by the international job opportunities that Beijing presents and the prospect of living away from family influences.

The Future of China

One further area that we explored with the participants about their futures was to probe their thoughts and feelings about the environment in which they live and work. China as a nation experienced extremely turbulent change during the course of the entire 20th century. For those who were highly educated and had exposure to the international community, there have been numerous and specific attendant risks. Even greater challenges have confronted those who have attempted to pursue a vigorously individualistic life path and many who have attempted to evade the prescriptions of either traditional family values or government policies have experienced set-backs or persecution resulting from their chosen course of action. At the same time, since the reform era began, a far greater range of life opportunities has existed for Chinese citizens. The Harmony students have embraced those opportunities open-handedly - some, as we have discussed, with something of an uncritical grasp. By choosing to study in a private sector college, the participants have increased their differences from the vast majority of China's population. Their hopes and dreams for the future seem to seek to further that differentiation. Such a course of action possesses its own risks and concerns however. For example, the *tongxue* or classmate network is traditionally the setting for the development of important lifelong social and professional contacts. The participants' view of Harmony's community is that the very diversity of its community mitigated against the formation of an equivalent system for those who studied there. In a personal and professional world such as that in China which is governed by the collective through such phenomena as *guanxi* being too different or separated from one's peers is potentially a factor which could reduce opportunities for success in the future. This is not to over-emphasize the point. It is clear from many participants' accounts that their families, in secure or high-status jobs, could ease the potential difficulties of difference that the participants might face. However, it also seems possible that the domestic work system might be as uneasy with the prospect of a lack of conventional "fit" that the participants possess as they themselves felt uneasy about working in domestic firms.

Taking all these factors into account, the participants views about China and the future identify the *guanxi* system - whereby individuals gain social and professional opportunities through personal relationships in favour of any other professional attribute - as the main potential obstacle for them in the future. Thirty-five percent of the accounts carry some comment about *guanxi* as a negative factor, for example:

> You know the word, "guanxi". It's always a big problem in China. Maybe you are so great, you are outstanding, you are talented, but just because you don't have a good relationship with your boss, maybe you cannot get promotion, you cannot be recognized. So you have to look for another way. It's always a big problem, even though the government always tries to get rid of this. The government does a lot of things to get rid of this kind of guanxi. But it still exists. (C, p.8)

> In China, you need to get the government to allow you to do something. They give rules and regulations or something. You cannot break the last, they just can keep it fixed. Sometimes, it is really hard. You need to know somebody. They really have authority or you must do something

excellent to get their permission. … It's much harder than to do business in foreign countries. (M, p.15)

[An obstacle] is with the government, I think.   Not just with the government, but with relationships, with *guanxi*, I don't know, but it seems to be easy to just do some here and to do business and then the government actually just cheats them. (N, p.8)

For many, this concern about the way that relationships, through *guanxi*, govern work and life extends to concerns about the level of official and business corruption that they perceive as part of the contemporary Chinese dynamic:

I worry about [China], much more than a little bit. The Chinese still have communistic politics - it is still a very strong and traditional way of managing the whole country. I don't think that it is good because now the system in the communist party it very corrupt. It is very easy to generate corruption because the system is very corruptible. Corruption is created by the system. … Central government controls many things, many businesses. In a simple way, in a foreign country, you just open a company and operate it. In China it is different. When you do a budget, you have to include many fees inside for the intangible corruption. You have to. There is no cure for this in China. The system still exists and I don't think it is curable. (A, p.14)

Let me speak about what I most dislike about China. The first thing I don't like is the relationship pattern, *guanxi*, especially in Beijing. When my aunt came here to do business last year I was a negotiator for her with a state-owned enterprise and we had to find so many relationships. What I found out was that there are some parts of Beijing that are so corrupt. … I really like the American and UK freedom and democracy where there power is not corrupt. In China we have centralized power, but in more decentralized structures democracy can happen. (AA, p.15)

For others, *guanxi* emerges in the form of regional discrimination for those who come from less developed parts of China:

I think it doesn't really matter if you are male or female. It is that people come from different parts of China that isn't so simple. … Some cities discriminate against people who come from outside. … When I look for a job, there is discrimination. Another thing is the people, Beijing people don't like people who come from outside, from another province. (O, p.8)

For others still, *guanxi* emerges in the development of family relationships as a support or constraint on individual life:

The only thing I'm sure [about] is that I will not maybe always be supported by my parents. I want to get some independence. ... In the education I took previously, [it was] just in the university where I live. That is one factor. And another is that my parents are so caring of me, and although they give me some space to let me think and do things, I think it is not enough. Often they just tell me what I should do and not do. (E, p.16)

Maybe [a barrier to success] is the relationship of the family background. If my family is very rich, I can be successful more easily. Because maybe my parents put money into their children to have a good education, and if they are rich they can invest more money into their children's business. You know there are many bad things in society that prevent me from being successful. ... Maybe someday, if I am successful somewhere, I will go back to [my hometown], but if I am not successful, I will never go back. ... That is why I always stay in Beijing and never go back home to visit. I have only visited my family once since I came to Beijing. (I, p.7)

Nineteen percent of participants noted in addition, the turbulence, control and confusion of the Chinese environment as a factor that could undermine their success in the future, whether this is manifested in political controls, the pace of regulation or the burgeoning population:

Now I am afraid of the number of people in China. I feel unsafe because of the people. Because we are in a changing system, if we change the system right, all the conflict will change in the political way. And if we do something wrong, a key point, it can change into maybe, civil war. A cultural revolution. That is a possibility. I'm afraid. I'm always afraid. (L, p.13)

Everything is changing and changing so fast. Maybe after five or seven years you can see a big difference. So that leaves us in a very confusing relationship. For me, I think it is really a big mess in China now and a confusing relationship in every aspect. Just for example, if you ask somebody, "What is your job, what are you doing now?" he will tell you exactly what his job is and what he is doing. And you will think it should be "this and this," but actually it is totally different. When he is talking about is not what he is doing. But he is honest with you. The thing is he cannot explain what he is doing exactly. Another example is, I have a friend...He has a very good job in a computer company, doing IT and the internet...But you know, the internet is a new thing in China, it has just been here for three years, so there are no mature regulations and rules for how to do it. So [my friend] told me that "If I said that this advertisement is worth three million, they will believe me. If I say it is worth five million, they will believe me." So, you see, this business is so interesting.

They just try and do their best, even the manager. He says, "We are doing a very good job here and we do not make any profit." So he just told me that their object now is to open their company on the stock exchange and "then we can earn a lot of money. In that way, we can realize our plan, our purpose". ... Like my mother, she is an editor in the television station. She used to go to her office just twice a week, just show up. At that time, the Chinese were just experiencing personal selling, so my mother went to do it - a salesperson. At the same time, twice a week she would go to work and then after that, she was a saleswomen and would do that for herself. So it is really confusing. (J, p.11)

Two participants express a direct concern about the way in which they have become different to other Chinese and they are concerned about the possibility of a return to the old pre-reform style, where their international learning would make them politically suspect:

The biggest concern for me is that the current policy will change in the future. Right now we are open, China has an open door for everybody. But there is the possibility in the future that the leadership will change and the policies will change too. Then we will close the door, or we would not go as fast as now, or we would retreat a little. This worries me the most. And especially for people like me when I have some foreign background after I graduate from the UK - that will be trouble for me if we return to the old China picture. (U, p.11)

I think, I don't know, but if I stay here, I think people don't understand me, some of my behaviour, they don't understand me. Like [my classmate from Harmony], he criticizes me. Every night, I go to a bar. He says, "good girls don't go to bars. They should stay at home and read, watch TV, listen to music, things like this." Now I think some friends - before they are good friends - think like this. One day I might want to go to live in another country. (T, p.14)

For others, concerns about China's future lie in its continuing status as a developing country, with poor education and the limited perspectives of local business people:

[My worry] is the businessmen. I mean the Chinese boss, his education level, his view of the world is very limited as well. I am worried about that. (V, p.8)

I think China needs quality education. Not to behave like a misbehaved person, to smoke and speak a lot of bad language and spit everywhere. I want my family to be this way, very polite, like foreigners. I think they call it, "gentlemen". (A, p.14)

Of the whole cohort, only two participants felt that there were no issues or obstacles that could potentially impede their progress. For the rest, they are preoccupied with high levels of concern about external environmental factors, which they feel could seriously derail their hopes and ambitions. A level of anxiety is pervasive in the majority of the stories in spite of the upbeat and optimistic tone of the accounts of individual ambitions and outlines for personal success. This apparent contradiction emerges as a somewhat fatalistic acceptance of the likely continuance of confusion in the Chinese environment for some time to come and a resilient determination to find fulfilment whatever develops in society at large. It may be that this anxiety about the environment has some influence on personal views of success, shaping them as inward reflective goals instead of external material objectives.

Individual Lives, Individual Paths

Overall, then, this group of people show a strong association between success and social position, which is not always related to wealth and is tempered by worries about what might happen in China in the future. They believe that fulfilment lies in the level to which they can determine their own futures and meet the objectives and aims for happiness that they have set for themselves. In these ways, the degree to which the participants as a whole group are seeking to differentiate themselves from conventional life and work patterns in Chinese society is, perhaps, significant. It is difficult to make a clear assessment about the degree to which Harmony is solely responsible for the drive to pioneer change through the nature of personal choices that the participants are making. As we have noted before, the group may well be predisposed to change, coming as many of them do from the first generation of free-market entrepreneurs in the PRC. However, their own perceptions about their experiences at Harmony seem to hold that the College was the pivotal mechanism for directing their personal and professional energies in specific directions within the new Chinese system.

The predominance of their views about the pervasive nature of the *guanxi* system in China is well supported by the literature, as are their commentaries about the confusion that exists in the political and business environments in the country. Interestingly, none of the participants suggest any attempt to work personally towards changing existing custom and practice, however uneasy they feel about it. In choosing to move themselves towards the international private sector, they are making a tacit commentary, perhaps, on the difficulties of integration that exist and making a pragmatic choice in that light.

Women

In other chapters of the book, we have woven a subtext of gender analysis, focusing on the similarities and differences in experiences for the men and women in the sample and their families. What emerges from the stories shared by women is that they feel strongly motivated to participate in China's new economy and see that it represents numerous opportunities for them, opening up a new legitimacy to share not only in prosperity but in the changing dynamic of power-sharing that seems to be taking place in China today. At the same time, the women in the group seem to be moving away from the accepted social and family roles that have traditionally existed for women in China. Many are ambivalent about marriage and child rearing. A number note the difficulties of managing career and family or talk about the pressures they feel from parents to move into the responsibilities of wives and mothers. Necessarily, these are not concerns, which affect women exclusively. However, the degree to which women appear to be eschewing traditional responsibilities instead of struggling with them as competing pressures to their personal ambitions is interesting.

Running through the accounts, we can see the gender narrative revealed not only in the stories of the men and women who take part but also through the stories they tell about their families. For example, the patriarchal social structure in China is implicit in the career profiles of all the participants. In every case, the fathers have higher education levels and more prestigious careers than mothers. Where we have information about parental ages, mothers are younger than fathers. At the same time, the domestic power of matriarchy in China is revealed in several of the stories. For example, one participants' account of the grandmother's power to control the size of the family:

> My parents had my brother first and at that time, my grandmother was still alive. My grandmother did not want another grandchild and so my parents didn't do that. After my grandmother died, because my mother really wanted to have a girl, so they just had me. After 12 years. (Z, p.3)

Looking again at the stories and the analysis, therefore, reveals extensive information about the role and statues of women in China. That investigation mirrors the general view expressed by, for example, the UNDP Report (1999), that characterizes China as a country where issues of women's equality have not been fully addressed and the dilemmas of identity and social position for young educated women remain unresolved.

During the course of the study, however, we also asked some specific question about women and their role in work and business in order to develop our understanding of gender dynamics. The answers are revealing. Of the total population, only two participants expressed the view that the world of work presented equal opportunity for men and women. Sixty-eight percent made specific commentary about women's lower status than men's in society, specifically concerning job opportunities and in obtaining work:

> In real life, men don't like strong women. Husbands don't like a wife who is stronger. Even in income, they don't like this. They say maybe it's OK, but really they don't like it if their wife's income is higher than theirs. (T, p.14)

> China is like Japan, a male-dominated society. You know, fifty years ago, the social standard for women was quite low. At this time, a man could marry several women as lesser wives and have concubines, so it is a cultural background problem. ... The real case for [women] is that it is difficult for them to find a real good job, more difficult than for men. They have to make an effort to adapt to this society. Maybe they have to start from a very low position, maybe a secretary. (R, p.12)

> There is a difference. Just like in a company. They always hire male employees and prefer men. ... I think we cannot get rid of our culture. They think men can do better than women. I think related to the culture and history, long history. You just cannot get rid of it, so that's why I want to do better in a career, not family. I think females always can, also can do a better job. (M, p.15)

> There are not many women in China working in the business area. I think that Chinese people still have the traditional idea that women couldn't do better than men. I think in a company all the managers are men and unless you have a very specific ability, it is hard to get promotion, especially in government companies. (Z, p.11)

> When you apply for a job, some positions are for men and some are for women. ... Maybe it is how Chinese culture perceives the position. If they want a secretary, they think, "Oh, it should be a girl." If it is a manager or senior manager, it must be most of the time a man. Probably they don't need to write it down, but people think this way. It is part of the relationship between people. The ideas of a job have developed over a long period and have become fixed. ... It is changing. I think people make the difference. If a woman has ability, then she can apply for that

job of senior executive or whatever. But the common person thinks that this position is for a man. When they see that she is a woman, they will think it strange. [But] they can accept that the woman has ability. The system is already not stable. (AE, p.11-12)

If you are a successful businesswoman, everyone will think you have some support from your family. Actually, my father doesn't like women who are stronger than men. He said it the first time when I was ten years old and I still remember it. At that time, I saw a movie talking about a female ruler in China, and my father said a woman couldn't be stronger than a man. "Oh," I thought, "Why?" But I couldn't argue with him. I thought, "Why not?" ... I think I can be a businesswoman and I have never thought that I am weaker than a man. If men can do it, then why not a woman? (H, p.11)

In addition, participants asserted an employment climate where not only was it difficult for women to find good employment opportunities but managers would actively discriminate against women when promotion opportunities were available:

You can see that most of the company's managers are men, not women. Women can only get promotion to a certain level. Above that, a woman cannot go. One is if a woman gets married, has a family, they have to think more about their family, so they have no time to contribute to the company. Another thing is that most Chinese women just think that they are not good, they are not better than men, they are not as good as a man. So, they just accept the level they are in. I think they lost confidence in that. (X, p.16)

In China, it's different to be engaged in business for a man and a woman, I think. For example, in the state-owned company, my boss, the president would tend to promote males rather than females to high-ranking positions, even though the male and the female have the same ability, even if sometimes the female possesses more skills than the male. (W, p.15)

Further, a number of participants noted the conventional view that even if a woman had became successful, the common view of her situation would be that she had support from a powerful male personality behind her - or had only succeeded in her work because of her *guanxi* not because of her skills.

A clear implication of this aspect of work is the idea that women in the workplace would be held in suspicion and even considered "dangerous".

> Women will have to do more to achieve the same as a man. ... You know, in the Chinese traditional picture, women are always weaker than men. They always depend on men to make up their minds for them. So if you choose a road of your own to compete with men that means you have nobody to depend on. This picture is very opposite to the traditional Chinese picture. If you get too strong or capable in your own field, then maybe they will say, "She is clever, it is OK for me to be her friend, but it is not OK for me to be too close to her." So women who are too successful always have this danger, not to be close with anybody, nobody wants to be close to them. (U, p.11)

Explicit in this assessment of the difficult climate for professional women is what seems to be an overt sexual politics in the Chinese workplace. For example, several participants noted the way in which people would ascribe the use of sexual favours for the success of a woman at work:

> The women's position has in the law become the same as men's, but in traditional personal ideas in people's minds, the woman should still be lower and cannot do some jobs. They always consider the man first if they want to give you an assignment or give you a position. For a receptionist or something, they will consider a woman first. In China, they say to be a woman is misery because most businessmen are very bad people. They just make money through any chance open to them, no knowledge, no education, so they treat women like tools. For example, in a job as a receptionist or a waitress, they think the girl is attractive to attract customers. That is the way the woman is treated in China. I see this in a bar, in a restaurant, in a hotel or in a company even. Sex is very important to the manager or the head of department. ... If women are successful in China, they must get a good relationship or even sacrifice their body, to be successful. You can get a car, you can get a house and you can get a high salary. That is not a joke. There is no other way. If you have a good relationship first, then maybe you can still show you are good quality, but many women graduate from university but still act in the same way. They sacrifice their bodies. (A, p.15)

> The important thing is to pay attention to the meaning of success of a man or a lady. If a man is a success in business, everybody will say, "It's OK, he's a hero." But if a lady is a success in business, they have a bad background. Not everybody, but maybe they have some background or, for example, some man supports her. (G, p.18)

Not all participants ascribed a negative connotation to the sexual dynamic of the workplace, however. One woman, in fact, noted that she felt this traditional view about women at work would give her, as a woman, an advantage in getting and maintaining her position in the workplace:

[Being a woman] should be an advantage, because men will pay more attention to you from my experience. And you are respected if you can deal with the situation - if you have a good attitude about doing work together and not other feelings. The most important thing is for a woman, she should make that kind of feeling, a very obscure feeling...Don't be open all the time to men, but make them feel you have something very interesting to hide from them. That is the most important thing. Don't smoke and be open and wear very colourful clothes, just keep yourself to yourself and they will discover that maybe you are more interesting. (K, p.12-13)

Overall, however, the picture of women finding it very difficult to excel in the workplace and to move into high status careers emerges quite strongly. Unsurprisingly, this issue centres on a prejudice about a woman's ability to manage the responsibilities of marriage and career simultaneously:

[My boyfriend] works in the marketing department as a sales manager of a Singaporean company in [our hometown]. ... [We] don't want to spend the rest of our lives in [our hometown]. That city is not good for young people, so in the future maybe we will move to another city. ... We look forward to being together. Maybe when I'm 27, we will get married. First, I want to do something with my job. If I get married early, then maybe the company will not accept me. ... Here there is nothing but relationships, which guide work. If you are a good drinker or dancer or something like this, especially if you are female, then you can establish good relationships between your company and another company and do a good job. Otherwise there is no future for you. And when you apply to a company, if you are a woman and just married, they will ask you when you are planning to have a child, so you have to be honest with them. If you will have a baby in the near future, I don't think you will get a job. (J, p.10)

When women get married and have children, they cannot concentrate on their jobs. (F, p.13)

The clear implication of all of these accounts is that women in the conventional work system in China experience numerous obstacles in the quest to access professional opportunity. It seems that, in spite of the efforts made by the government, traditional attitudes about women persist and it is open to question whether opening-up is necessarily providing more opportunities for women or not. Indeed, given that the largest group of foreign investors in China are from countries such as Taiwan and Japan, which possess an even stronger neo-Confucian tradition than mainland China and where workplace equality is even more challenged, it is possible to argue that opening up is closing down opportunities for women in China in the world of work, just as it is in the state education system, as we described in Chapter 2. Certainly, the issue is one which figured as important and of concern in all of the women's accounts in the study.

From the perspective of education, it is clear that the women in the study see their careers at Harmony College as a liberating and a differentiating force. As we have noted in our discussion about group working in the teaching and learning dynamics, many of the female participants make note of the learning that they have undergone in developing more assertive behaviours to the men they encounter in their study groups. As a group, they also attach high levels of importance to education itself as a passport to a better, and freer life which allows them a greater say and higher levels of self-determination than would other wise be possible. For example:

> When I was young, I thought my father was a hero in my heart and wanted to be like that. But now I think he is not perfect and also has shortcomings. But he is my father and has more experience than me, but sometimes this does not equal to his always being correct. Yes, I should listen to his advice, but it doesn't mean I must obey his order. (H, p.9)

Certainly, this force for individualism is something that includes the male participants in the study, but in the women, it is a more pronounced characteristic and one that figures more frequently in their accounts.

The Elusive Nature of Fulfilment

Given that the majority of participants, both men and women, show strong associations between happiness and fulfilment in life and professional achievement, it would seem that the female participants in the study might encounter a greater number of potential challenges before they are able to find the fulfilment they seek. As a group, they are universally motivated towards work outside of the domestically owned sector - even though some of them have been bruised there also - and the majority are seeking education and/or work experience outside of China. Perhaps the commentary that their stories provide on the gender dynamic of contemporary China, therefore, is that the forces moving against equality are marshalled so strongly, that it is only by moving into the external community that women have any chance to find real professional opportunities. What that implies for the future balance of Chinese society is difficult to foresee, but it seems to stand as a contradiction to the integrated and equal society that the government has articulated as at the heart of its domain. For the individual participants in the study, however, it seems as though some elements of heartbreak and frustration are firmly embedded in the system, which will force them to make hard choices and personal sacrifices along the way.

8 Chinese Students in British Universities

Changes in higher education funding in recent years have encouraged British universities and colleges to look increasingly to overseas students, both as a method of revenue earning, and as a way of increasing the diversity of the university community. International offices have never been busier it seems, as they try to meet the challenge of recruiting a growing number of new students world-wide and at the same time meeting the academic standards demanded by departments and faculties.

The challenge to maintain student numbers became even more pressing after 1997 when a number of the long-term sources of international students - the rapidly-developing economic powerhouses of Asia - collapsed under the weight of regional economic crisis. Not only did individuals in those countries see their personal wealth disappear but a number of governments have subsequently taken significant action to rebuild the domestic economy at the expense of international migration. For example, in Malaysia - long a good source of international students for Britain - the government imposed monetary controls that made it very difficult for Malaysian nationals to take money abroad, including for educational purposes. As a result, UK universities and colleges began looking to newer markets and China has loomed large in this picture.

There is no doubt that an increase in the number of full-fee paying Chinese students in UK Higher education is potentially good for the bottom line of each institution. There are a range of implications that attend this increase in numbers, however, that require careful attention if Chinese students participating in UK Higher Education (HE) are to get the best out of their learning experience. A body of literature over many years documents the difficulties experienced by a variety of international students in the UK Higher Education system. It concerns the achievement of both their initial expectations of the university experience and in performing adequately within the system itself (McNamara and Harris 1996, Elsey 1990, Jones 1999, Kinnell 1990, Mortimer 1997, Shotnes 1987; Hayter

1996). Many of the issues affecting overseas students impinge on a basic approach to academic equality in UK HE. This questions the extent to which both institutions and the people within them are aware of or equipped to ensure that culturally different student groups receive real equality of access to the apparent educational opportunity. It is interesting to note that the *Times Higher Education Supplement* reported recently that the UK's global share of the international student market has fallen substantially - perhaps reflecting perceptions about multi-cultural insensitivity in UK institutions compared to other global players (February 2000). It is also interesting to note that the *Times Higher* also reported that anticipated numbers of Chinese students in British universities for 2001/02 are predicted at more than 10,000 (April 2001). This group seems set to become far more visible and vocal a presence within the overall academic community than it has been in the past.

In order to understand the needs of Chinese students effectively as a foundation for enabling provision, it is useful to take into account the extent to which previous learning experiences in China may influence student behaviour and development as learners in the UK environment. Such an investigation would involve a discussion of what has been termed a learner's "implicit theory" of learning (Claxton 1996). Such a discussion represents aspects of the practical outcomes for us as educators of this research project. This section of the book, therefore, compares and contrasts the Chinese and British education systems in the light of possible issues that might confront participants in the reciprocal teaching and learning environment at university level. It compares viewpoints expressed in the literature about the ways in which Chinese students are perceived in their orientation to study with information reported by study participants.

UK Perspectives: how people typically view Chinese students

From the descriptive information derived from the educational stories told by the study participants, it is possible to map some of the notional skills, experiences and attitudes that a "typical" Chinese student might possess on entry to the UK system. Examining insights drawn from our study, from the already-existing literature about Chinese students in the UK system and from literature about the teaching and learning paradigm within the UK system, it is possible to plot a set of educational values and practices from the UK system against the student and identify the gaps (Figure 8.1).

Chinese student - "model" experience	UK system expectations about "model" student behavior	Perceptions about Chinese student performance in UK Higher Education
Experienced in developing techniques for processing large quantities of data	Experienced in taking a critical approach to complex problems and literature	Experienced in rote learning and memorization of data
Students accustomed to individual-based approaches to learning and assessment	Students accustomed to working in groups and alone	Students do not make contributions to group work
Students accustomed to expressing knowledge as unitarist ideas and factual truth; knowledge as conformity	Students' understanding is achieved by reconciling conflicting opinions; knowledge as iconoclasm with the past	Students do not understand how to build an argument or reference; find it difficult to express complex ideas
Examinations accurately measure academic accomplishment	Examinations are one of many different methods of assessment	Students poor at assessments other than exams; they do not take coursework "seriously"
Lecturer is the "expert" who conveys absolute knowledge and truth	Lecturer is a mentor who opens up the doors to reflective, independent thinking	Students ask lecturers to provide "all the answers" to learning development
Learning happens to the young; maturity should bring full understanding	Learning is a lifelong process	Students want to "get through" their education; they want "all the answers"

Figure 8.1: Chinese Student Experiences and Perceptions vs. UK Higher Education Attitudes

From the information drawn from study participants and the literature about education in China, it is possible to suggest that the level of academic adaptation Chinese students are required to undergo when they arrive in the UK system might be extensive. Lectures will be a form of teaching that they feel comfortable with (though they may feel uncertain about how to document the learning outcomes of the lectures) but much of the UK university experience, both academic and social, is something that would be extremely alien to students from the People's Republic. The overall style of independent self-directed learning, the lack of individual pastoral care and support available, the approach and style of student-centred methods and course assessments all present daunting challenges. The extent of academic and personal stress that Chinese students seem to go through during their studies might be likely to disadvantage them both personally and academically.

The study participants from Harmony College indicated strongly that they perceived a high requirement to change in orientation to learning on entry into the "western" learning environment. In addition, on commencing their studies in the new environment, the interviewees felt enormous pressure to make significant personal and intellectual adjustments very quickly in order to maintain educational performance. The interviewees also noted that the familiarity of a known home environment and relationship network was influential in coping with the stresses of the change. For Chinese students entering the UK system in the Britain, however, the challenges could be more specific, since they would be confronting cultural adaptation in all areas of life.

Rote Learning: a deeper approach for the information age?

Overall, it is interesting to note that a common assumption about Chinese students in the UK system is that they are competent at rote learning but do not possess critical thinking skills (Chan and Drover 1996). Certainly, this may reflect the previous opportunities to develop skills that the students have received in China. It also implies a value assumption prevalent in the UK that critical thinking is somehow more "useful" or "important" as an indicator of higher or deeper learning than the ability to process large quantities of data.

This assumption may be somewhat limited in its perspective and represent a cultural notion of learning and knowledge. Since the ability to manipulate large volumes of data may be in itself an important capability in the "information age" in which we live, and also may have some implications for the development of the lifelong learning society, it is worth considering this aspect further.

Facility with the use of intellectual techniques and constructs for learning new information is a generic skill underlying the level of rote learning required in the Chinese education system, where content of information is consequently de-emphasized. In itself, this may impose a limitation on an individual's ability to deal with conflicting information content or contexts. However, it is certainly a competence that is highly transferable into a number of different environments, since it is not dependent on the content of the learning itself. It may enable an individual to experience lower stress in new learning situations, since the ability to progress a "sense-making" activity in organizing structuring for remembering and articulating learning inputs as a prelude to considering the implications of their content may promote confidence to move forward in the learning experience. This technical notion of learning that seems to dominate the Chinese system, then, should not perhaps be devalued as a contributor to higher and deeper learning experiences. Instead it may be viewed as one of the skills that Chinese students possess in enabling them to move quickly up the learning curve of new learning environments (Chan and Drover, 1996). Certainly, it is sympathetic to the view that Chinese intellectuality has evolved differently to the "western" in its orientation more than the basic content of intellectual ideas (Allinson, 1989). It may also account for what Marton has called the "Chinese learner paradox", whereby Chinese students are able to adapt and perform well in the international educational environment in spite of the extent of adaptation they must undergo as part of the process (Marton 1992).

Formality and Social Isolation

In terms of attitude and construct about the learning experience, a number of possible insights emerge from the study participants' perceptions which may impact on performance levels during assessment. Chinese students may well engage with the educational experience in a more formal way than their UK counterparts and confer a greater authoritative legitimacy on their lecturers. At the same time, they may have an expectation of greater personal engagement in the student learning experience from university academics and administrators and anticipate very high levels of personal and academic support than other groups of students. Certainly anecdotal stories of Chinese students studying in the UK in conditions of complete social isolation are not uncommon. All of these factors merit both further study and attention from those involved in educational design in the UK system.

The Importance of Curriculum Design

Many universities have already begun to experiment in the design of orientation and support programmes for Chinese students and other international groups in order to help them assimilate socially and culturally with a minimum of difficulty. Given the government's agenda to increase international students' participation in higher education markedly during the next few years, there is also an important read-across to curriculum and programme design inherent in this broadening multi-culturalism of the student community. The enrichment of the university community brought by international students is perhaps limited currently to the social aspects of university life or individual research outputs. A closer examination of the strengths and differences of the learning orientations of the different cultural groups and individuals participating in UK higher education could pose important challenges and opportunities to UK educators. It may be useful to consider the degree to which UK education is heavily conditioned by a cultural paradigm. By doing so, UK universities might be able to develop programmes not only meaningful to a broader international community of students, but one also containing important additional elements that would enable the majority - the UK students - to approach change and the global information age with an intellectual flexibility. This facility for change that the existing paradigm may be forcing upon international students who choose to participate in it certainly does not exclude the UK student.

The Learning Process and Skills

Further differences begin to emerge between the UK and Chinese systems when considering the practical processes of the learning experience. As implied above from the policy emphasis on standardization, it is clear from the accounts in our study that Chinese students will typically have experienced an extremely formal and didactic approach to teaching and learning during their years of compulsory education and at university. Although the Chinese government has been attempting to reform the system, overwhelmingly, innovation in the classroom has been unsuccessful and the environment remains very traditional in style. Practical classroom dynamics will inevitably influence a student's continuing behaviour in the educational environment.

Questions and Participation

As our participants have pointed out, in the Chinese classroom, the teacher speaks and the students listen. Asking questions in class is actively discouraged. Should a student provide an incorrect answer, they tend to receive some kind of rebuke or punishment from the lecturer and can become the victim of ridicule from classmates after the class. During the class, the teacher will provide the students with structured notes - usually on the blackboard, which the students will copy and learn verbatim - students are not encouraged to take notes independently.   Active participation in learning, then, is something that can be highly emotional for Chinese students. It may be particularly challenging in the UK system, for example, where student participation and opinion sharing occurs openly in many seminars and lectures. Interviewees noted that they were often very worried about looking stupid or losing face in the classroom environment. In addition, "basic" skills, such as the ability to organize matrix notes or aids for revision is something that can be bewildering for the Chinese student simply because they have no prior experience.

Lecturer Support and Extra-curricular Relationships

Outside of the Chinese classroom, however, there is frequently a warm and friendly relationship between lecturer and students. We have noted from the study participants that the personality of the teacher is an extremely important factor in determining the positive or negative motivation of the individual students. Students freely approach lecturers outside of classes - and are often encouraged to do so. The real level of personal contact time and individual support that a lecturer will give to a student is very high compared to the UK system. Lecturers are generally available to students, have low teaching hours and often few other academic responsibilities. Students will be accustomed to finding staff ready willing and able to talk to them privately - and at length, without an appointment. There is also an important social and personal dimension to the lecturer-student relationship - something that is less frequently found in the UK and often discouraged. Students and lecturers may eat dinner together, go out together and develop close personal mentoring relationships, very much reflecting the Confucian master/disciple tradition (Cheng 1994, Cua 1989). Lecturers often take on a mentoring role for students, which lasts long after the formal educational relationship has ended.   Parents also expect to get highly involved in discussions about all aspects of student work and performance.   The insistence of direct communication only with the student about academic and associated matters such as is usual in the UK, is, therefore, puzzling to many families of Chinese students and to the students themselves.

Individuality, Assessment and Competition

Owing to the competition for places in Higher education - and driven by the strong examination system - students tend to view the educational experience extremely competitively. As we have drawn out, student work in China is entirely individual, and almost completely examination-based. Students will have had little experience in working in groups, for example, and, therefore, group activities may be difficult for them. Interpersonally, they may find working in a peer group intimidating and may also find it difficult to understand the learning benefits of such exercises. A number of interviewees noted that they who felt that group activities were "just playing, not learning" because the learning style was far removed from the formal mode to which they were accustomed. All stated that they found group working activities one of the most difficult aspects of studying in the "western" framework. In addition, Chinese students are not accustomed to the notion that is it technically possible for all students to achieve equally well or badly within the system. In China, class performance lists are produced each semester and students streamed according to their place on the list - there can only be one student at the top of the list, the place on which matters enormously for each student's career and future. If you are at the bottom of the list, you are almost inevitably condemned to ridicule and humiliation from classmates - and sometimes lecturers - as well as being down-streamed or deprived of future educational opportunities. This extreme approach to selection may have the potential to reduce the level of co-operation and sharing with other students that they may feel comfortable and has further repercussions for how students might operate in groups. Certainly it injects a high level of performance stress into the way in which Chinese students may approach the learning environment.

Formative versus Summative Assessment

The emphasis on examinations in China has a clear set of implications for study patterns. Students are unlikely to have experienced assessed course-work, though they will have received large amounts of unassessed "homework" every night - in the form of structured exercises, reading and memorization - and will be willing to work very hard at it. The Chinese government is currently attempting further reforms in education to address the stresses that such high levels of non-assessed "homework" is having on the development of young people (Kuhn 2000). Students will, however, typically not have experienced the idea that coursework can somehow have an important role in determining final marks for the course. For many students, coursework, therefore, is viewed as unimportant compared to the final exam.

Academic Writing and Critical Skills

The form of examinations in China is typically factually based, with extensive use of multiple choice questions. It is interesting to note that writing, in the form of how to style, structure and present a piece of writing is not taught in China, where the emphasis is on calligraphy - learning to write complex Chinese characters correctly. Students, therefore, are unlikely to have encountered essay writing to any extent, certainly not written assignments of the challenging 3000 to 5000 words typical in many undergraduate courses in the UK or research papers of any length. Nor will they have any experience of using references or multiple sources of information to inform their written work or their thinking. Even at university level in China, courses are driven by single course texts (with supplementary materials in some subjects such as languages), as noted above. The teaching method emphasizes the correct memorization and reproduction of teacher's notes or textbook information - referencing is not used, since almost the entire question response a student makes is likely to be in the form of memorized sections of text. Information is viewed in a unitary way: the teaching of facts, a direct reflection of the wider unitarism of the intellectual and political environments (Woo 1993, Meissner 1995, Little 1992, Hayhoe 1996). A strong emphasis in the Chinese system lies in the development of a student's ability to grasp structures and systems, which enable the learning and reproduction of information. Given the highly unitary approach to intellectual life in China, this ability seems very developed - techniques for remembering information content are valued and rewarded through the assessment system more highly than reflection on the value of the content of the data itself (Chan and Drover 1996).

Performance Standards

A very important aspect of difference in the two systems lies in the area of the style of assessment and grading. Not only is assessment confined to examinations designed to produce a list of student capability from first to last in the class, but also the pass mark is set at 60% or "B". A good student in China would expect to receive grades at either A/B level or 80-100%. It is extremely difficult to persuade a student that a "C" or 2:2 level is an average grade in the UK system or that 50% is "not bad" or "average" for a piece of work. Unfortunately, cultural issues concerned with face and ideas about failure mean that it may be very difficult to re-motivate many students once they begin to feel they are "no good" - whatever the average performance of the rest of the cohort, for example. This is caused in part from the pressure that students will have experienced in the Chinese system to maintain a consistent level of performance throughout the educational career and fears about the possibly damaging long-term consequences.

Progression and Performance

Students in universities confront more extreme perceptions about grading and assessment. Getting into university in China is so difficult that it is virtually unheard of for a student to fail, and should this happen, it is usually associated with a significant personal set-back, illness or something similar. Students are also allowed multiple opportunities to re-take examinations in which they have been unsuccessful, and this does not affect their progress through higher levels of the degree programme. Frequently, students will be studying for third or fourth year courses without having completed the requirements of all first and second-year courses. Some students studying in the UK, therefore, may find it difficult to take the first attempt at an examination seriously - they may regard it as a "practice run" to see what the form of the examination might be. More seriously, the high levels of pressure that exist in the Chinese system to ensure performance derive from different stems than within the UK system. In the UK, student motivation may tend to derive from the direct effects of performance in the formal assessment regime. For Chinese students, the pressures are arguably more intangible. These pressures are connected with "face" and "shame", with perceptions of class positioning compared to the rest of the group, with meeting personal and parental expectation and the wider pressure that society brings onto students to perform well educationally and then be able to become valuable and "productive" in their role in the community.

Peer Relationships

Socially, there are a number of factors that may be culturally different from that of the UK for Chinese students in the HE environment. In terms of working style and patterns, the Chinese class and university runs in a much more tightly structured pattern - the idea of *tongxue*, classmate, is socially very important in China. Connections that form at this stage of life are regarded as binding and lifelong. Students are also accustomed to working with the same relatively small group of people throughout their school or university careers. The looser organizational form and the larger numbers of people in the UK system can leave Chinese students feeling isolated and without the social and academic support network in which they would tend to rely for help. Once in the UK system, other ways of meeting British or other students can be difficult - walking into a crowded student union can be a daunting experience for Chinese students, as it is for many students who come from cultures where going to "bars" is not necessarily regarded as a socially positive activity, especially for the young. In China, the social environment is controlled both by the authorities and by the peer group - students live in same-sex dormitories on campus throughout their university careers, typically sharing a room with six to eight other people. Social activity tends to be limited, take place in the daytime and is often related to studies in some way. This trend is changing in China in the large urban universities but remains a consistent pattern through most of the rest of the country and will certainly colour the expectations of the increasing number of Chinese students participating in UK education who have not spent much time in the urban environment in China.

Youth and Competition

In terms of academic background, the Chinese system presents very different challenges to the learner than the European one. First, as we have noted in earlier chapters, there are only places in the public domestic system for 7% of eligible students (China Daily 1998). Many students will value university education very strongly, therefore, and their initial motivation in the learning situation tends to be very positive. A strong parallel perception seems to exist that HE - and education generally - is aimed exclusively at the "young", concomitant with both entry requirements and the policy notion that HE exists to develop future leaders of the country. The extensive network of part-time adult education options available to people in China challenge this assumption somewhat. However, the dominant preference study participants expressed was for participation in the formal system, owing to the strong institutional hierarchy in China and the status that a formal university education would confer to an individual's future life.

Conclusion

As education practitioners the process of carrying out the research project that has been the subject of this book has been very much within the spirit of action research and an active commitment to make changes to our professional practice. The themes we have listed above represents a range of issues which we feel we can practically take into account in the design and delivery of courses and assessments in our routine work as teachers. As a response to the stories that the study participants have shared with us, however, we have also engaged in extensive reflection about the cultural and professional values and assumptions that we have tacitly acted out in our careers.   We have tried to explore the implications that those assumptions have for our students.   Inevitably, this is a continuing process and sits within the broader professional context in which we work and study. There are some fundamental questions which influence the degree to which any individual, institution or education system will want to make changes in response to the increasing inter-connectedness of the world and to the processes of economic globalization. The pragmatics of the situation, however, seem to pervade all aspects of the philosophical debate. If we see education as an increasingly global market-led activity, then sensitivity to our international customers needs makes commercial sense.   If we see education as the facilitator of social globalism, an increasing sensitivity to the needs of different cultural groups within its context will enable the celebration of diversity that is inherent in the global perspective.   Even if we see education as the preserver of national culture and exclusivity, we can see our own values in sharper focus through a lens that compares it to others. At the most human level, developing a better understanding of the perspective of a group of students with whom we have significant contact has improved our empathy with them and has allowed us to find reasons for behaviours and values which otherwise we would have found odd or inexplicable.

For us, then, as researchers, the process has been very rich, full of discovery and insight, and enormously rewarding because of the openness and trust with which each of the study participants treated us in the telling of their own histories.   The re-telling of the stories in this book will inevitably provide a different and less personal experience for the reader. However, by including so many extracts from the interviews and by selecting a small number of the stories in complete form at the end of the book, we hope to have conveyed something that has some connection to the process of the work as well as its outcomes. For it is in the stories themselves that the stimulus for making change lies.   The accounts come from a group of people who exist in a tremendously dynamic environment and who for the most part have turned the meeting of different educational traditions from culture clash into serendipity. It would be enormously valuable if both educators and institutions could take that fortunate happenstance and shape it to achieve more consistently fruitful and positive ends.

9 Their Own Words

The following stories have been edited down to provide a summary of the interviews with these participants. While some of the words are answers to initial questions we asked the participants, mostly they are in explanation of "tell us about your life." We feel the words of the participants may more fully display the individual personalities within the lives they describe.

"The Unambitious Woman"
Female participant

Background

I am 23 years old, and I was born in 1976, that year was the end of the Cultural Revolution, which is very significant. I was born in Beijing and I am an only child, so somehow I am quite spoiled by my parents. ... About 6 months ago I moved out from my parents home because my father, got another apartment from his company, so I live alone now. You know, this is the first time I have lived independently and I wanted to try this kind of life. I think it's quite important for me and for my future.

Family Background

My father is a general manager of a food company, the Number Fourteen Food Company Limited. It is located in Longtan. It makes biscuits and chocolate and candies, things like that. My mother is retired now but she used to work in the train station. She was responsible for buying stationery for her colleagues. She worked there for 24 years. We lived in one house while I was a child - it came with my father's job. But we moved once or twice since then, only in Beijing.

My father graduated from university in light industry, his major is fermenting technology. My mum graduated from high school. My dad comes from Hebei Province and my mum from Shandong Province. How they came to Beijing is quite a long story. Actually, after my father graduated from university, he came here to find a job, and my mum came here with my auntie. So both of them, how do you say? Actually my father is my auntie's neighbour, and my auntie thought he was a good guy, so she introduced my father to my mum and then they got married. They were married for two years and then I was born.

Elementary Education

I first went to school in 1983. I was seven years old. When I started school, all the students were about the same age as me, six or seven years old. My school was not near my home. I first went to school in Dongcheng District. I lived in Chaoyang and my parents thought that the quality of the teaching was not so good. My parents wanted me to get a better, a higher quality of teaching, and the teaching in Dongcheng District is better than other areas in Beijing. This was not a private school, but a government school. My auntie lived there so I went to go to school and stayed with her. I lived with my aunt until middle school when I came back to my parent's house.

When I went to the primary school, the entrance requirements were not so strict. Not a very strict examination, you just went there and the teachers asked you some basic questions, just some basic maths questions and something like that. Actually as long as your IQ is not so low, you could enter. It was simple. ... I'd stay with my auntie during the week and at weekends I went back to be with my parents. In those days, we just had a one-day holiday each week. So on Saturday, my dad came to pick me up to go home and on Sunday he brought me back. My aunt has a son and he is 12 years older than me. When I stayed at her house we were always fighting. He was kind of like a brother to me. ...

Actually, my school life was, ermmm, it did not make me feel so excited. Because, you know, in the Chinese traditional teaching system, students are usually forced to listen and forced to sit and do something required by teachers. Students are required to do a lot of things, even the first year I went to school, I had a lot of homework every night. So it was hard for me to get time to relax and play with my friends. Actually, I think my childhood is not exciting or fantastic, just hard work. I have this kind of feeling.

At school, the teacher was very strict and the classroom was arranged, I don't know whether you have been to a traditional Chinese classroom? It's arranged, just like when we take an exam, with the desks and chairs in rows, the classroom is arranged like that. The teacher stood in front of us and just dictated the information to us and wrote something on the board. We were not allowed to speak freely without raising our hands or we would be punished. So I thought our communication with the teacher is not so good. I did not like school!

Middle School

I left elementary school to go to middle in 7th grade, 1989, three years middle school and three years high school. Altogether six years elementary school and six years of high school. I took an examination to go to middle school but actually the examination was quite easy. You know the events that took place in 1989? So at that time, I remember, we just could not concentrate on our studying...and our teachers had to go out to, how do you say? Support those er, students, and so that year the exam was quite easy for us and I got high marks. This made it easier for me to go to the good high school, which I went to. I went back and lived with my parents at the second year of middle school. That felt good.

Middle school was the same as elementary school. I think it was the same, all the same. The teacher was very strict, very serious and with thick glasses, always, always [laughter], scolding us students and telling you what to wear and how to walk. Everything, everything we did, we had to listen to them. It's quite hard for us, and you know actually my teacher who is in charge of my class was the teacher who taught us maths. Actually my maths was quite poor and I was quite afraid of the maths teacher. She was very strict even though she was quite young. At that time, she was only 24 but she was quite strict. She was always near you, always like that [leans over], and so every night I cried because I was still with my auntie and I had no one to tell my feelings [to]. It's different feeling to tell my auntie, than to tell my mum, you know. Actually our relationship is close but just does not feel as close as to my mum. It's different. ... There were some teachers in the school that I liked, though, the teacher who taught us Chinese. She was quite kind and encouraging and helpful for us, in our studying. Especially students who were quite poor at their studying, she was willing to spend extra time after work to help them. Quite kind - just a few teachers. The rest were just for the traditional teaching method, and made us lose interest in our study.

High School

From middle school to high school, I also took an examination. Actually I did not go to a high school, it was called a specialized professional school. It was for four years. Like my dad, I studied fermenting technology, for making yeast for bread and that kind of thing. I couldn't make good beer, though! ... Actually when I graduated from my middle school, I had 6 choices to go to high school. I had 6 choices, but I didn't get a good result in the exam. So, you know, that professional school, was my last choice. I had to go there. No choice. The school was located in Chaoyang District.

The teaching there was quite different from middle school and the teachers treated us like adults. They didn't force us to do this or to do that. I think it's quite different. I felt we could have our own right to control our daily lives. Because of my major, I had to do a lot of experiments in the lab, so almost half of the time I spent in the classroom and the other half in the lab. At this time I thought my study was quite interesting because it was not just simple knowledge you could get from the classroom, but also you could combine your knowledge with practice, it was quite interesting. The teachers were kind and helpful to us. Also the class in our professional college was quite big, our college is quite big. They had one library building, one laboratory building and two teaching buildings. There were around 1000, about 30 to 40 in each class.

Every parent wants their children to go to university. Actually, my parents were disappointed with me because my results were lower and I could not go to college. But when I went to this specialized professional school, my study was not so bad, so they became happier. While I was studying in this school, I had more interest in my study than in middle school. I was able to study actively not passively. The teachers did not force you to study, instead they encouraged you and supported you. They encouraged you to do some other activities instead of just studying at home and in the classroom. In my high school, we also had a lot of outdoor activities like football matches and things like that. They organized us to go to some society, to go to some old people to do some kind things for them and things like that. ... We also had a lot of inside activities in school. We had a student association. I was a member of that. I think the function of this association was to prepare you as a leader for the future, to prepare you in your managing ability and in your co-operating ability.

Group Work in Chinese Schools

When I was in the laboratory I worked with my group. Each group would be around 3 students. I worked with the same students in each subject. We had fixed groups in each class and six or seven different subjects, so different groups. The teacher chose who would be in each group. There was no special way of allocating groups. They just chose students according to the attendance list.

As part of the student association, I also used to work in a group. We would socialize, we went out to some old people who had no children to go to their houses do some housework for them. Everyone could participate in this activity, no special person organized you to do this or that. ... It made me feel that everyone had the responsibility. Every week we co-ordinated and came together. We had a meeting. It was a bit like leadership training because in this group, you still had your own responsibility, you still had to arrange a lot of things, such as who should go to do this and who should go to do that. ... There was no teacher involved. We could arrange some activities based on our own minds. We did not need to listen to our teachers. Our teachers, you know, gave us free right to organize these other activities. I felt I could be my own leader.

Harmony College

I left high school at 19 and came to Harmony in May 1996. Actually my parent's colleague knew the previous principal of the College, Dr Zhang. Dr Zhang and he were good friends, so my father's colleague introduced my father and introduced him to Harmony. At that time the College was quite near, just ten minutes walk from my home. My father told me about the College. He told me that there was a school that was operated by foreigners and all the teachers were foreigners. He just gave me the information and let me make the decision. And I thought it sounded OK and I was quite interested in English. It was my favourite subject when I was at school. So I made the decision to come here. I made the decision. It was not my parent's decision. They supported me financially. My parents wanted me to do this because of the fierce competition in China. You need higher education, otherwise I probably could not get a good job. And my parents hope for me to have a bright future. ... I had never been to a college and my parents wanted me to have this kind of experience.

When I came to Harmony, I was quite afraid. I had never talked to foreigners before and was quite frightened. I remember at first I was interviewed by a foreign teacher called Stephen, a guy. He just asked me some basic questions but I just didn't know how to answer and I remember my face turned quite red. I continuously said "sorry" [laughs] and he said "No, it's ok, it's not your fault". I did not even know how to say something like, "thank you, ... OK", something like that. I just repeated words I remembered from inside my mind. The teachers maybe did not even understand what I was saying, but ... the first impression in my mind was good because I remembered he let me sit on the sofa and was very relaxed. He made me feel not so nervous and gave me a cup of tea. We had just a relaxed conversation. I never had this kind of this interview before, especially in a school! I thought maybe he would be like a Chinese teacher, very strict - sitting in front of table and a lot of books and a lot of papers - asking you very difficult questions. But he asked me about my family and my friends and my background. And after five minutes, I became more relaxed and my English more fluent.

When I started at the College, I felt better because no matter what, in terms of the classroom, it was not the traditional Chinese classroom with the tables in rows. Here the chairs were in a circle. In that way we felt we had close communication with our teachers and we always played a lot of games. I thought it was fantastic and made me feel, when I woke up in the morning, that I desired to go to school. I really desired to go to school. When we finished our class, we felt the time was so short, we even wanted more time to talk to the teacher and to study. That kind of feeling we never had in Chinese school. Even though English was my favourite subject in school, in Chinese school, the teachers teach us like, er, they just taught us grammar or memorizing something to pass exams, just like that. They never let us talk. So we had no time and no opportunities to talk English in the school at all. But the Harmony English programme offered us this opportunity to develop our oral skills very fast.

The business programme, was not as interesting as the English programme. Generally, it was fine, you could say, but communication with the teachers was less than in the English programme. Probably my reason for feeling this was because in the English programme I was supposed to be the best student, for grammar and speaking. I was quite proud of this and I wanted to talk more to the teachers. But when I studied in the business programme, there were more foreign students and they had better English ability; they could speak better English than me, so I felt so shy to speak with them, and, I don't know how to say this. I lost my self-respect. So this is why I didn't like to talk much in the class.

The main difference between Harmony and my previous education was something in the way of teaching. The major difference is the way of teaching. As I told you before, in Chinese high school and middle school we did not have our own right to decide what to do. We were always told by teachers what to study and what to learn. I once read an article about western education. It said that in western middle school, the students have the right to choose their favourite subjects. They don't have to study the things that the teachers arrange for them. But in Chinese school, we didn't have that right, and teachers used to judge a student just based on their exam results and nothing else. After the exam our results was always read to the whole class. Somehow it was not a good thing for the students whose results were not so good. In school, competition was very strong. I thought that the teaching style in Harmony was different to what I had experienced before, so the way I approached my study was different as well. I think it was quite helpful for me to study and before at school, after class, I didn't have time to read actual books to study and to learn things in my own way. But in Harmony I had a lot of time to read and I read some books, some novels, some English novels and some English articles for my English. At Harmony there was less homework, less enforcement and more independence.

There are some disadvantages to this way of learning. I think the main disadvantage is because the teachers didn't treat you very strictly as Chinese teachers, so we could not manage our time. I think this is a problem we got from Chinese school because we didn't have that habit to manage our time by ourselves. I also think relationships with my classmates at Harmony were not as good as my relationships with my Chinese middle school classmates and so on. Because my classmates from Harmony were from different situations, different places, areas, they had different backgrounds. But in Chinese middle school, we all had the same background. We had not been out into society. We all stayed in the same area; we all stayed at the school; our minds were quite pure. But at the College a lot of students had working experience and some of them were quite sophisticated. I felt at the beginning of studying at Harmony, I felt it was quite difficult to communicate with them because I started to feel it is too difficult to, whenever you say something, you had to be careful. Do you understand what I mean? I don't know. Just like you feel you cannot speak, how I want to speak in Chinese school, but here, at Harmony, maybe I would say something wrong, they would get upset. Still, it was not a serious problem, but...

Group Work at Harmony

I think group work at Harmony was quite helpful. Everyone contributed and we treated one group as just one person, and er ... I think my co-operating ability began to improve a lot. I liked group work. I don't know. In a group I don't feel so afraid, just in the class. I don't know maybe I have psychological problem [laughs]!

I think the difference between group work at Harmony and in Chinese school is that in Chinese school, when we did our group work, we still worked individually. Even though we were in the group, we didn't like to work with each other. Actually, we never did group work like we did at Harmony. We just did experiments. ... Each person did their own part, not like giving group presentations or conducting interviews for projects things like that. The meaning of "group work" is different. What I learned at Harmony was about how to co-operate together instead of working individually. I learned this by thinking about my experiences, doing more in groups, more than before and then summarizing the experiences I had, getting rid of a lot of bad disadvantages from before. For example, thinking "in this way we do group work is bad", "and this way is good", "and then in this way." ... Before exams I still like to work independently, otherwise I cannot concentrate on my studies. But if I came across some problems, I would discuss them with others to get some answers.

The Future

I finish at Harmony in a couple of months. After that I have no real idea of what I will do. I really don't know. I have no plans. Actually I am quite afraid of my future life because I have never worked before and I don't know what a job is going to be for me. I don't know if the knowledge I learned from Harmony is suitable for me to work in a company. I feel a bit nervous. And now I try to call my friends who are working and my cousins to try to gain some information from them to release my nerves a bit. They tell me the good things about going to work, not as frightening as I thought. I will get a job in some company. I think it should be a foreign firm because in a foreign firm, foreigners do things actively and they are not lazy. ... They know how to get their job done in time, how to manage their time; otherwise, they will be fired. They have very strong pressure on them. But in Chinese companies and factories, they have the mind such as, er, they always put off doing things and erm, and as soon as they go into the office, the first thing they do is not work but reading the newspaper and drinking a cup of tea. They don't have too much pressure, so I think it's meaningless to work, just to earn money but without contributing any effort. It's meaningless. I think a foreign company would be more stimulating and I want to combine the knowledge I have learned at Harmony with practice. I really want to fulfil myself.

Success

I think success is not something that means you have to achieve great things. You just have to set your own personal objective and try to achieve it step by step, and you decide the time you can achieve it and then I think the success will come to you. I think for now, the major success for me has got to be to get a good result and to get a better degree. That will be success for me. In my future, I don't expect to gain a high position in a company as soon as I begin work. I don't think I will be a manager or a manager's assistant. ... No, I have never thought that. I just want a basic job to learn from basic things and to progress step by step and to learn by myself and to improve step by step. That's success. I don't know about getting married or having a child, maybe in ten years. I don't know. It's not my present plan.

When I get older, I think I will try to remember some very good things from my life. But I'm not an ambitious woman. I just want to have a common life, just as everyone has now. I'm not interested in wearing suits and attending parties and dinners or meeting famous people. I'm not very ambitious. Everyone has their own personal goals and abilities; they have their own condition. I cannot count on myself to be the chairman of G.E. or Motorola. It's impossible, I think. I just want to, I just want to fulfil myself as much as I can, you know, without so much pressure on me.

Women in Business

As a Chinese woman in business, it is still more difficult for a woman to find a higher position I think. I think this is partly still because of prejudice against women. I think that's it. But now there are more and more women that are in higher position in companies in China, chairmen or general managers, but still very limited, very few. You have to be very, very outstanding, very great. It's hard.

I think maybe everything we learnt in the College or in the school is still different from the things that we are going to face in companies and in society. It is still quite different to the reality, so maybe when we go to face some very serious facts, I cannot adjust to it very quickly.

The Environment in China

China has a lot of problems. Now, more and more students graduating from Chinese colleges want to study in foreign countries because they think if they work in a Chinese factory or Chinese state-owned company, the opportunity they have to fulfil themselves is quite limited. I think I agree with this idea. I think most of them who go to foreign countries to study will come back. I think China is still their roots, is still the place they were born. Even me, I have always wanted the opportunity to go to a foreign country to study; it's always been my desire and I think I will try. To study or to work in a foreign country for a different experience, then to learn advanced knowledge and ability and then to come back and to contribute to my country. No matter if it's is good or bad, China is still my responsibility. And you know the word *guanxi*. It's always a big problem in China. Maybe you are so great, you are outstanding, you are talented, but just because you don't have a good relationship with your boss, maybe you cannot get promotion, you cannot be recognized, so you have to look for another way. It's always a big problem even though the government always [tries] to get rid of this. The government has done a lot of things to get rid of this kind of this *guanxi*. But it still exists.

"The Book Worm"
Male participant

Background

I was born in 1972 in Beijing. I'm 27 years old. And I don't have a wife -
I'm not married! In my family, I have my parents and one younger brother,
aged 25. My father and mother met when they were classmates in the same
university. My brother is studying at the Foreign Study University. He
studies Business English.

Family Background

My parents worked in the same institute, the Chinese Academy of Science,
for about 20 years and then my mother went to a new office - the patent
office, the Patent Office of China. I think she did better than my father, and
she changed career at the right time. ... When they first graduated from
university, they did not have a choice about where they went to work. They
were appointed to a position by the government. And after that they just
had to work and work.

   Actually, my mother was forced to go to a new position. But now
she's happy. She works at the patent office information centre. At the
beginning, my father's work at the institute was some research on satellites
for military use. Then at one time they wanted to export from China, but
because of competition from outside, they could not contend with foreign
companies who had higher technology. And the government thinks that to
invest in technology development and to do the basic research is too
expensive. So there was no new research to do. My father had to change.
At first, he worked in the institute, but the institute established two systems.
They just said "there are now two systems in the country. In one, the
company is the name and in the other, there are research institutes. So we
will adopt the dual system. One is working in the market, and the other is
working on pay from the government." So my father had to work for the
market. And they organized a new company, but it was dominated by, it
was invested by the institute.

   I grew up in the dormitory of the Chinese Academy. The
environment was very good. Not about the material things, I think the
material things were poor. But I really enjoyed the atmosphere of the
people. They were civilized, or something like intellectual. I enjoyed that.
... My parent's main fields were computerized automation. It is very
difficult to explain. Originally, they were cultivated to major in automation
in the atom bomb. They graduated from the Harbin Institute of Technology.

At that time it was called Military Technology Institute of Harbin. They came to Beijing when they were awarded a job by the government. And if there, if the Cultural Revolution had not happened, they might have been sent to the West, maybe into Xinjiang or Sichuan. Those are poor places. I would have been born there and then lost everything I have already got.

So I grew up in an intellectual atmosphere. We lived near the Friendship Hotel. Along in there, outside the dorm of the academy there was some agricultural land. And the people who lived there, in front of the dormitory, were people who worked on the buildings, in construction. So maybe because there were a different group of children, we did not play with each other. There was a line there, yeah. It divided people. People could not even talk to each other. They would fight with you or steal something. ... I was told about them in that way. And sometimes, sometimes, we did play with them and I would always be fighting. (Laughs.)

Elementary Education

I started school when I was six. In first class, I was about six. I studied in the primary school attached to the People's University. That primary school was a national important primary school, a key school. It was open to all students, even if you lived in different places, even if you live in Xicheng District, you could apply. The local farmers' children did not go there. So the students of competence could apply. You took a test. If you passed the test, you could enter. At that time, people could not get into primary school when they were six years old. They have to wait until they were seven years old. But I would have had to wait for another half year, and I do not want to do that. I was supposed go to a place called PT primary school near my home. This school accepted me first, but it's not ah...ah...a key school. But since I was accepted by that local school, my parents said to the key school: "you see they have accepted him although he is not of that age, so maybe you could give him a chance to take the test." And the people gave me the test, and I passed.

Middle School

I went to middle school when I was 12. It's the Zhongguancun Middle school. At that time it was not so good a middle school. I took the test for entry to middle school and I was not so good at that time. It was maybe my third ranking school. They gave you a choice. It was my third choice. You have to pass the exam. At that time I was very nervous, because we only took Chinese and Mathematics. And because mathematics was easy, everybody could get 100%. Chinese was difficult for boys, because they are not so good at writing on paper. What I got was only, the two tests together were, 191.5 out of 200. 0.5 is very important at that time. If you do not get the 0.5, maybe you will … you will be put into some high school and that high school will, they will ruin you.

I think in middle school and primary school I was lucky. Although the middle school was not so good at the time, middle schools were just beginning. It was a middle school and, and the students all came from the Academy. That was important. The teacher's level was ordinary, but the student level was okay. So when we graduated, about 20% of our graduates entered key high schools. I think in my class maybe all students were able to go to a high school.

High School

I studied in the high school attached to Peking University, Beida Fuzhong, which was a key school. I was about 15 when I went there. I studied there until I was 17. I lived at home. It was very near, a five-minute walk. Then I graduated and went to university. I went to Beida, Peking University I studied meteorology. The choice of subject was not made on purpose. I just wanted to do that because it was a good university. And, and in middle school and high school I was interested in mathematics. It was a good link with mathematics, and I wanted to go to Beida.

University

When I got to Beida, I distrusted it. The atmosphere was changed. People maybe had a lot more choice and did not want to spend their life in an academy, just like their mothers and fathers. At that time, the reform showed its consequences. The money was there and we thought about our future. I went to Beida in September 1989. I had to go to military training first. That was the first year they had military training. We went to the military training for one year. The reason for that was about the, the June 4th. Yeah. They thought it was dangerous for students to come direct into university and be talked to by the older students there. The training lasted for about 10 months in Shijiazhuang. There were no teachers there, just military training teachers. We changed our mind. Washed my brain. They told you the politics, the Chinese Revolution history. And some military training about … It would destroy your health. And something like discussions. I studied English by myself. There was a teacher there, in Shijiazhuang - it was a military college. There's a teacher, but I did not feel that teacher could teach good English. We didn't have English classes.

The main class was politics - about the history of our revolution and something like that. We talked English, though. But at that time, when they talked, when they taught, taught us about the revolution, all of us, about all of us read English. I think some of our classmates after one year they came to Beida and they got TOEFL score 677, and went to Columbia! I knew when I went to Beida that I would have military training. I signed an agreement. Now I think it was not a good choice. But at that time, ah, I was, I thought Beida was more important than military training.

People's attitudes to the conditions at the camp depended on the people. Some people came from the rural land, they thought it was okay. But I could not accept it. It's mainly because of the atmosphere. I think that students from, from urban areas, especially big cities found it unacceptable. It's about the atmosphere. It just made you think many things when you knew they were not true. It's a, a, because I was not a person on the street. I was a conservative person at that time. Before the crash, about one month before the crash, I told my classmates that the students would not win. But even me I could not accept the situation there. I felt that, ah, you lost all your freedom. That is maybe, maybe I did not realize at the time, but now I think I was brought up in the atmosphere of freedom, and I like freedom and liberty best. I will not let any, thought or theory say that if you do this you will fight for freedom.

When I arrived at the Beida campus, I thought the education system was changed from before. The government had changed the principal. They gave us a severe mark system to leave no time for us to think, or to read. Every morning I had to walk two times around Beida. That was to take into account about your physical marks. And because the military training - it still changed some people's minds. Especially from small places, like I said before. From my observation, I believe their thought would be shaped. If they had come to Beida first, they would have been shaped as a human rights fighter or a freedom fighter. If they came to the military training first, they became a good party member. On Beida campus they tried to keep some military system. But I was not changed from the military training. I was still the same. Sometimes I think my going to Beida, some part is my parent's fault. They wanted me to do that. Even if it meant military training.

I was 17 when I went to university. When I was entering primary school, from that teaching system, I could have got into university when I was 16 - according to that system. Then they changed the system. At the beginning the system was five years of primary school and five years of middle school. Then when I was in was in primary school it changed into 6 years of primary school, three years of middle school and three years high school. So I studied an extra year in primary school.

Work

I graduated after four years [in university] in 1994, when I went to the meteorology centre, and then to a computer company. The government assigned me to the meteorology centre, but I didn't want to do that, so I decided to go and work for a computer company. It was just a small company in Zhongguancun [the technology district in Beijing]. At that time, I really couldn't call it a company. It is more like some classmates working together. We decided to do this in the last year of university. The others in the company were mostly from the meteorology department. At first my parents thought maybe it was a loss of security to begin this company. But after about two months they both accepted it. ... There were four people in the company. We sold all kinds of computer parts. We sold all parts to the government, and we made computers by ourselves, because we had the parts, so we could make computers just by ourselves. The money for the business came from our work in the last year, just before graduation, in our spare time. We just worked and got money. And, you know, to make the guarantee, to get the license from the government, we had to do something, we had to draw up a paper to give us a high valuation for our computers - maybe it was only worth about 10 yuan but we would say it was 100. That is maybe the principle to get a license. It's impossible to get a bank loan.

I worked in the company for three years. But we did not grow up, (laughs) we did not grow up - and this was a problem. So I thought I still could learn something new. If we just worked there, we could get money enough to live. It was also good. But, I decided to learn more about English. I feel my English is okay, but to learn something new in a foreign system, it could be a help to a small company. After that, I thought, maybe I could take a place in a foreign company and still have the small company. That small company is still going but I could not take care of the communication well. Sometimes I go just to help but I will not take a profit now because my contribution to the company is down. It's not so good.

Harmony College

At first I went to the College for English and then for the teaching system because it needed only two years of study. And I thought that people would see a diploma or degree from a foreign country as important. I supported myself at BIMC from my savings, and a little help from my family. It was because of the business problems. Though that was a conflict. Some of my colleagues thought we could do something better, but when I talked about the situation, I thought in 1997 the market was not so good. I thought the price was cut down. We needed new customers and our old customers had already bought their computers. At that time they did not want to change. We also invested…one of my partners invented a small program. And he said this program could do very well and make us money. We tried but we made a loss. Because you know programs in Chinese language are very difficult. As soon as you invent a good program, suddenly there is a copy on the market because someone will steal it. It's difficult.

The College was near my home and I went to have a look. I started in September 1997 in the first semester of the degree programme. When I went to the College, especially in the first semester, I felt content. I felt this school was good. There were no facilities but I thought the teachers were good. The atmosphere though, I did not really think the students' language level at this school was good. I thought that it would be good for this College to keep a language level standard but maybe the teachers have to pay a lot of effort to do that. But in some ways, it was not like a college. The College looked like a mixture of high school and college. I thought that mainly from the language level and age of students at the college. I mean the students in the language program looked like they maybe are not fit for college. They should study in the high school for awhile and then when they come to the college, the college would provide business training.

The main difference in the teaching style was that some knowledge did not come from the teacher. You have to attain some knowledge first and then you can develop your own thought. At Beida and elsewhere from my former education, you were taught Knowledge and teachers would say "When you have the knowledge, you can think after that. But now you have to remember what I have taught you". Knowledge gives you a base. I think that it was good that the students used their skills but I think that some of the students did not have a base, and when they used knowledge, they did not use it properly. They do not have a notion of what a good job is like. They just tried their thinking and give sometimes, just their own thoughts, not from a standard answer.

The main differences were about the teachers, the thought of teaching. In our high school, the ultimate aim was to enter university, so they gave us the same right answers. If you wanted to learn more, that is your job. But the teachers' job is to tell you what is right, what is wrong. And the examiner will ask what they tell you. And we will practice. That is the education system. In university, because I studied mathematics and physics, the important thing is the theory itself. You have to understand it first and then you can use it or apply it. So it still emphasizes knowledge. We thought if you want to do something yourself, it will be in graduate school, as a graduate student, then you can do it yourself, you can use your mind, your own thought. But in the undergraduate education you must first grasp the system of this knowledge and after that you can do what you want.

At Harmony, teachers gave students the chance to explore their own mind. But sometimes I think the students did not know anything about basic things. They just used the way and it looked creative, but this did not form a base, they did not form a knowledge base.

Group Work

I had never experienced group work before I came to the College. I thought group work was a waste of time, in the beginning. At university and high school, some teachers would say: "you should help." ... Especially in high school, they thought that group work is just for good students to help the downside students and what group work was that the good student just wrote a question and gave it to the other one. This was because the good student did not want to waste his time because the [university] entrance exam was most important. But when the teacher asked, "how did you get on", the poor student had just copied the answer. And the teacher said, "okay, it's okay". It's the best way to save time and meet the teachers needs.

At the College, I think group work was different because the subject was different. The subject was about people and group work is what we have to learn. Though I am not someone who likes group work. I'm a person, not such an open person. I do not want to share feelings with other people. But I understand that business is about sharing feelings, sharing resources - for use - business is taught that way, so I have to learn. I have to accept that. I know this, but it is very difficult to do in practice. It is still a little difficult. You know I was taught by my parents when I was very young that, "You grasp knowledge, and we grasp knowledge, and some people grasp us who grasp knowledge. To use knowledge is not as good as use the people. And it's important to get the power." My parents told me some leaders in the institute did not have any good knowledge but they were in a very high position. So my parents did not feel happy. I did not understand. But when I was about 25 years old, I could begin to understand a little. The most important thing is not what you are yourself, your individual quality. It is about the quality of how to use others.

In a group, I tried to avoid conflict (laughs). I know conflict can generate creativity, but sometimes if the conflict becomes chaos, people aim at people and not at work. So in those situations, I would think, "okay what you said is fine. And I know that you are wrong, but it's okay, I accept you." So sometimes I gave in because I didn't want to tell the truth and tell them that they are wrong.

After Graduation

I have almost finished my studies. After that, I will pursue my master degree in Britain. Because I am not young and I think time is important. And then I would like to join a financial organization, a foreign organization, which has invested in China. Finance is a much higher layer in business than computing. Now computers, especially in China, are just like retailing. Like retailing anything, like vegetables. The only difference is because the product is more important. And maybe in finance there is still a lot of use of computers, so if possible I can link the two together. I want to work for a foreign company because my degree is more accepted in foreign countries. And I think the Chinese bank system is changing due to reform. They want to provide the good things they used to provide, like houses but they cannot. Now they do not provide houses - the most attractive thing to us. And I think about the money I'll get because foreign companies pay more. What I have learned can be directly used in a foreign company because they use this system.

Success

My success is too ambitious. (laughs) If possible for, its about the style of life of retiring. And it's living in the beautiful countryside and a garden made by myself in the Chinese style in the old Chinese style like in Suzhou and like that. And sorry, I do not worry about money. (laughs) Then I could read what I would like to read, not the things that I have to read. I would most like to be remembered for, I think for the education I have received. It's about, you see I am a quiet person. I am very quiet and do not want to communicate, and I do not want to violate others. But when I was a very small child, the whole institute know me for my, for my doing something extraordinary. As a person who did not obey any rules. I was very naughty. But I was changed. I was changed by beatings from my father and by books. From my father a severe beating. He used this, a belt.

As for love, when I was young, love was something very subtle and needed to be cultivated and protected carefully or everyday life could destroy it. So I think success will be a guarantee to love. I think love is, is something, it is in conflict. I know in the real world people use love as a way to go up and they are very pragmatic about love. I understand this. And maybe I will laugh at the romantic love. On the other hand I feel love should be something that you really enjoy. You do not think about what is good, what is not good, think about advantages. There is a conflict.

China Today

I think there are too many people in China. I understand my goals are only of a single man. They could not last long in Chinese history. The longest is about a hundred years. There will be war. We will lose everything. Too many people. And I'm afraid of, I am afraid of the number of people in China. I feel unsafe because of the people. And I will, because we are in a changing system, if we change the system right, all the conflict will change in a political way. And if we do something wrong, a key point, it can change into, maybe into, civil war. A cultural revolution. That is a possibility. I'm afraid. I'm always afraid.

"The English Teacher"
Female participant

Background

I'm from Inner Mongolia and everyone, my parents, my grandparents lived there until now, but last April my parents moved to Beijing. Right now I am 28 years old. I'm not married yet and don't even have a boyfriend. I think this is the biggest concern for my parents, especially my mother. They think for a Chinese woman at my age, well at least to be married is important. Some other women at my age already have their own babies, so my mother always worries about me in this area. Recently I am being pushed from every direction of my family, not only my parents, but my uncles, my sisters; they are all using different ways to try to push or persuade me into marrying somebody. Right now I feel that it is okay. If I can find a suitable guy, to get married is okay. But if I have to get married just for the sake of marriage, I don't like the idea.

Family Background

I have three sisters and I am the youngest one. All of them have already got married and have their own children. I have one sister living here in Beijing. She has lived here for almost 20 years. She was in university in Beijing for almost eight years, and then after graduation she was assigned to a big company here in Beijing. It used to belong to the foreign trade economic department and now it has been changed but it is still quite big.

She is, we call it a kind of middle manager. She is doing the importing of machinery from other countries, especially developed countries like Germany, the U.S.A. or Great Britain for the enterprises in China especially the oil fields or the power plants. It's a Chinese company. Since being appointed, she has been working in that company without moving to any other companies. My other two sisters are still in Inner Mongolia. Both of them work in a bank but not in the same place.

My eldest sister was able to come to Beijing because she passed her entrance examination with a very high mark and then she got permission to study here in Jingmao Daxue - Trade and Economics University. My second sister studied trade, foreign trade as well, but unfortunately after her graduation, she doesn't work to use her major. And as for my third sister, her major in university was English Literature, but after her graduation, she also didn't find any suitable job for her to use her English so she was assigned to a bank to work as an accountant. Right now she is working in the import and export department for the bank to issue certificates of credit, things like that.

My father was, well, his education was something like high school, but higher than high school, but lower than college. In Chinese we call it *zhongzhuan*, a middle technical school. And my mother only graduated from a primary high school, a middle school, but she used to be very brilliant when she was at school. You know when she went to school it was very late compared with today's standard, so she could not go for the examination of higher school because she was older than the limit. She didn't have the right to proceed in education. After she left her high school, she began to teach for some years until she met my father and got married. Now she works as an accountant like my father. My father had been working as an accountant for many, many years, and then he worked for a bank and became the president of that bank.

Education

I got my college education in Baotou City, which is famous for steel and iron. I was born and raised in a very, very small town even further west than Baotou. My town is very near to Yinchuan Province. Before I got my college education, I really never left my hometown. Oh no, I left my hometown. I got my high school education in another town which is as little as mine, but that high school was very famous for a high rate of college acceptance - *gaokou fenshu*. That school is very famous in my area, so I left my home to study there when I was in grade two of high school. After one year I graduated from that high school and went to study in my college for two years. My major was English teaching. That school was actually called Baotou Teachers' Training College, just for training teachers in different areas, mine was English.

A funny thing is well, (laughs) at that time I think I was a little stupid and I really didn't know what I could do, but I had a very grand dream. My sisters were my models and their majors had something to do with English, so my interest in English began when I was very young. Before the entrance examination, I had a very strong dream that I would like to study English, or something connected with English and maybe be a business person after graduation. When I filled out the college form I chose some of the best colleges of China, most of them are in Beijing, but after the examination my result wasn't so good and my marks were only enough for my teachers' college. I went there and I felt very disappointed. The first day when the teachers asked all the students to introduce themselves, their backgrounds and their interests, anyway, do you know what I said? I said I hated to be a teacher but I had no other choice. My teacher just smiled and thought I was very funny. Now when I look back I think I am very funny and stupid.

During the years two years I studied there, I experienced the biggest movement, the democracy movement. Besides that my college life was very, very quiet and I spent most of my time in reading and studying. I worked very hard and little by little I thought to be a student in this college isn't that bad, and finally I even found that well, to be a teacher was not so bad. I think those two years were very good preparation for my future career although I didn't realize it at that time. I spent most of my time in studying English because I like English very much, so little by little I became one of the best students of our department. And that is the end (laughs).

Actually, I think those two years were the happiest time for me. There are a lot of good things for me to remember. The funny thing about the movement, well, Baotou compared with Beijing is very small and very remote although I thought it was a big city. When the June 4th happened, and before that a lot of students were trying to go on strike and things like that. Some of my classmates came to Beijing to see those students who were on the hunger strike, but I didn't get the chance. I really wanted to go, but I didn't get a chance. The biggest thing that happened that day was that the students of our college and all the other colleges in Baotou decided to have a strike. All of us went to the railway station to try to travel to Beijing. But this news was leaked before we got to the railway station, and all the trains which passed by Baotou or leaving from Baotou stopped. They dare not to go to Beijing. If the trains had been running, we would all have gone to Beijing. We stayed there almost a whole night, and a lot of people especially from the city bureau went to talk us into going back to our schools. I remember very deeply that when one of them who was talking to groups of students said, "well, what do you think you can do if you succeed in going to Beijing? You can do nothing, except watch. In my opinion, because I am older than you, the best thing for you to do is concentrate on your study. Learning something is more important. You are concentrating all your time on democracy but do you know what is going on?" We all got very silent because we didn't have a clear idea of what was going on in Beijing, so since there were so many lobbyists around us, we returned to our school. I was among them. It wasn't because I am not active in this movement, but because of what that person said. 'Get some effectiveness.' I thought for us the most important thing was to study. We could do nothing unless we got some things like knowledge or wisdom to arm ourselves with. We cannot change the situation if we are not strong enough. So after that I focused all my time on studying.

Work Experience

Even though I had a very happy time in my college, I still think to return to my home town to teach for my whole life isn't the best thing for me, for my life. My hometown is very remote and it's very hard for you to find the chance to speak even one or two sentences in English. I felt since I had spent so much time studying English that I wanted to use it. I wanted to get a better chance to use it. Even though I had such thoughts I still returned to my hometown because I had been assigned there. I began to teach in my mother's school where I had graduated. That was in 1990. I taught there as a middle school teacher. The first year I just taught as an English teacher and the second year I was a head teacher. My former teacher who was then head master, thought it would be better for me to be a head teacher, to take charge of one class, so he assigned me to a class without even notifying me. I didn't think I had very good preparation for being a head teacher, but anyway I began to work at it and I found it was very hard. Because in one class we had almost 60 students and some of them were really very naughty. I have to admit now that that one year was a complete failure for me. My teaching was quite successful because I like to put new ideas into my teaching and I like to put reforms into place within my own range of power, but I was not good enough to be a head teacher and I made a mess of it. That year I became very disappointed with myself and thought I wasn't suitable to be a teacher, so I thought about quitting.

Then after two years I changed my job to be a government worker in my hometown. I worked for an employment agency. Actually, my work should be to train the workers in some skills. People said I should train them in English, but actually English is useless at that place, at that time.

For my department, the whole department was very idle at that time. We had nothing to do because if people wanted to find a job, they just found some relation or some connection to find a vacancy, not through us. I stayed in that work and just sat in my office and did nothing but read my books. At that time I felt so crazy and thought maybe teaching is better. (laughs) That was in 1992 and I was 21 years old. I had nothing to do and I thought it was better to be busy. I thought what I had learned should have something to do with my work, so I thought maybe I should be teaching, but since I had changed already, I had no way to return to teaching. I spent most of my time reading different kinds of books. I stayed in this way for another two years until 1994.

Then I changed my job again and started to work as a bank accountant in my hometown. You know I don't think I am very good at numbers, especially working as an accountant. I thought it was very dull, and I was never good at mathematics in my high school years. At that time we had a common belief that if you worked in a bank, you have a better, higher salary and a better position. So I changed my job just because of that. I worked in my father's bank. There for the first time I began to work with computers. Very simple things only - my job was as a computer operator to book keep all the happenings of different businesses and then at the end of the year, I would make a balance sheet. This job wasn't so interesting but at least I was busy and didn't feel so useless. ...

In my hometown it is not so usual to change your job so many times. Well, it is not so easy I should say. If you want to change your job, you have to have some connections, somebody to help you; otherwise, it is completely impossible. I was lucky. I should say my father had relations to help me with it. My parents supported me a lot at this time. (Laughs) you know my problem is that I am always shouting, "I want to use my English and want to make good use of it." So my parents got really upset and they always said, "you should be content about your situation. Now you are working as a bank clerk and have a better salary. You should be satisfied." Something like that, but I said no, I want to use my English. Still what I had learned had nothing to do with my work. During these six years, I had been thinking and thinking about whether to stay in my hometown or leave to go somewhere like Shenzhen or Beijing, bigger cities, where I could be sure to use my English. I kept thinking of this for many years. During my work as a government worker, I heard a lot of news of some of my colleagues leaving their jobs, their teaching jobs, and going to some other places, so I was always considering if I should choose this way. I was thinking about whether the time was good, but I wasn't brave enough to take any risk.

Reasons for Moving to Beijing

I finally came to Beijing for several reasons. First of all, that year when I was in the government, I suddenly got the crazy idea of going abroad to study. I began to prepare for TOEFL test, but it was impossible for me to stay in my hometown to prepare for this test. There was no information about the test or how to prepare for it. I need to have specific training for that test. I went to Beijing and asked for my sister's help. She found a place in Beijing Foreign Language University in 1994 and I began to join the course to prepare for this examination. That was my first time in Beijing. That year I passed the TOEFL test and I was admitted to a college in the USA and I tried to apply for a visa, but I was turned down. After that I stayed in Beijing for 6 months to prepare for this examination, so I got a clearer idea of the difference between my hometown and Beijing. It convinced me that if I stayed in Beijing I would have more chances to use my English, so that half year helped me to make up my mind to go to Beijing finally, and finally quit my job as a bank clerk.

I made up my mind to come to Beijing in the summer of 1996. At that time it still was not very direct. I mean in that year my mom got a very serious illness and she went many places to try to find a good doctor to cure, but it didn't work very well. I accompanied her to Beijing and during that time we visited lots of different hospitals to find a good doctor, but still it wasn't so effective. We stayed in Beijing for two months maybe. Then my mom went back to my hometown. I decided to stay here to try to find a job. I stayed with my sister. You know my first job was … I went to the town market and there was a shop in Liulichang that was trying to recruit some people to work for them. Liulichang is quite a special place since most of their customers are foreign visitors, so this job is actually a shop assistant, but this assistant must speak English. I began to work there in August 1996 as a shop assistant. You know my parents always thought that if you have a stable job, the position must be stable and the salary must be stable, otherwise it is not a stable job. They always advised me to find a better job. But for me I found that I liked this job very much because actually my major interest isn't only to make money, to sell goods to tourists, but to talk with people. Everyday I met people from all over the world and if they could speak English, I liked talking with them, not only about the goods in our shop, but about everything. As long as both parties are interested in the topic. I found the job very interesting. Each morning you can not imagine what will happen on that day, so it made me very, very excited. I think that is my happiest working experience although it was very short.

I stopped working there because at that time my parents thought it wasn't a stable job, and they think that if you go to Beijing, if you don't find a stable job, then you had better go back to your hometown. This always pushed me to find some other job although I liked working in Liulichang very much. I finished working there in December 1996. Then I went to teach primary school in New Century School. Actually, I got the information about the school, so I went to try it because I heard they were recruiting and they needed people no matter what your major was. So one day during my leisure time I went to the school and found the personnel department manager and I asked him very directly if he needed any English teachers. That person was very kind and said okay and he arranged an interview with the head of the English department. The same day I met with the head of the English department and that girl was really kind-hearted. She had studied in the USA for over a year and spoke fluent American English. We had a very good talk. You know when I went to look for this job, I thought I had nothing to lose even if they didn't need English teachers. I can still work in Liulichang. I had no stress at all and just talked with the head of the English department freely and friendly. Then I think she was impressed so she asked when I would be free to teach a class. She gave me a textbook to refer to and set up a day for teaching.

I went away and prepared the lesson and on the appointed day, I went to the school and taught. After that the teacher said it is okay but the problem is that it is in the middle of the semester and there is no vacancy for English teachers, but we do want you to work here as a teacher. You will have to wait for some time. I said okay and then I quit my job in Liulichang and began to work there. I worked there full time, but since New Century is a private school, it is a little different from those public schools. All the students have to stay in the school for the whole week from Monday evening to Friday afternoon. In this situation, the school needs not only teachers, but also teachers in charge of the evenings, what do you say a house mother. So I became a house mother before I started teaching. I began teaching there one semester later, in September 1997.

I have quit my job there because that school is really, well, it has a very silly environment. I mean when the teachers working there, a lot of them are not happy with the environment because the people don't trust each other, especially the boss to the subordinates. They always press you and press you but never try to understand you. I used to think one of my reasons to study at Harmony College was to find what the reasons for the problems in my former school were, the problems with the management. It has been the tradition for the teachers in that school to quit in a very special way. At the end of the month is the payday, so teachers would get their money and leave without saying a word to the headmaster. So a lot of teachers left in this way because if they don't leave in this way, the school will punish them by deducting a whole month's salary. Besides that, we also have a deposit, so that if a teacher leaves in this way, all the money, the monthly wage, will be kept by the school. In order to minimize their own loss, most teachers choose this way to leave. One day they get their money and then the second day they leave.

Meaning of Education

In 1997 I had been in Beijing for some time and I realized that English is not the only skill for me to change. You know later on, I felt that really I am still supposed to be a teacher, but maybe my aim is not only for being a high school teacher or a primary school teacher. Because if I teach English only, I really cannot get the chance to improve my English. In Chinese high schools all teachers use the textbook without changing anything. When I first began teaching back in my hometown, I used the textbook that I had learned when I was a student. Right now the situation has changed for the better. There are some changes in the textbooks but not so many. If you teach in a high school, that means that you have to review the same things over and over again, without any improvement in yourself. Some teachers just save their own time and use the former year's teaching material to teach this year's students. It is very simple.

For me I don't think it is a good way; it isn't fair for the students you are teaching presently. I think if you want to practice on speaking, talking and giving presentations, then to be a teacher is very useful, but if you have been a teacher for three years and have taught the same material from the same textbook, it is really very, very dull. I have seen some of my former teachers continue in this way and finally become professional teachers. They just teach and don't love their students because they feel they are all the same. And they don't want to improve their teaching skills because they have the same textbooks and teaching materials. Maybe at first when they graduate from their school, they have great enthusiasm to be a great teacher, but after two or three years, they have lost this enthusiasm. They regard teaching as a kind of living style. I don't think that is good.

I always think it is very romantic to be a business person, travelling around the world and negotiating with different people, from different places. It is still a little stupid.

You know my major in my first college is English and I worked as an English teacher for some time, and after I came to Beijing I found there were so many people who could speak English. You know I came from a very small town in Inner Mongolia and it is very hard for you to find anyone who can speak English. So I felt very good about being able to speak English. After I came to Beijing and began looking for jobs, I found that English isn't my advantage because it is very common, so many people can speak English. So if all I know is how to speak English, I think I am completely illiterate. I need to study something. I told you that my big dream was to be a business person, especially to do business internationally. I think also I have been influenced by my sister because she does this kind of job and I think it is very interesting. I began to look for such a school, but it is hard for Chinese students to continue their study if they don't have a very high score on their national entrance examination. That was last year or the end of the year before last when I was reading the newspaper and saw an ad for Harmony College that used very attractive words like "you can study in Beijing but get a BA degree from the UK. You need only pay a very small amount of money to get a high quality education." I thought it was good because the school was teaching English and Business. I thought it would be good to improve my English and gain some skills for doing business. I visited the school. First of all I just phoned them and they told me the same things as the advertisement. I was not so convinced since I thought it was a big thing for me to stop my teaching job and go back to school. I asked some friends who were in the UK at that time to check the cooperation Harmony College had with the UK university. I was cautious enough. He got the same information as the advertisement. I also wrote e-mails to the UK university, but they were answered by someone in the marketing department at the College in Beijing.

Harmony College

I went to Harmony College for the entrance examination that Amy supervised in August 1998. I didn't tell anyone in my school about my decision because it was not 100% for sure until I got the letter of acceptance from BIMC. That is when I started my resignation. They were not very happy about my leaving because it was the beginning of a new semester. The school leader said even if you are leaving, you should tell us in advance so that we have time to find a new teacher to take your place. I told them I wasn't sure that I would be accepted, so I couldn't tell them before. If I had told you, you would not have given me any job because you would think I was leaving soon. It was really a bad situation for me. I had to explain to them, but they were not very happy, so they deducted my whole salary for the last month that I worked. I should get that salary. It was the summer holiday salary but they refused to pay me. I also lost my deposit, so I lost a lot of money. That is why when I came here and began my study, I felt really very disappointed. It was not what I had imagined. I had thought that this environment would be very exciting because all the teachers were from abroad and they taught in English, ...but when I came here it was very different.

For a long time I couldn't find the feeling that I was a student again. It seems the school does nothing to help us feel that we are students and that we are students of Harmony College. And the teaching method used would depend on who is teaching. Like Amy was exactly like what I want, what I hoped for. We can learn from her how to learn, and that is what I wanted. But for some other teachers, I really feel very disappointed. They just give us notes and tell us to keep on writing, keep on writing because that will appear on your examination paper. It was the same as Chinese college, the teachers really didn't know how, especially now, I think the situation is worse. All the teachers just keep us writing, maybe there is one exception. She is trying to make us research and discuss some things, but others just keep us writing notes.

The most important thing is, especially for future business people, what we need most is to have the ability to deal with different, unexpected problems. I think what Harmony College lacks such kinds of lessons for us. They can give us different roles and let us to play out the roles to enable us to learn. We never have these courses and I think it is a big thing. Now, I want to finish my study in the UK. I think studying in the UK will be very, very helpful for me. Especially for doing business, you have some international or at least UK background and that will be very helpful. I think my studies in the UK will be very different. First of all the feeling of being a student is very important. I must find this feeling of being a real student, and I am studying something. I think I can find this in the UK and it is very important to me. The second thing is ...I hope I can find, is to get joy from study. I can enjoy the procedure of studying.

Group Work

I think it is a very fresh experience for me because I had never done it before in my former schools. I think it is very helpful for me, but the problem for us, especially the students at Harmony College, is that there are many, many students who are very strong minded and have strong personality. They are hard to work with. But for my group, like when we were writing the report, it was fine. I think group work is useful in the study of business. It is quite a Chinese way. I must learn to compromise, especially when I meet those strong personalities. I must learn to compromise. I do admire some of them that have a very special way to deal with problems, and I can watch and learn from them. I watch what they are doing about a certain situation. My former situation used to be simple and pure because I only deal with some students, so I never had such chances to deal with different problems. Right now I think these students give me different aspects to look at the things from different angles and I can learn from them, but sometimes we just spend too much time quarrelling and we cannot reach any kind of solution. It is also always the person who can speak most and who can speak loudest that always takes the leading role and we do things according to what he or she said.

The Future

My family is funding me partly and then partly my funds for overseas study come from my savings. My parents are happy to help me out, but they are a little hesitating, especially my mother. She always says you are almost 30 years old so you should stop thinking about studying and start thinking about other things like marriage and starting your own family. Things like that. I do want to get married and have children. I think that is quite a natural thing, but I do not want to force myself because other people say it is time for you to get married, so I will try to find a person to marry. I do not think that is a good way. If I don't get married, I will be upset I think. I hope after my study in the UK, I can get married and settle down somewhere, probably in China. I really like ...(laughs) well, you know Chinese people always say if you don't become a wife and a mother, then your life isn't so complete, so people always keep on telling me so. Sometimes even now I feel very bad because all my good friends have already married and I am the only one that is left. This gives me a very bad feeling. It seems that no one wants to select me.

Success and Ambition

I think success is most of all an inner feeling: you are very satisfied with your life and most of the time you are happy with your life. That is success. And at least one thing is for sure. At least you yourself will feel that you are not poor materially or spiritually. You yourself feel you are rich. That is success.

Well, probably my own tendency will be to be a teacher. A teacher who is liked by most of the students - that is one aspect. Another aspect is that I do become a business person, and I can be very capable, and good at solving different problems. I know that will be very stressful, but if I do become a business person, I hope I will do my job very well.

Maybe I can put the two together. I do feel I like teaching very much and I believe I can organize myself very well and express it in my own words. I do think the most ideal way for me, the career, will be, after graduation, I will become a business person for some years and then I will turn back to school to teach, maybe teach college students.

I myself am such a person that does not plan a lot. If I think it is the right road for me, then I just go ahead. Whatever problems I meet I just try to solve them on my way, but I never think yeah, before I even walk on this road that I will meet this or that and have it cause me to stop.

The Environment in China and Women in Business

The biggest concern for me is, is the current policy will change in the future. Right now we are open, China has an open door for everybody. But is there the possibility in the future that the leadership will change and the policies will change too and then we will close the door, or we would not go as fast as now, or we would retreat a little? Yeah. That worries me the most. And especially for people like me when I have some foreign background after I graduate from the UK - will that be trouble for me if we return to the old China picture?

The situation for women and men in business in China is not equal. Women have to do more to achieve the same as a man. You know, in the traditional Chinese picture women are always weaker than men. They always depend on men to make up their minds for them, so if you choose a road of your own to compete with men that means you have nobody to depend on. This picture is very opposite to the traditional Chinese picture. If you get too strong or capable in your own field then maybe they will say, "yeah, she is wise; she is clever; it is okay for me to be her friend, but it is not okay for me to be too close too her." So women who are too successful always have this danger, not to be close with anybody; nobody wants to be close to them.

"The Mature Student"
Female participant

Background

I am 36 years old. I was born in May. I am already married. I have been married for over 10 years. I married when I was 24 years old, just after I finished university. My husband is in the government and we worked together so we got married. And I have one child, a girl; she is nine years old and goes to school. (shows a picture) - oh, she has really long hair. Isn't she cute? Yeah, I'm very proud. She is in the first grade. My husband is a journalist and he is back in Beijing now. My mother and father live in the countryside outside Beijing. And my parents, yeah, how do you say, both of them are retired. Before they both worked in the army. My mother was a doctor and my father, oh, I don't know how to say that position, but it was a high position in the army. They are quite old. When I was growing up, we moved all about China, because they got married in Korea. You know in history, China went to Korea to help them fight the other countries, the Americans (laughs). They got married there and came back. My parents have three other children. My older brother, my older sister, me and my younger sister. My brother and my younger sister both work in university as English teachers.

We lived all over, about ten cities. I was very young so I don't really know. I went to maybe about ten different schools, I really don't remember. When I studied in primary school, I always jumped from this school to this school, so when I was 16 years old I finished high school. It was very early. When I was younger I jumped two grades. At that time I didn't know if I studied hard or was a good student, I just jumped levels. In general I think the level of the schools' education is similar. But the quality was absolutely different, especially between the city and the countryside. The quality in the countryside was very low because of the teachers. For the army, there were special schools before 1949, then after that it was cancelled. When I think about it the primary school in Beijing is much better than in other cities.

Educational and Professional Background

I finished high school when I was 16. After high school, I went to technical school for two years. Then I worked for one year. Then I went to university. I studied car manufacturing in technical school. And then I worked for one year as a, I should say engineer. It was like an engineer. Then I went to an adult university here in Beijing. I studied there for about four years. I studied, well, not exactly part time, it was full time. After I worked for one year I went into the government. The government asked me to study. The government supported my study. So at that time my job was to study full time. Ahh, I worked in the Beijing government. The department is hard to describe. It is like the party branch. I worked as, can I say it in Chinese? Beijing *Tuanshibei*. I don't know how to translate it into English. When I was in technical school, I was a leader, and when I went to the company to work also I was a leader. So at that time I was not very old and wanted to change the job. We often had meetings with this government department and when they asked me if I were interested in going to this organization, I said sure I would like to. Then I went to that organization. My parents did not help me.

I have been a party member for a long time. But my husband is not a party member. He is angry with me for joining the party. If I work in this organization, in the Beijing government, I must be a party member. When I finished my degree I went back to work in that department for about six years. I met my husband when I went to university. He had just graduated from this university. We were in the same department.

After I worked in the government for six years, I changed jobs and worked in another company for three years. Then I changed jobs again and worked for a Canadian company - this company worked with a Chinese company and the bank to develop a major office building in Beijing. I worked for them for about a year. Then I changed jobs again. I still sometimes have to go back because a contract hasn't finished. I cannot say I have completely stopped my work because I am still with that company.

I use Harmony College as a reason to stop your work. Whether I get a degree or a diploma, it is not very important. If I go to another company, I can also find a job. Before I worked with that Chinese company, I used to work for an American company, as a sales woman. And then I worked in another company and in the government. I think people will look at my experience more than my qualifications. Sometimes I think the experience is very, very important. I have become interested in the business studies at the College, but some of the courses I find not very interesting. You know before I studied Chinese literature, so the study is very different. In university, I studied Russian, Chinese literature and car manufacturing, but the Russian and Chinese literature were just intro courses, the car manufacturing was my major course, and also some Chinese management.

Now my parents disagree with my study. Absolutely not. They want me to stop and get another job. In their opinion, study is unnecessary. Why bother studying? If you get a good job, you can also study. You have studied there for a long time. And your daughter misses you. It takes up too much of your time. But my husband is okay. He wants me to study here and finish this degree, and then we can look for other jobs and do other things. As for me, because I am used to working in a Chinese company, it has been for over six years, so I think it is better I for me to continue like that. I don't want to work in a foreign company. I think I am a Chinese and I love China. I want to learn something and do something to support the companies of my country. (laughs) It is my opinion. I think maybe my studies here will help because sometimes in China, ... You see I worked in a Chinese company and I know Chinese training. I can't get more knowledge and technology and something, so I think here I can get more new business skills and learn things that are special for me. Also you see when I was working in the American company I got two months of training in every year. It was according to my level. When I was at a low level, it was basic skills training. It was education to teach skills.

Reasons for Study at Harmony College

For me the background is not normal. I am not the same as other people [at this College]. You see I already graduated from a Chinese university about 10 years ago. So my purpose in coming to this school to study is just to improve my English--because before I studied Russian in university. I have never studied English in school or university. So when I worked in the company, I found English was extremely important. That is one reason I had to improve my English, so I came to this College. At that time, I planned to finish at the highest level of the English programme because I needed to go back to work. My boss was not happy with this because I was wasting time. Also at that time I was in charge of a training department. So my boss asked me to stop, and I said yes, I can stop.

At that time something was happening in my company. Sometimes younger people come to this company and do some things illegally. That means they get commission from the contract. It was a Chinese company. So I knew this was happening, but I didn't know how to solve this problem. Also my boss knew these things, and also another company called and said some bad things about it. So I didn't know what to do. I asked my boss whether my boss could give me a period of time to stop work because, and another reason was that my husband had travelled to England, so at that time, I was very tired. I studied, I worked and I took care of my daughter by myself. So I asked my boss for some time off. She said it was impossible, there are some contracts that you have to control. I said okay, maybe I can work here to follow the contract, but when the contract finishes I want to stop. At that time I was really ill, also there was a lot of pressure. Strange people called me and told me things but I didn't know what to say, what to do. I called my husband but he wasn't in China and also my parents were angry with me and told me to stop working in that company. But I had a very good relationship with the boss. She was an old lady who I had worked with in the government. We had worked with the same organization. You know in China, the personal relationship is difficult to change, so I did not know how to talk with her. I just kept saying, "oh, my god. I have to stop." For this reason, I still stay at Harmony College to study. It was not a special reason that I came to Harmony College to study English. I could have gone somewhere else to study English. I just got the paper advertising this university. The advertisement said there were English teachers, not Chinese teachers, so I thought it would be better for me, so I just tried it.

Harmony College

I began my study at the intermediate level of the English programme at Harmony. You know I think it isn't a college. It cannot compare it to the Chinese college. It is poor quality, not all the teachers, but some teachers are really at a low level. Sorry. (laughs) Maybe I just understand it in Chinese. I am familiar with the Chinese way, so when I came here I just thought what are they? Are they teachers? They just come here and go back to their countries quickly. They don't know their students. They don't know whether they are good or not, which parts they are good in and which parts they are not, or whether they can understand you or whether they can't. This isn't for you two. I think this is just in general a problem.

When I first came to the College, I felt nothing. It was boring. I think compared to the Chinese university, the environment is not good. I mean maybe on the wall in the Chinese university there are some symbols or logos or notices, but here there are some papers which are not helpful to the students. It is nothing. The environment is not good for the students. Also I think the teacher must have enough education. And second I think they should be responsible for their job. Responsible...for example, when he or she is teaching the class, I think most of the students don't understand. Maybe for the teacher he or she knows, but she doesn't want to spend time with the class, so they just pass through the material quickly. I think it is just a waste of the teacher's time and the students' time. Both of them are guilty. I don't think it is just the teacher's problem. The problem comes from both the teacher and the students.

I think sometimes it is a language problem. And sometimes I think there is a different idea that the teacher thinks and the students sometimes, especially Chinese students, they are used to studying in the Chinese school. They don't want to talk. They don't want to ask a question. In Chinese school you don't talk much, and you don't ask questions. What believe for the teachers, first for me the standard of that teacher's own education is important, and whether they can teach us. I know this about a teacher because sometimes the college introduces the teachers and the backgrounds. Not a lot of the background, but at least that the teacher comes from which university and where he worked before, so we have already some information before they come to the classes. So then we know after the class begins what is good and what is bad. Some teachers teach so that the students understand. The other teachers teach in a different way and the students don't understand.

The students here are very different. I think the students can learn differently. They are different levels and different ages. Sometimes I understand the teacher's meaning, the real meaning, but some students just cannot. I don't know whether they understand very well what the teacher wants to teach. So I think in the beginning, I must divide it into two levels: one, is that they just graduated from high school, and the other level is that they have gone to university or worked. I think that the students from high school feel it is just like attending class and they do just what the teacher tells them to do. I don't think they have a very clear purpose in attending this class. It is my opinion. Maybe some of them are very good, but for me I think I am older, and if I come here it is not always useful.

I think in Chinese universities the teachers give the students direct answers. Here they don't. Sometimes the teacher doesn't give you an answer, there is not an answer. It is very different. For example, if I studied in a Chinese university and didn't understand a question, I would ask a teacher to explain in just one sentence. It is okay. I get this one sentence and I can understand the book. But sometimes here I cannot get information from the teacher, so I feel confused. Maybe the problem is with my English. Sometimes the course is different, the teacher should know the answer, but they don't tell me. With some courses like business skills, different people have different skills and must understand the course in a different way. I don't know whether I am right, but some courses I should get a direct answer. Other courses, especially like your course or Yvonne's course, I think maybe we should think about how to deal with the situation ourselves.

I continue to study at Harmony College because first, I think I have a situation that I can't change. I cannot go back to my company. I have to stay here because my company and my boss already know that I study here. If I change to another university, she will ask me why and something and whether I can come back to work. And second, I have already studied for three years and I want to continue to learn some business courses and continue to learn some English. If I change to some other university, I don't know whether I can continue from the same level. Also the university will not give me any paper yet that will help me get into other universities.

The good things I have gained from my study are one, I have improved my English. And the other is that I have studied some business courses - those are the two good things. The bad thing for me is that I have probably lost the chance to get a promotion in my company. The other is that I have maybe wasted time here. Maybe this isn't the same as other students, but I am old and so when I am here I cannot work.

Group Work

I never worked in groups in any other part of my studies. Never. I think the group work here is okay. When I was in a group, I thought our group was much better than other groups. We can communicate and there was no conflict. Maybe they were younger so I can understand, maybe we can understand from our experience. I think it is good, so I quite understand your meaning. Sometimes I think the conflict, especially when you work in a company or in an organization, is a serious matter. Working in a group was sometimes helpful, sometimes not helpful. Sometimes it was according to the group level. Some students didn't want to say anything. Some students wanted to talk a lot. Some students wanted to talk a lot about other things. In this university, I think the quality of students is very, very poor. But the group work experience is definitely helpful for working in a company. You can understand some of the conflict.

Success

I can't say that I'm a success. I think I have failed in my life. (laughs) I thought when I had just graduated from university, I was a success. I worked in a company and I worked hard and I got a promotion quickly. Then I went to a different organization and it was better than the factory, so I was moving up. When I stopped working in the government and went to a foreign company, then I felt, how do you say? I just felt nothing. I think it is maybe the same for Chinese in a foreign country. If I work in a foreign company, I can't get a high position. First, I am a lady, I can understand that, but the second, I am Chinese. These two things kept me from getting a high position. When I worked in a foreign company, I thought I was quite good. When I was in a Chinese company, I was younger, and I was in charge of a group of people and most of them had graduated with a master degree and had already worked in a foreign company as well. That was difficult and is why I am studying. When I stop studying here I will go back to a Chinese company. It is difficult to say now. I just want to be a normal person. I don't want to be very famous. But my husband wants to be very famous. We always argue. His ambition is very, very strong.

The Environment in China and Women in Business

There are still problems in general, still problems, especially for women in China. Second is that maybe there is a good chance to get promotion, to achieve your goals, but there are personal relationships, connections. Also I think in China this is very, very important - your connections. Being a woman is the first problem though. A lot of young women don't realize this; they haven't worked. When I was their age, I also had very strong opinions, but after I worked in a factory then I knew that maybe I cannot move up. I had pressure, especially in the car manufacturing. At that time maybe there was something I couldn't do, and they would call a boy to do it, and I would feel oh, I can't do this job. Also I think this was very important that I do this job, but others would say no, you cannot do this job because you are a woman. Another example is when I studied in the technical school, there were a total of 100 students, but only four of us were women. At that time I couldn't do anything. To be a successful woman in business, first, I think education is important. Then experience, your achievement, your relationships, your chance, and your different jobs all make a difference. Many factors affect it. But if this department wants to look for a manager, a good manager, and you go there, even if there isn't a good person, they won't choose a woman.

In general the situation in a Chinese company seems to have changed a lot over the past few years, but if you examine it closely, it has changed just a little. If you are a woman and you just work in a company, it is okay. But if you get promotion, then gender is very important. Also in government and politics too. Actually in my job with the Chinese government, well I should have got a promotion, and I didn't get a promotion, so I was angry, you see. So I thought to go to the university to study English. At that time I also got some money from the government, so my boss knew it was unfair that I didn't get the promotion. So I just stopped working and didn't say anything. At that time I studied for about half year in university, I studied English. And then my boss asked me whether I would come back but there was no position, so maybe I would have to wait for one year. I discussed this with him and said no, I'm not happy. I just want to go. So the government gave me another job, but I didn't like that job. At that time, I had a friend from Hong Kong and he asked me to work with this company because this company needed me. So I think okay, I'll just try this company. So for one year I worked in the foreign company and I didn't tell the government. I didn't stop my job. After one year, they think I'm good at my work so they persuaded me to stay, and I think, okay, I'll stay there. So at that time I talked with my government department and left the government job. I think I was wrong to do that, but you know at that time nobody cared if you did something else.

The Future

In the future I want to go to outside to study. But the problem is that I'm older so I worry whether the university will accept me or not. My other problem is my family. I want to leave the college after semester six, but I don't know whether I can. Then if the government allows me, I will go back to do something. If it is impossible, then I will go to a company to do something. I prefer to work for a Chinese company, but if a Chinese company says no, then I will just go to a foreign company.

"The Construction Kid"
Male participant

Background

I'm 23 years old and come from Heilongjiang Province in the Northeast of China. I was born in 1976 the same year that Mao Zedong died and Zhou Enlai and Zhu De. I have a large family; there are 13 people: I have two brothers and a sister, and my parents and my sister-in-law and my nephew, and then the other sister-in-law and another nephew, and my brother-in-law and my nephew. No girls in my family except my sister and mother. I'm my parent's youngest son.

Family Background

My family is actually from this area, Hebei Province near Beijing. My parents are both from here but went to Heilongjiang Province when they were young students. So both my father and mother's *laojia*- family home - is Hebei. My mother graduated from high school and my father just finished middle school before they both went into construction work. They are both 56 years old now. They actually work for a company but then they organize groups of workers from the countryside to undertake a project like constructing a building or other projects. My mother and father pick the project and organize it; it really has nothing to do with the company. The company processes the information about where to get the project and then you go through the company to pay the tax. Actually, my mother works in the construction department and my father works in the maintenance department of a factory. Their construction business they do outside of their jobs, like a private business. We lived at my father's factory and I went to the school attached to my father's factory, where he works. That factory is where my brothers and sister work now.

My brothers didn't go to college. They finished high school. My sister finished college. They all work in the factory in my hometown; a factory that manufactures paper especially for newspapers. My mother decided I would come to Beijing and study for a college degree.

Elementary Education

I went to a government school near my home. It was very strict. I started when I was seven years old. The teachers were very strict and would punish students by making them stand in front of the class or in the corridor and the scores on examinations were very important. We had to have 60 to pass and if you failed, you had to stay another year to see if you could pass. I started school a year before you had to because my mother was very busy so she wanted me to go to school. She said some good things to the headmaster and then he allowed me to start school.

Yeah, elementary school was very strict. You had to sit with your hands behind your back and very straight - all the time you had to sit like this. And if the teacher asked you a question, you had to stand up to answer and then sit down when the teacher told you to. I didn't ask questions though because I felt I was not very clever. I could see other people understood, but I didn't. I just thought I would read the books again later to see if I could answer my questions.

In elementary school, we all wanted to join the Young Pioneers. The first batch (of students) who joined the Young Pioneers were very admired by the other students and the teacher also said some good things about the student. You joined the Young Pioneers based on your performance - the teacher would choose based on your academic performance. It all depended on your scores. The purpose of the Young Pioneers was to give a good image to other students, to practice good behaviour, to be a model student. We also had the *sanhao xuesheng* - the three-goods student.

Middle School

Moving into middle school was very important - there was a very important examination before you went to middle school. The examination decided whether you could go to middle school or not, whether you had to stay in elementary school longer, but it also divided the students. The middle schools were divided into three levels: very good schools, so-so schools and not very good schools. It depended on your score. If you scored high, you went to a very good school and so on. I went to the not very good school near my home. I lived at home and walked to school. It was the middle school for the children of the paper factory. All the parents of the children in the school worked together. I studied there because of my father's work in the factory.

I went to that school for three years. There were about seven or eight classes with maybe 45 students in each class, a lot of students. I felt middle school was very confusing. The teachers did not control the students. The students had their own thinking. In primary school, the students just listened to the teachers - whatever the teacher said, it is just like a rule and the students had to obey, and the students liked to obey! But in the middle school the students were a little out of control. In the classroom the teacher would have the lesson and the students would be talking to each other having their own conversation. The teachers always felt very bad about that. And there were a lot of conflicts between the teachers and the students. I have learned a phrase, "the generation gap" - with that I understand what was happening. The teacher always said you have to study hard to get knowledge and then have a nice job in the future. The middle school teachers did not explain very well, because in the old days their education was not very good. They just said the school is good so study hard.

Most of the teachers had the university background I think, but the important thing is that China developed very fast and the students' thinking also developed very fast and their behaviour varied a lot. I think I was very, ah, my character is very silent, so I didn't have any conflicts. I can feel the conflict, but I didn't have any conflicts with teachers.

The teachers tried to be strict and it was not allowed to leave class. You had to go to school everyday. If you didn't come to school for three days without any reasons, you were cancelled. In China students have the right to nine years education, but if the student goes against the rules, they were not allowed to go back to school.

In middle school there was more participation from the students. The students are a little older and we know how to communicate with the teachers. For me if I like the subject, I like to ask questions, but also I always considered whether it was worthy of asking or whether I should do it myself. Sometimes if the question was a stupid question, because the students have many different ideas and if you come out with an idea that is, ah, what people think is strange, then maybe it is not worth asking. And the model school student we had in the second year of the middle school. The students were encouraged to join the league, become a League member. We didn't know the reason, but we wanted to join. They didn't know why they wanted to join. I thought it was a good thing, so I joined in my second year. If you scored well, then your name was written on the blackboard, and all the students would write it down and would know who got the high marks. Actually, it was very confusing. Once the teachers said they would choose League members and then the students would have a meeting. It was decided which candidates and most of the candidates were the monitor of the class and the study chairman, the very important persons in the class. And also some people who had performed very well and were respected by the other students, so they can be the candidate. After that the candidates names were written on the blackboard and the students wrote down which one they choose to hand in, that was an election of the members.

High School

OK, nine years of education was finished. Some students can enter society if the student does not want to continue studying. And other students who do well and don't have any other things continue to senior high school. Senior high school lasts another three years. There were also other high schools that trained the students to have special skills - technical high schools. So students can go all sorts of different ways, usually based on examination marks. Actually most students have more potential, a really good future, if they go to high school, not technical school. I was 16 when I went to high school. It wasn't near my home. My home was in the southeast of the city and the school was in the northwest of the city. I travelled everyday. It took me about half an hour by bicycle; it was about six kilometres. From my middle school class, there weren't others who went to my high school. All the students in the high school came from other schools. It was a very good high school. It was the distinguished high school in the city. There were only three distinguished high schools in the whole city.

I studied *wenke*, art, in high school. I decided that in my second year, in the second half of my second year. The set up of the school was like the middle school - there were 45 students. The students were very excellent students who had scored very well. I think I learned a lot in that school. I learned from other students, and from the environment. People were studying very hard and they know a lot of knowledge. I think the teachers were very knowledgeable and they make the class very meaningful. All the students pay a lot of attention to the teachers. I think the pressure came from the environment because all the students knew that study was important to the future. Whether you liked it or not, you had to study. They actually did very well. They think that every student studies, so if you don't study it was very strange in that environment. When I was at that school, I preferred to work in a group. We shared information and copied each other. Actually, I think you learn a lot from sharing ideas at high school. You have a lot of opinions to share. It was an informal group. We were all friends. You didn't really choose a group, you just joined with people who were friends. If you had a question in high school, you could ask the textbook or share the opinions with friends. You could also go with your group to ask the teacher after class, but the teacher never put us in groups to work during class.   All of my homework and marks were individual.

The decision to study *wenke*, I didn't decide for myself. At the time when you had to choose between studying *like* and *wenke*, I went somewhere to travel. When I came back, they had already been divided. My teacher said you should study *wenke* and I said OK. I thought about it and shared my opinions with my father, and we said OK. Then after three years of high school, I took the university examination. The most important examination is the university examination. Almost every student in China doesn't sleep during the nights before the examination. We did the same thing, all the students in my high school. On the 7th of June the exams started and it was very hot. I took the exams in 1994. It was a very hard period. I even find it very hard when I think back on that period. During that period everyone just studied, recited. We had to understand seven subjects. There was lots of work to do for the examination. Actually, after the score comes out you can choose your university and the major you want to study.   The universities are all over China, many cities. I chose a university in Xinjiang. I could go there because my score was enough, but my mother chose the position for me again. She told me to go to Beijing and I agreed. I wanted to very much. She thought studying in Beijing would be better for me.

Actually, after the examination I waited for the scores and waited for the university to send offers. Everyday I visited my classmates and we just enjoyed ourselves. Then my mother suggested we go to Beijing to see the universities in Beijing, because the good universities are in Beijing. So my mother and I came to Beijing together to look at the universities, to do some research.   Everyday we went to universities and visited the headmasters to talk about my scores and see whether I could go to the university. Actually, I couldn't because I didn't choose these universities as the real ones on my form, so I couldn't go there. So one of my relations introduced Harmony College to us and my mother and I visited the College. They said a lot of good things and I thought and my mother thought it would be good for my future, so I decided to stay.

Harmony College

The marketing people at Harmony College at that time said you can learn English and you can get an overseas education. That is very attractive to students. It was attractive to me and most importantly it was attractive to my mother.

Study at the College was very, very different from any of my study before! I started at the intermediate English level. In my opinion, studying in Beijing is an attractive thing. And I got to know many students and we picked classes. I felt the classes were very interesting. Sometimes I was a little nervous but very excited. I remember my first class at the College was given by a lecturer from Australia - his name was George and he had a moustache and beard. In the first class he asked us to stand on the tables to see whether we can understand his words. And when we stood on the table the class became very interesting.

I think most of the aspects [of studying at the College] are advantages. At present I don't feel there are disadvantages. Probably there is something but I personally cannot identify any now. You gave me difficult advice about my English level, but you encouraged me a lot. I like pressure sometimes. If the pressure is not in front of me properly, I do just everyday effort. If pressure comes, I have a goal to strive for, so I will do my study fully. Hmm…some people say there is a lack of pressure at the College. It really depends on the person. Some people like pressure; some people don't. Yes, pressure is also good, but sometimes not good. Freedom also has advantages. I can learn English freely. You know if you are very relaxed you can learn very well sometimes. If you imagine it is hard, then you feel "I cannot do that". It could become a disadvantage.

Oh, sometimes I feel that the Western way I learned in College doesn't always fit with my situation in my company. Actually, I would like to work in a foreign investment company because that is more fit to what I studied in Harmony College. But I didn't have a chance to go there, so I chose a company that is Chinese.

Group Work at Harmony College and its Influence

I think the main difference at the College was group work. We were divided into groups and the members were committed to the group. You have to share your opinions otherwise you couldn't finish the work, the homework. You had to communicate. Sometimes it was important to ask the lecturer's advice and for suggestions, so you become important and you share information to overcome the conflicts between group members. It is important. I learned from this. Not only learned knowledge, but also learned the way you get knowledge. I think my group work experience from the College does help me in my job. I know in the group your position is, you can be in one position or another position. Your behaviour is important to the organization. If you do something, it actually makes a difference, either a big difference or a small difference, to the improvement of the business. I feel what I can do is just do my job very well, and get the recognition from my colleagues and from my manager. I feel recognized and I feel it is useful because I get lots of encouragement. I feel good about going to the next step.   Most importantly it helps me understand the organizational structure.   You can do something in the organization to smooth it, or to make people know how important you are to the group organization.

I think the group in my high school were just friends.   We liked each other; we respected each other.   If others weren't our friends, then they couldn't enter the group.   But in Harmony College's group, we didn't know each other, and weren't friends, but we had to do it; we had to get a result.   You can be friends if you know each other, but even if you don't like the person, you can work together to achieve something also.   My thinking changed after I joined this kind of group.   In the company you can have very close friends.   He or she works with me very often and we cooperate with each other and get to know each other well.   And sometimes the organizational structure, the big structure, you feel you are doing something good for the improvement.

After Graduation and the Future

Now, I work for the Construction and Redecorating Project Company.   This company mainly works on projects undertaking interior decorations.   They need lots of materials like marble, granite, floorings and wall coverings, lots of materials that are not available in China, not available at a high quality, so we import from overseas.   I mainly do this importing.   Actually my job is to assist my manager in joining the meetings with the foreign material providers to discuss what terms to buy the goods.   Most of them come from Europe: Germany, Italy, Spain and Greece.   We do a lot of very nice quality materials. ...   I use English a lot; I act as an interpreter at that time.

My family didn't help me get this job.   Actually, I saw an ad in the newspaper.   I went to visit my manager and he said OK, let's have a try.   So I tried it out and my manager felt that it was OK.   Later I found it was related to my family's business; otherwise, I wouldn't stay long.   There is a connection to my family's business.   My mother and father will bring their business to Beijing soon.   I won't work with them really; they work quite close to my company; they pay a tax to my company.   They sub-contract from my company.   When they come to Beijing they will do the same thing, but will network in Beijing to get information.   I will stay with the company probably, but I'm not sure.   I think my family doesn't feel that what I have learned is fully used in this company.   Now my position is administration assistant.   Sometimes I work as interpreter, sometimes I administrate, or do some office work.   Now, I feel I have to learn another skill, like computer or some other skills, more English or other things.   I will probably after a time…my mother wants me to continue with my studies. Hmm, I think if I choose I will choose to study overseas, but I'm not sure if I can realize this. My family has always been important to me. I have been supported since when I was born until now. My family will support my future study otherwise I cannot go. My mother wants me to study overseas. She always thinks that going abroad is a good thing.

Success

Success means probably in a very good position, like what I have learned some administration, probably like something in the management field. Having a position in management, this is one aspect. I think it is different depending on how I perceive it. If my family is around me and my life is very busy, it is also success. I think I will be very late to get married and have a child. I will get married when I am much older. I will make my family become more successful. I don't want my parents to work very hard anymore, so I want to support them to a happy life. Probably I will stay in China because my parents are here and I don't want to leave them to do the hard work anymore to support me. I think being in Beijing or in my hometown doesn't matter. I just must support my family because they have paid lots of money for me. I want to invest in them so they don't have pressure. If I am successful in my business, in my career, then I can support my family, help my family members have a better life.

The Environment in China and Women in Business

In China, I think, to be in society, I have been thinking about society in a more realistic way, how to be in society, the politics, the economics. I think the politics are a bit heavy in China. When you do something, if you don't pay a lot of attention to politics, then you cannot be successful. It is not easy to be successful. If you don't know how to network, how to know the government, how to have relationships, then you cannot be successful. Yeah, *guanxi* is very strong here. I think this will have an influence on my career, but I don't know if this is better overseas or not because I haven't been there.

Whether women and men in China have an equal opportunity in business in China depends on position. When you apply for a job, some positions are for men and some are for women. Maybe it is how Chinese culture perceives the position. If they want a secretary, they think it should be a girl. If it is a manager or a senior manager, it must be most of the time a man. Probably they don't need to write it down but people think this way. This thinking is part of the *guanxi* system. It is part of the relationship between people. These ideas of a job have developed over a long period of time and have become fixed. The situation is changing. I think people make the difference. If the woman has ability, then the woman can apply for that job of senior executive or whatever. But the common person thinks that this position is for a man. When they see that she is a woman, they will think it is very strange. They can accept. They can accept that the woman has ability. The system is already not stable.

"The Self-Made Woman"
Female participant

Family Background

I was born in 1971, that is 28 years old. I was born in Jiangsu Province, in a small city. I have five brothers and one sister, two step brothers and three brothers. Four brothers are older than I am and then I have a younger brother and an elder sister. I am almost the youngest. My family background is quite complicated. When I was 13 my family lived in Jiangxi. My father died of cancer, stomach cancer. It was kind of a sudden situation. I was in my first year of middle school, 13 years old. It was in the wintertime. At that time we were required to live at school and at the weekend when I came home, my father had moved into hospital. My mother had to take care of him. Before that my father seldom got ill. He was very strong that way. Then for about one month around the Chinese New Year, my father got ill and the day before the New Year, my father died. Before that day, he said he wanted to go home because he didn't want to stay in hospital. My brother was only ten at that time, so my brother and my situation were the worst. Three of my older brothers were already married. My mother was a primary school teacher, a Chinese teacher, and suddenly this. Also my mother and my father were not originally from that city. My mother was originally from Jiangsu, Wuxi County. My father was from Jiangxi but not from that specific place. You see in China if you are not a person born there, you have some difficulties sometimes, but now the situation seems to be getting better.

My father had a very interesting background. My father was a countryman; he was born in the countryside. And he was quite bright, I think. He was the first person from that little town to be accepted to a university. He was 18 years old and my grandfather and all my ancestors were all farmers, peasants. My father got the chance to have a college education. He first went to a teacher's training college in Jiangxi. He was born in 1929, so just after he got into college the war began, the war between Jiang Jieshi (Chiang Kaishek), the former president of Taiwan. Because Chiang Kaishek's son was originally from my hometown in Jiangxi Province, so that was very important. His son was sent to that place to manage and the education system was very good in that province. They had a Christian college and according to the museum - now if you go to that place there is a big museum that shows you the history - there were quite a lot of foreigners, mostly teachers, who were mostly Christian. They had both a Christian girls' school and a Christian boys' school in the 1920's. Also in the beginning of the 1940's they were still there. ... My father wasn't a Christian; it was just that the education system was very good in that province, so my father got the chance. Every year they had an open examination. If you are really poor but could pass the exam, you could get a scholarship. After the war, he joined the Guomingdang (KMT) army. Because he was recruited, not just recruited, maybe forced to join the army. Then he was sent to Taiwan for training for eight months; he learned the, how do you say? He worked the radio. He did this kind of secret job. After that he was sent back.

When he returned to China after training in Taiwan, the army was appointed to Shanghai. Then the situation changed a lot. Mao Zedong was going to win, so the head of the army was, how do you say? He would go over, to the other side, to the former enemy. The other side didn't accept them without any caution, so my father was in a specific position with the radio job, so he was sent to a re-education camp in Anhui. After re-education he was sent to a university. His major was economics. He graduated from university in 1954, and he had quite a good job in the transportation department of Jiangxi Province. In 1958 the revolution started, not really a revolution, but a campaign, a *gaizao*. In the anti-rightest campaign of 1958 my father was the first or one of the first to be criticized because of his complicated background. Then he was sent to Jiangxi to a factory city to work as a kind of mechanic. It was quite difficult for him then. He was in the revolution, the Cultural Revolution, and they treated him more severely. He was sent to a farm, to work. That was in 1964. He stayed in the country for five years, and returned to his city in 1969. In my memory, my home in that factory city was quite poor. The situation was quite poor. The living condition was quite poor. We never got rice for dinner. Until I was 16, I lived in the same house in that place. It was quite historical, that place. The house we lived in was built around a circle and every family had a room and would cook in the corridor. Eight families shared the courtyard. My two elder brothers had already married, but six of us lived in that house.

My father married several times. First, you see, in China it was common to have a wife that was older than the husband. My father had a wife that was four years older than him. The mother of the boy would buy a young girl who was two or three years old from another family and then the girl would do the housework of the family. It was a common kind of arranged marriage. My father's situation was like that. Before he was 18 years old, he had his first son, my eldest brother, so my brother's daughter is as old as my younger brother. My mother wasn't his second wife either; she was his step-wife. In the army he married a colleague and then that woman died when she was giving birth to my second brother. He had divorced his first wife; she is still alive in her hometown.

My mother was moved by the government to be in the same city as my father. At that time, every job was assigned by the government. Only if the government allowed a worker to move would the person have citizenship there, in that place. I was the first child born in Jiangxi. A few years after my father died, my family moved to Shenzhen, in 1986. I was 16 years old. My mother, my sister, two other brothers and I moved to Shenzhen. Only my two step-brothers and their families live in that town in Jiangxi now. My mother decided to change the situation and she got a job in Shenzhen. At that time Shenzhen was new and the government was recruiting some experienced teachers, so my mother had many years teaching experience. She had a teacher's college education and had taught for many years.

No one in my family went to university. Going to college is my dream and my mother's dream. All of my brothers completed high school because they had to, but my two eldest brothers only had two years of high school because that was all there was at that time. My sister only graduated from elementary school, five years schooling. My other older brother graduated from high school and my younger brother went to a vocational school after middle school graduation. He said he didn't want to waste time. He wanted to work. All of my brothers except the younger one are married and have children. My sister is also married. My step-brothers work together running their own transportation business. They bought a big bus and transfer locals from Jiangxi to Canton. Many, many people go to work in Canton, migrant workers. My sister moved to Shenzhen but then she married someone from Jiangxi and moved back. She lives in Jiangxi now. My younger brother still lives in Shenzhen. My mother died in 1993.

Educational Background

I went to school in Jiangxi, through middle school. You see in that kind of factory city, they have a school that is just for the factory children. I went to that sort of school. The children of the workers of that factory didn't have to pay. The school was almost free. I started school when I was 8 years old. That was the common age. There were more than 50 students in a classroom. Actually, before I entered the elementary school, I went to kindergarten, mostly with factory children. I have a very good memory of that teacher, a lady. She was not married at that time and she was very kind. She would take us outside and would organize some games for us, and then she would ask us to have a handkerchief. It was quite expensive for some of the kids, and she would ask us all to have one and put our name on it with a needle - to embroider our name there. Every day she would check to see if it was clean, and if it wasn't, she would send us to clean it (laughs). I remember we had two classmates who couldn't afford to buy the handkerchief, so she bout it for them. Everyone had to have a handkerchief.

I don't have a good memory about the teacher in my elementary school. In middle school I had one Chinese teacher who also taught us the basics of biology, how a tree would grow that type of thing. Most of my classmates liked him very much. I liked him very much. Then I was very motivated. I always received the top score. That is why my mother tried to let me study and not make me do housework. My sister had to do that sort of thing. I remember after class that teacher was also in the class. He was in charge of our class, so he would organize some activities after school. Usually you would attend but it was not required.

I finished *chuzhong*, junior middle school, in Jiangxi. Then I studied *gaozhong*, senior middle school, in Shenzhen from October, although the other students had begun in September - I was late. Since my high school was in another province, I was a little uncomfortable because I couldn't speak the dialect. The students, because during those years there were not many outsiders, it was 1986, and there weren't many students from other places, so I was quite alone. I had also lost interest in studying. I wanted to find a job right away. My mother was still teaching in a primary school, a government school. And we lived in a small apartment with two bedrooms, but shared a kitchen with two other families. It was my mother, sister, brother and I. Anyway, my mother didn't want me to quit school. She said I had to at least finish high school, and then she would let me do what I wanted to do. I was quite honest and open with my mother and told her I couldn't concentrate on my study. I told her that money was very important for me to concentrate. She said at least I had to finish high school; she would not change her mind. At that moment, in high school we had to be separated into art or mathematics in high school. Since I was quite interested in biology, I felt mathematics was okay. I was in *like ban*, the science class. You see the math and the algebra were very difficult if you were not concentrating. If you missed some lessons, then you failed. You will feel it very difficult to catch up.

Usually the study was individual study both at home and in the class. I just couldn't concentrate. In my second year in Shenzhen, my mathematics grade was very low, below the average. My mother was so angry with me. She said that if I dare study this way, her heart would break because she had supported me. She really pressured me. I said okay and tried to struggle with my studies. I tried hard to manage the examination, so my grade was still above average. Grades were based all on examinations. We had homework exercises, but they were easy and the exams were difficult. The exams were what you had to concentrate on. Then the last year, I told my mother I was not going to go to college; that I was not interested in going to college. Because my situation was not so good, I didn't want to go to college. She said okay but that I should at least attend the high school graduation examinations. She wanted me to go to college but at that time, my grades were not so good, so I couldn't get the top colleges, maybe enter some provincial universities, but not the top ones. So I just attended the graduation examination. I didn't even attend the college entrance examination. That was 1989.

In Shenzshen, I always was feeling very pressured and didn't enjoy my studies. I learned some of the language and made friends, but I was not really okay towards others. I didn't make many friends in class. My best friend was my younger brother, also not my mother. I couldn't tell her what I felt. At that time, my mother thought I was quite naughty. She couldn't understand me.

Professional Background

So I left school and started working in a hotel, the Excelsior Hotel. I was a clerk in the library. I would get the newspapers and take them to my desk. Then I would put the room numbers on the papers and let the lobby boy send the papers to every room. I got the job through an introduction. The vice-president of that hotel, his son was my mother's student at that time. I worked at that hotel for a total of eight years. When I was working in the library, I found the books were very interesting, mostly I would read the books. Then I realized that a college education was important to improve your job, to survive in a real organization. Hmm...mostly I studied English. I studied English by myself at that time. My English was not that good. The first textbook I read was a copy of an American textbook, *English for Today*, and then I studied a British one, *New Concept English*. I tried to recite from book one to book three, but book four was quite difficult because it was all about scientific discoveries. I also went to an

English club at the Shenzhen library, which was free. I had a very interesting experience. I studied English from textbooks in Chinese, all published in Chinese. Then a guest in the hotel, a regular guest in the hotel, a man from a small family-run business from Hong Kong, he introduced me to *Reader's Digest*. And then the Shenzhen library had some old copies of *Time Magazine*. When I had the chance to read these magazines, I was fascinated by all the information, by the technology that had improved so much in other countries. Also in Shenzhen we can watch the Hong Kong television programs, and they had English tv programs. They had a lot of English programs. I am also interested in 20:20 and BBC.

I didn't receive much training from the hotel, just on the job training. I read some secretarial book when I was promoted. I received job training. Just some regulations or something like that. Since the hotel was a government organization, we had some political lessons. For example, after a big meeting of the government, then the personnel department would organize a training class to tell you the political issues. The education was different than in high school. In high school you really want to learn something for your examinations to get high grades, but for hotel training most of the time I felt it was kind of routine, just another routine.

I had three promotions during the eight years I worked at the hotel. The first was from the library to the marketing department, as a clerk. Then the second promotion was from marketing to secretary. I stayed in the first job from 1989 to 1992, and then in the marketing department until 1994. Then I worked four years as a secretary. As a secretary, I would write the reports, and just the routine. Usually once a month the report had the market view. It had three parts. An introduction of this month's work and then an analysis of the occupancy rate at the hotel. How much compared with the previous month and then with the same month in the previous year, just this kind of style. Then the last part told what the plan was for the next month. I had no training. When I started to write this kind of formal report, I studied on my own and my manager accepted it.

Chinese Teaching/Learning Styles

The competition in Chinese schools was very severe. The teachers from elementary school to high school just liked the good students who got higher grades. They would usually ask more questions of the top students. Then the top students would receive more respect from the other students. Just the normal students would not attack the top students. The classroom was very disciplined. When I was in middle school and elementary school I would sit this way (indicates straight back with hands behind her back and head up). In the morning when you went to school, you usually had a meeting and then you had to write poems, Chinese poems, and in high school you had your English class. It was half an hour before the real classes started. The teachers would come to the class to supervise the students reading. We sat at our desk and read a book. And the teacher would just walk around and have a look. After that we had morning exercise and then we had the first class. Usually we had four classes in the morning and in the middle we had body exercises at about 10:20.

Mostly I was interested in Chinese and Mathematics, so I paid a lot of attention to these two teachers. I found that Chinese teachers are usually very emotional. When they are talking about the articles, they tell you this is what is behind the article, the meaning of the article. I think for the Chinese teacher, we were taught to tell not what was true. Before the lesson, they asked us to find the main idea of the article, what the thought of the article was. We had to write it down. It was a kind of homework, an exercise. The next day the teacher would ask some of the students to read what they had written about the main idea of the article. Then we were using very patriotic, very political thought - just this sort of thing. It is interesting because when we were so young we really didn't know what this author wanted to tell. At that moment maybe the writer was really emotional. There was no patriotism, but when the teacher asked you to tell the story, the main idea of the article, you had to tell the accepted thought of the article. It was difficult for us kids to deal with this situation. Lover of country was very important. That was in 1978 and most of the articles in my textbook were about the revolution, about Mao Zidong fighting with somebody. It was too much criticism about the other side. I had a feeling when I was in middle school, that Hong Kong and the western world was so bad. It was dirty and what. Then when I got to Shenzhen and had access to tv programs from Hong Kong, I thought, and then I listened to the songs, the music from Hong Kong, and I thought, how can these people be so dirty if they have such emotional feeling. I started to think back to the articles I had studied and I felt I was cheated. They didn't tell all the facts of the situation. But now I look at my niece and nephews' elementary school textbook and they have changed a lot. The articles are not so political. They write about nature and about going somewhere and having good feelings about these places. I think this is better for a young kid to develop.

A College Degree

To receive a college education was my dream - all the time. In 1993, I was thinking about going to college, but, I was thinking about going to Beida. At that time I had an elementary and middle school classmate from Jiangxi who was studying at Beida. He was the second student from my province to be accepted to Beida. He was accepted in 1991 in the Biology department. I told him I was interested in going to the school. The adult program only offered three majors: business, English and politics. I was interested in English. The quality of the training class would be, the English quality, would be better. Then I was not interested in their business training. I am not interested in politics so I was interested in going to Beida for the English.

I was saving my money all the time. At that time it wasn't too expensive at Beida. Then when I was thinking to go, my mother died in 1994. So I suddenly go. I was in a very bad mood. I couldn't understand why the situation was like this. I also knew about Harmony College at that time. I had seen an advertisement. My former classmate went there to have a look, but they didn't advise me to go at that time. He went to the College when it was in Chaoyang. He told me that there wasn't a very good situation there. He met a man who was swaying a lot, and seemed drunk, a Chinese man. He said that it didn't seem like a real college at that time. So I was thinking about going to Beida, but then everything changed. So I kept doing my job.

My company supported me a lot. Some guests in the hotel, some businessmen were interested in my going to their company. They offered me a good position in their company, but I was not interested in a job first. I was interested in education first. Then the salary was okay in my company and they treated me well. But I think if I wanted to self-educate while in a stable situation and with a well-known job, it would save my time. In the hotel, I was familiar with everything and could do the job and go back home to study. It would save my time. I didn't have to think too much about the job.

Then in 1996 I took the TOEFL. I was thinking about going to America. I was also not satisfied with that kind of degree. You see in China if you want to receive a real degree and not just a training certificate, it is quite difficult. Even in Beida or something they offer a different sort of degree. I was not satisfied with that kind of degree. So I thought to go to America, but money was a problem. I told my brothers I needed money and I also invested money in the stock market. Then it was a good situation, maybe I was lucky because I earned money on the market. Shenzhen had the first stock market in China; it had just been started for three years at that time. It was very prosperous and then fell out. I went to Beijing to take the TOEFL and took two weeks leave from my company to take the test. My score was not really high, it was only 593 and the writing part was only a 4. I was not very well prepared for that examination. First there wasn't a good living condition. I was living in the Beida dormitory in the room of a colleague of my former classmate. I took the exam in August. The lady supervising the building was helpful because she allowed me to stay so that I could take the exam. Definitely I wouldn't pay a hotel bill to take an examination, not for two weeks. Then I was just living in the room.

After the examination I began contacting universities in America. I was very interested in going to America. You see my former classmate received a full scholarship from Rutgers in New Jersey, so maybe we could support each other. He was my only friend from before. After the examination I was quite sure my score was high enough to enable me to apply to a university course, so I wrote letters to America. I went to the American consulate in Guangzhou; they have a library that offered college entrance materials. I wrote to many American universities. After the TOEFL result came out I had the centre send my score to the University of Louisiana and also the university in Mississippi. I was accepted at both. These were the only two universities I had applied to because I had to pay an admission charge of $20 and $30 dollars. I received the acceptance letter in 1997 and in April started to apply for a visa. My citizenship is in Guangdong Province so I didn't have any trouble getting a Chinese passport - that was straightforward because my attitude was very obvious, I had an acceptance letter, and my company recommended me. Then my visa application was rejected three times in 1997, and I realized it was useless to continue trying. The officer advised me not to try again.

Harmony College

I decided to enter Harmony College in May 1998. At the beginning I felt very motivated. I was trying to not say much to my classmates because I didn't feel very open with them. I was quiet during my first semester. Now I feel I can speak very directly with my classmates. I think the organization of the classes was good. I liked the assignments very much. I hadn't had this kind of experience before. From my experience in high school, we didn't have assignments, just homework exercises. In the first class when you were teaching us, I thought the teaching style was fascinating. And I was very impressed by Mr. Spear. I always called him Mr. Spear. He gave me the impression that he really cared about the class and the students. I won't say anymore because maybe it wouldn't be polite. My strongest feeling is that the teachers in BIMC are not as responsible as those teachers I had in high school. It is just a feeling. The lecturers would come to the class late. You see I had Tony Howard and he was quite disappointing. He really didn't prepare class before he came. Sometimes he would take the wrong book and teach from that without realizing it was the wrong book. In class we wouldn't talk about the content of the class but about other things. Maybe he thought it was relevant, but the textbook was very useful.

Group Work

I didn't enjoy group work at the College, but I really think it is important for me. Sometimes it is quite interesting. From your project in the first semester, I had group work experience. I had Sheila and Lynn and who else…and then you see, some of them don't care about the education. But me I am paying my own tuition and I really care about it all the time. And then it was group work, so if other group members do not participate and do not care, for example, if you said let's meet in the library and you went to the library, you would discover you were the only one there. Then you waited ten minutes but nobody showed up, you felt very upset and uncomfortable, but you still had to finish the project. I would try to calm myself down and try not to be angry and try to talk with them to finish the project. Group work is good for me because I learned how to deal with the situations; like when others didn't agree with my idea, or when you as a group member had to write the whole project and do everything yourself— you overcome the unfairness that it was group work but the others didn't pay attention. Also now, I understand myself better. That is the most important thing. I found that sometimes I was quite selfish and I would feel it was very unfair if I did the whole job. And sometimes I would find myself very bossy.

The Future

First, I want to finish my school and after that I want to work for a company for some years, at least three or four years. And then if I have the chance and meet a really good person, I will get married. Marriage is important to me. I see my future in China. I think in my opinion there are a lot of opportunities in China for business development, even for entrepreneurs. I believe I have this kind of sense of discovery. I see this kind of business opportunity, for example once I had this idea of opening a shoe repair shop. It was an investment of $200,000. It had a big machine imported from Japan and there was a shop. Then the shoes prepared were very expensive in Shenzhen, sometimes 40 yuan for one pair. And the business was really good. Even now, that business is really doing well.

The Environment in China and Women in Business

I think that in China for me, I think it is good. I think that if you are a businessman, China is a really good place. The problem is whether you can see the opportunity or not, and overcome the problems and have a good attitude, and not think that you will make a lot of money all at once, and don't think you can cheat and then leave. I think this kind of attitude is not good.

I think it should be an advantage to be a woman in business in China today - because men will pay more attention to me from my experience. And you are respected if you can deal with the situation - if you have a good attitude about doing work together and not other feelings. The most important thing is for a woman, she should make that kind of feeling, a very obscure feeling, how to say? Don't be open all the time to the man, but make them feel that you have something very interesting to hide from them. That is the most important thing. Don't smoke and be open and wear very colourful clothes, just keep yourself to yourself and they will discover that maybe you are more interesting. Sometimes when I, when some people invited me to dinner, I would not drink even though I can drink, but I was not lying because at that time I could not drink. You always have to pay attention to the situation.

Glossary

We have used the pinyin system for translating the Mandarin into English. The government of the People's Republic of China accepts this system in its own use but does keep some historically accepted spellings such as Peking for Beijing and Canton for Guangzhou. This glossary gives you some translations of terms from Mandarin, and some names of places, people and terms important in the Chinese context.

Anhui	=	east central province of China
'banjuren'	=	classroom teacher responsible for a group of students
Beida	=	short form of Beijing University
Chaoyang	=	a district in Beijing
Chengdu	=	city in Sichuan Province
'chongyang meiwai'	=	worship and have blind faith in things foreign
'chuzhong'	=	junior middle school (3 years)
Cultural Revolution	=	a time of political upheaval from 1966 to 1976 that radically changed the substance of education in China (also known as The Great Proletariet Cultural Revolution)
Deng Xiaoping	=	political leader who brought in the reforms in 1977; he died in 1997
Dongcheng	=	a district in Beijing
Four Modernizations	=	Deng Xiaoping's reform agenda for the army, science and technology, the economy, and agriculture
'gaizao'	=	a political campaign
Gang of Four	=	four leaders of China, including Mao Zedong's wife, who had most power during the Cultural Revolution
'gaokao fenshu'	=	university acceptance rate for a senior middle school
'gaoyi, gaoer, gaosan'	=	1st year, 2nd year, 3rd year of senior middle school
'gaozhong'	=	senior middle school (3 years)
Gongchangdang	=	the Communist party (mainland China)
Great Leap Forward	=	a national campaign between 1957-59 meant to push China ahead economically
Guangdong	=	southern province of China, near Hong Kong
Guangzhou	=	Canton, city in Guangdong Province
'guanxi'	=	relationships, networking
Guomindang	=	the KMT party (Taiwan)

Haidian	=	a district of Beijing
Harbin	=	city in Heilongjiang Province
Hebei	=	northern province of China, surrounding Beijing
Heilongjiang	=	northeastern province of China
Hohhot	=	city in Inner Mongolia
Hu Yaobang	=	political leader whose death in 1989 sparked the student protests
Hubei	=	east central province of China
'hukou'	=	official residency
'hutong'	=	narrow lane, alley
Inner Mongolia	=	north central protectorate of China
Jiang Jieshi	=	otherwise known as Chiang Kaishek, leader of the KMT party and later Taiwan
Jiang Zimin	=	present leader of China
Jiangsu	=	east central province of China
Jiangxi	=	east southern province of China
joint-venture	=	an economic partnership between foreign and Chinese companies instituted in the 1980's
June 4th	=	unofficial term referring to the 4 June 1989 government crackdown of student protestors in Tian'anmen Square
'laojia'	=	ancestral home
'laoshi'	=	teacher, often used as a title
Li Peng	=	present leader of China
'like'	=	science class, a subject differentiation in the second and third year of senior secondary schooling
Liulichang	=	tourist shopping area in Beijing
Mao Zedong	=	leader of the Communist Party and the People's Republic of China from 1949-1976
'maodun'	=	conflict - from a story of a soldier trying to sell his "best shield" and "best sword"
'minban'	=	privately-funded schools that have always formed the mainstay of rural education in China
Open Door policy	=	post-1978 process of opening China to the outside world for trade and exchange
Qinghua University	=	a leading university of China located in Beijing, well-known for its excellence in the practical sciences
Republican era	=	the period when the Guomingdang (KMT) controlled China from 1910 to 1945 (civil war = 1945-1949)
'sanhao xuesheng'	=	three-goods student: good study, good health, good character
Shandong	=	east central province of China
'shaomu'	=	sweep the grave, show respect for one's ancestors
Shenyang	=	city in Liaoning, a province in northeastern China
Shenzhen	=	a special economic zone near Hong Kong
Shijiazhuang	=	city in Hebei Province
'shuyuan'	=	academies for cramming for the examinations
Sichuan	=	west central province of China
Suzhou	=	city in Jiangsu Province

Tai'ping Rebellion	=	an uprising against the Manchu emperor lasting from 1850 to 1864
Tian'anmen	=	central square of Beijing
'tongxue'	=	classmate
treaty ports	=	port cities opened to foreign trade through treaties agreed between the Chinese emperor and different foreign powers after various military encounters
'tuanshibei'	=	meeting member, similar to a parliamentary member
'wenke'	=	humanities class, a subject differentiation in the second and third years of senior secondary schooling
Wuhan	=	city in Hubei Province
'wushu'	=	a martial art
Wuxi	=	city in Jiangsu Province
Xian	=	north central province of China
Xicheng	=	a district of Beijing
Xinjiang	=	far western province of China
Yinchuan	=	city in Ningxia, a western province of China
'yuan'	=	unit of currency of China
Yuyanxueyuan	=	Foreign Language Institute in Beijing
'zhongdian zhongxue'	=	key senior middle school
Zhongguancun	=	electronics area in northwest Beijing
'zhongzhuan'	=	technical senior middle school
Zhou Enlai	=	early leader of the Communist Party and Foreign Minister for the PRC from 1949-1976
Zhu De	=	leader of the Communist Party and head of the PRC's army from 1949-1976
'zifei'	=	self-pay tuition

Bibliography

Acker, A. (1991), 'Distribution of Educational Resources in China: a study of senior secondary schools in Haidian District, Beijing', University of Cornell (MA thesis), Ithaca, New York.

Ackers, J. (1996), 'Evaluating UK Courses: the perspective of the overseas student', in McNamara, David and Harris, Robert, *Overseas Students in Higher Education: issues in teaching and learning*, Routledge, London, pp. 187-200.

Agar, David (1990), 'Non-traditional Students: perceptions of problems which influence academic success' in *Higher Education*, vol.19, Kluwer Academic Publishers, The Netherlands.

Allinson, R. E. (1989), 'An overview of the Chinese mind', in Allinson. R. E (ed), *Understanding the Chinese Mind: the philosophical roots*, Oxford University Press, Oxford, pp. 1-25.

Altbach, Philip. G. (1996), *Comparative Higher Education: knowledge, the university and development*, Comparative Education Research Centre, University of Hong Kong, Hong Kong.

Alvesson, M. and Deetz, S. (1996), 'Critical Theory and Postmodernism Approaches to Organizational Studies' in Clegg, S. Hardy, C. and Nord, W. (eds), *Handbook of Organisation Studies*, Sage, London.

Arnowitz, S. and De Fazio, W. (1997), 'The new knowledge work', in Halsey, A.H., Lauder, H., Brown, P. and Wells. A. (eds) *Education: culture, economy and society*, Oxford University Press, Oxford.

Bai, L (2000), 'The metamorphosis of China's higher education in the 1990's in Keith Sullivan (ed), *Education and Change in the Pacific Rim*, Oxford University Press, Oxford, pp. 241-265.

Barendsen, Robert D. (1975), *The Educational Revolution in China*, Office of Education, U.S. Department of Health, Education and Welfare, U.S. Government Printing Office, Washington.

Barker, John (1996), 'The purpose of study, attitudes to study and staff-student relationships', in McNamara, David and Harris, Robert, *Overseas students in Higher education: issues in teaching and learning*, Routledge, London, pp. 109-123.

Beard, Ruth and Hartley, James (1984), *Teaching and learning in Higher Education*, Harper Education Series, Paul Chapman Publishing, London.

Bex, Tony and Watts, Richard J. (eds) (1999), *Standard English: the widening debate*, Routledge, London.

Biggs, John (1996), 'Western Misperceptions of the Confucian-heritage Learning Culture', Watkins and Biggs (eds) *The Chinese Learner: cultural, psychological and contextual influences*, CERC and ACER, Hong Kong/Australia.

Biggs, John and Watkins, David (1996), 'The Chinese Learner in Retrospect', Watkins and Biggs (eds) *The Chinese Learner: cultural, psychological and contextual influences*, CERC and ACER, Hong Kong/Australia, pp. 327-355.

Borgonjon, J. and Vanhonacker, W. R. (1994), 'Management Training and Education in the People's Republic of China', in *The International Journal of Human Resource Management*, vol. 5, no. 2.

Bray, Mark and Lee, W.O. (1997), 'Education and Political Transitions in Asia: diversity and commonality', Lee and Bray (eds) *Education and Political Transition: perspectives and dimensions in East Asia*, Comparative Education Research Centre, The University of Hong Kong, Hong Kong.

Britton, James (ed) (1984), *English Teaching: an International Exchange*, International Federation for the Teaching of English, Heinnemann.

Brock, A. (1997), 'China: opportunities in the education and training market - franchising and distance learning', British Council Report, British Council, Beijing.

Brown, P. and Lauder, H. (1997), 'Education, globalization and economic development', in Halsey, A. H., Lauder, H., Brown, P. and Wells, A. (eds) (1997) *Education: culture, economy and society*, Oxford University Press, Oxford.

Bruner. J. (1996), *The Culture of Education*, Harvard University Press, Cambridge, Massachusetts.

Burke, Crowley and Girvin (eds) (2000), *The Routledge Language and Cultural Theory Reader*, Routledge, London.

Chan, David and Drover, Glenn (1996), 'Teaching and learning for overseas students: the Hong Kong connection', in McNamara, David and Harris, Robert (eds), *Overseas students in Higher education: issues in teaching and learning*, Routledge, London, pp. 47-61.

Chan, David and Mok Ka-ho (2001), 'Educational Reforms and Coping Strategies under the Tidal Wave of Marketisation: a comparative study of Hong Kong and the mainland', *Comparative Education*, vol. 37, no. 1, pp. 21-41.

Chan, Luke M.W. (1996), 'Management Education in the People's Republic of China', in Brown, David H. and Porter, Robin (eds) *Management Issues in China: domestic enterprises*, Routledge, London/New York.

Chan, W. K. K. (1998), 'Tradition and Change in the Chinese Business Enterprise: the family firm past and present', *Chinese Studies in History*, vol. 31, no. 3-4, M.E. Sharpe, New York, pp. 127-144.

Chan, Y.M. (2000), 'Self Esteem: a cross-cultural comparison of British-Chinese, White British and Hong Kong Chinese children', *Educational Psychology*, vol. 20, no. 1, pp. 59-74.

Chen Jingpan (1994), *Confucius as a teacher: philosophy of Confucius with special reference to its Educational implications*, Foreign Languages Press, Beijing.

Chen Min (1995), *Asian Management Systems: Chinese, Japanese and Korean styles of business*, International Thomson Business Press.

Chen, T.H. (1974), *The Maoist Educational Revolution*, Praeger, New York/London.

Chen Xianda (1999), 'The Modern Value of Traditional Chinese Culture', *Social Sciences in China*, Spring.

Chen, Y. (1999), 'Tradition and Innovation in the Chinese School Curriculum', *Research in Education*, no. 61, pp. 16-28.

Cheng Kai-Ming (1994), 'Young Adults in a Changing Socialist Society: post-compulsory education in China', *Comparative Education*, vol. 30, no. 1.

Cheng Kai-ming, Jin Xinhuo and Gu Xiaobo (1999), 'From Training to Education, Lifelong Learning in China', *Comparative Education*, vol. 35, no. 1, pp. 119-129.

Cheshire, Jenny (ed) (1991), *English Around the World: sociolinguistic perspectives*, Cambridge University Press, Cambridge/London/New York.

Cheung Kwok Wah (1997), 'The Regulation of Pedagogic Discourse: relationships between the state and intellectuals after the Cultural Revolution in China', Lee and Bray (eds) *Education and Political Transition: perspectives and dimensions in East Asia*, Comparative Education Research Centre, University of Hong Kong, Hong Kong.

China Daily (1998), '21st Century Entrance Exams to be Reformed', vol. 5, no. 262, July 8, Beijing.

Claxton, G. (1996), 'Implicit Theories of Learning', in Claxton, G. and Atkinson, T. et al (eds), *Liberating the Learner: lessons for professional development in education*, Routledge, London, pp. 45-56.

Claxton, G. (1996), 'Integrated Learning Theory and the Learning Teacher', in Claxton, G. and Atkinson, T. et al (eds), *Liberating the Learner: lessons for professional development in education*, Routledge, London, pp. 3-15.

Claxton, G., Atkinson, T. et al (eds) (1996), *Liberating the learner: lessons for professional development in education*, Routledge, London.

Cleverly, John (1994), *'On the evidence before me...* Putting the Case for Educational Reform in China', *Comparative Education*, vol. 27, no. 1, pp. 53-59.

Connell, W., Christie, F., Jones, P., Lawson, R. (eds) (1973), *China at School*, Ian Novak Publishing Co., Sydney.

Cortazzi, Martin and Lixian Jin (1996), 'Communication for Learning across Cultures', in McNamara, David and Harris, Robert (eds) *Overseas Students in Higher Education: issues in teaching and learning*, Routledge, London, pp. 77-90.

Cua, A. S (1989), 'The Concept of *Li* in Confucian Moral Theory', in Allinson, R.E. (ed), *Understanding the Chinese Mind: the philosophical roots*, Oxford University Press, Oxford, pp. 209-235.

Davies, Alan (1999), 'Standard English: discordant voices', *World Englishes*, vol. 18, no. 2.

Davies, H. (1995), *Chinese Business: contexts and issues*, Longman, Hong Kong.

Davis, A.L. (ed.) (1969), *Culture, Class, and Language Variety*, National Council of Teachers of English, Illinois.

De Court, Erik (1996), 'New Perspectives on Learning and Teaching in Higher Education', in Burgen, A. (ed), *Goals and Purposes of Higher Education in the 21st Century*, Jessica Kingsley Publishers, London.

Deem, Rosemary (2001), 'Globalisation, New Managerialism, Academic Capitalism and Entrepreneurialism in Universities: is the local dimension still important?', *Comparative Education*, vol. 37, no. 1, pp. 7-20.

Dunnett, S., Dubin, F. and Lezberg, A. (1986), 'English Language Teaching from an Intercultural Perspective', in Valdes (ed) *Culture Bound: bridging the cultural gap in language teaching*, Cambridge University Press, Cambridge.

Elliott, Geoffrey (1997), 'Learning and Teaching in Post-Compulsory Education: a lifelong perspective', *Research in Post-compulsory Education*, vol. 2, no. 3.

Elsey, Barry (1990), 'Teaching and Learning', in Kinnell, M. (ed*)*, *The Learning Experiences of Overseas Students*, Society for Research into Higher Education and Open University Press, Oxford.

Entwistle, Noel and Tait, Hilary (1990), 'Approaches to Learning, Evaluations of Teaching, and Preferences for Contrasting Academic Environments', *Higher Education*, vol. 19.

Epstein, Irving (1988), 'Special Educational Provision in the People's Republic of China', *Comparative Education*, vol. 24, no. 3, pp. 365-375.

Evans, Linda and Abbott, Ian (1998), *Teaching and Learning in Higher Education*, Cassell Education, London.

Fagerlind, Ingemar and Saba, Lawrence J. (1983), *Education and National Development: a comparative perspective*, Pergamon, Oxford.

Flowerdew, Miller and Li (2000), 'Chinese Lecturers' Perceptions, Problems and Strategies in Lecturing in English to Chinese-Speaking Students', *RELC*, Singapore, vol. 31, no.1, pp. 116-137.

Fu, W. (1996), *Cultural Flow between China and the Outside World throughout History*, Foreign Languages Press, Beijing.

Fuerwerker, A. (1998), 'Doing Business in China over Three Centuries', *Chinese Studies in History*, vol. 31, no. 3-4, M.E. Sharpe, New York, pp. 16-34.

Gallagher, Tony (1998), *In Their Own Words: profiles of today's Chinese students*, China Books and Periodicals.

Glaser, R (1998), 'Education for All: access to learning and achieving usable knowledge', *Prospects*, vol. 28, no. 1.

Goldman, Merle (1981), *China's Intellectuals: advise and dissent*, Harvard University Press, Cambridge.

Goodman, David (1996), 'The People's Republic of China: the party-state, capitalist revolution and new entrepreneurs', in Robison, R. and Goodman, D. (eds) *The New rich in Asia: mobile phones, McDonald's and middle-class revolution*, Routledge, London/New York, pp. 225-243.

Gough, Leo (1998), *Asia Meltdown: the end of the miracle?*, Capstone, Oxford.

Gow, Lyn and Kember, David (1990), 'Does Higher Education Promote Independent Learning?', *Higher Education*, vol. 19, pp. 307-322.

Gow, Lyn, Kember, David and McKay, Jan (1996), 'Improving Student Learning through Action Research into Teaching', Watkins and Biggs (eds) *The Chinese Learner: cultural, psychological and contextual influences*, CERC and ACER, Hong Kong/Australia.

Green, A. (1997), *Education, Globalization and the Nation State*, Macmillan Press, London/Basingstoke.

Hannum, E. (1999), 'Poverty and Basic-level Schooling in China: equity issues in the 1990's', *Prospects*, vol. 29, no. 4.

Hawkins, John N. (1974), *Mao-Tse Tung and Education: his thoughts and teachings*, Linnet Books, Connecticut.

Hawkins, J. (1983), 'The People's Republic of China (mainland China)', in Thomas, R.M. and Postlethwaite, T.N. (eds), *Schooling in East Asia*, Pergamon Press, pp. 136-187.

Hayer, J. (1996), 'Overseas Scholarships: culture shock or learning opportunity?', Claxton, G., Atkinson, T. et al (eds), *Liberating the Learner: lessons for professional development in education*, Routledge, London, pp. 144-157.

Hayhoe, Ruth (1984), 'The Evolution of Modern Chinese Education Institutions', in Hayhoe, Ruth (ed), *Contemporary Chinese Education*, Croon Helm, London.

Hayhoe, Ruth (1984), 'Chinese-Western Scholarly Exchange: implications for the future of Chinese education', in Hayhoe, Ruth, (ed) *Contemporary Chinese Education*, Croon Helm, London.

Hayhoe, Ruth (1989), *China's Universities and the Open Door*, Sharpe Armonk, New York.

Hayhoe, Ruth (1996), *China's Universities 1895-1995: a century of conflict*, Garland Publishing, Connecticut.

He Zhaowu et al (1998), *An Intellectual History of China*, Foreign Languages Press, Beijing.

Henze, J. (1984), 'Higher Education: the tension between quality and equality', in Hayhoe, Ruth (ed), *Contemporary Chinese Education*, Croon Helm, London, pp. 93-153.

Ho, David, Y.F. (1986), 'Chinese Patterns of Socialization: a critical review', in Bond, M. (ed), *The Psychology of the Chinese People*, Oxford University Press, Oxford, pp. 1-37.

Hodge, Robert and Kress, Gunther (1993), *Language as Ideology, 2nd edition*, Routledge, London/New York.

Hollinger, R. (1994), *Postmodernism and the Social Sciences*, Sage, Thousand Oaks/London/New Delhi.

Holmes, B. (1984), 'A Comparativist's View of Chinese Education', in Hayhoe, Ruth, *Contemporary Chinese Education*, Croon Helm, London, pp.7-25.

Hong, E. and Leung, K.H. (2000), 'Preferred Homework Style and Homework Environment in High- versus Low-Achieving Chinese Students', *Educational Psychology*, vol. 20, no. 2, pp. 125-137.

Hu Chang-tu (1962), *Chinese Education under Communism*, Bureau of Publications, Teachers College, Columbia University, New York.

Hu Shiming and Seifman, Eli (1976), *Toward a New World Outlook: a documentary history of education in the People's Republic of China, 1949-1976*, AMS Press Inc., New York.

Jiang Wenying (2000), 'The Relationship between Culture and Language', *ELT Journal*, vol. 54, no. 4, Oxford University Press, Oxford, pp. 328-334.

Johnson, Robert Keith (1997), 'Political Transitions and the Internationalisation of English: implications for language planning, policy-making and pedagogy', Lee and Bray (eds) *Education and Political Transition: perspectives and dimensions in East Asia*, comparative Education Research Centre, University of Hong Kong, Hong Kong.

Jones, Alison (1999), 'The Limits of Cross-Cultural Dialogue: pedagogy, desire and absolution in the classroom', *Educational Theory*, Summer.

Jones, Phillip W. (1998), 'Globalisation and Internationalism: democratic prospects for world education', *Comparative Education*, vol. 34, no. 2, pp. 143-157.

Kachru, Braj B. (ed.) (1992), *The Other Tongue: English across Cultures, 2nd edition*, University of Illinois Press, Urbana/Chicago.

Kachru, Braj B. (2000), 'The Alchemy of English (1986)' in *The Routledge Language and Cultural Theory Reader*, Routledge, London, pp. 317-329.

Kempner, Ken and Misao Makino (1993), 'Cultural Influences on the Construction of Knowledge in Japanese Higher Education', in *Comparative Education*, vol. 29, no. 2, pp. 185-199.

Kinnell, Margaret (1990), 'The Marketing and Management of Courses', in Kinnell, M. (ed), *The Learning Experiences of Overseas Students*, Society for Research into Higher Education and Open University Press, Milton Keynes.

Kipnis, A. (1997), *Producing Guanxi: sentiment, self, and subculture in a north China village*, Duke University Press, Durham.

Kirby, John R., Woodhouse, Rosamund and Ma Yamin (1996), 'Studying in a Second Language: the experiences of Chinese students in Canada', Watkins and Biggs (eds) *The Chinese Learner: cultural, psychological and contextual influences*, CERC and ACER, Hong Kong/Australia.

Klein, N. (2000), *No Logo*, Flamingo, London.

Kobayashi, F. (1976), *Education in Building Chinese Socialism*, Institute of Developing Economies, Tokyo.

Kuhn, Anthony (2000), 'Chinese Re-examining Schools', *The Post and Courier*, January 20.

Larsson, Y. and Booth, M. (1998), 'Attitudes to the Teaching of History and Use of Creative Skills in Japan and England: a comparative study', *Compare*, vol. 28, no. 3.

Lee, W.O. (1996), 'The Cultural Context for Chinese Learners: conceptions of learning in the Confucian tradition', Watkins and Biggs (eds) *The Chinese Learner: cultural, psychological and contextual influences*, CERC and ACER, Hong Kong/Australia.

Lee, W.O. (1997), 'Changing Ideopolitical Emphases in Moral Education in China: an analysis of the CCP Central Committee documents', Lee and Bray (eds) *Education and*

Political Transition: perspectives and dimensions in East Asia, Comparative Education Research Centre, University of Hong Kong, Hong Kong.

Leung, Y.M. (1991), 'Curriculum Development in the People's Republic of China', in Marsh, C. and Morris, P. (eds), *Curriculum Development in East Asia*, Falmer Press, London, pp. 61-87.

Leung, Y.M. (1995), 'The People's Republic of China', in Morris, P. and Sweeting, A. (eds), *Education and Development in East Asia*, Garland Publishing, Connecticut, pp. 203-263.

Lewin, K. (1995), 'Basic Education amongst National Minorities: the case of the Yi in Sichuan Province, China', *Prospects*, vol. 25, no. 4.

Lewin, K., Xu Hui, Little, A. and Zheng Jiwei (1994), *Educational Innovation in China: tracing the impact of the 1985 reforms*, Longman Group, Harlow.

Li Peng (1994), *Report at the National Conference on Education*, Department of Foreign Affairs, State Education Commission, People's Republic of China, Beijing.

Lin, Jing (1993), *Education in post-Mao China*, Praeger, Westport, Connecticut.

Little, Angela (1992), 'Assessment and Selection in Education in China', Institute of Education working paper.

Liu, Ben (1998), 'Communication and Culture', *Social Sciences in China*, Winter.

Liu, Sandra and Williams, Gareth (1995), 'The Contemporary Trend of Marketing Chinese Universities in Hong Kong: an incoming rival to British counterparts', *Higher Education Quarterly*, vol. 49, no. 1, pp. 4-15.

Maley, Alan (1986), "Xanadu - A miracle of Rare Device: the teaching of English in China", Valdes (ed) *Culture Bound: bridging the cultural gap in language teaching*, Cambridge University Press, Cambridge, pp. 102-111.

Martin, Elaine (1999), *Changing Academic Work: developing the learning university*, Society for Research into Higher Education and Open University Press, Milton Keynes.

Matsul, M., Ma, Y. and Cornbleth, C. (1988), 'Making Women Visible in the Curriculum', in Willson, Grossman and Kennedy (eds.), *Asia and the Pacific: issues of education policy, curriculum and practice*, pp. 99-108.

Mauger, P., Mauger, S., Edmonds, W., Berger, R., Daly, P., and Marett, V. (1974), *Education in China: Modern China Series No. 5*, Anglo-Chinese Educational Institute.

McGinn, N.F. (1997), 'The Effect of Globalization on National Education Systems', *Propsects*, vol. 27, no. 1.

McGreal, I.P. (1995), *Great Thinkers of the Eastern World*, Harper Collins, New York.

McNamara, David and Harris, Robert (1996), *Overseas Students in Higher Education: issues in teaching and learning*, Routledge, London.

Meissner, Werner (1999), 'New Intellectual Currents in the People's Republic of China', in Teather, D. and Yee, H., *China in Transition: issues and policies*, Macmillan, Basingstoke, pp. 3-24.

Montaperto, R. and Henderson, J. (eds) (1979) *China's Schools in Flux*, M.E. Sharpe Inc., New York.

Mortimer, Kathleen (1997), 'Recruiting Overseas Undergraduate Students: are their information requirements being satisfied?', *Higher Education Quarterly*, vol. 51, no. 3, pp. 225-238.

New Star publishers (1996), *Development and Reform of China's Educational System in the 1990's*, Beijing.

Partington, Geoffrey (1988), 'The Concept of Progress in Marxist Educational Theories', *Comparative Education*, vol. 24, no. 1, p. 75-89.

Pennycook, A. (1994), *The Cultural Politics of English as an International Language*, Longman, London/New York.

Pepper, Suzanne (1991), 'Post-Mao Reforms in Chinese Education: can the ghosts of the past be laid to rest?', in Epstein, I. (ed), *Chinese Education: problems, policies and prospects*, Garland Publishing, Connecticut.

Pepper, Suzanne (1996), *Radicalism and Education Reform in 20th-Century China: the search for an ideal development model*, Cambridge University Press, Cambridge.

Price, R.F. (1970), *Education in Modern China*, Routledge, London.

Priestley, K.E. (1961), *Education in China*, Dragonfly Books, Hong Kong.

Reich, R. (1997), 'Why the Rich are Getting Richer and the Poor, Poorer', in Halsey, A.H., Lauder, H., Brown, P. and Wells, A. (eds) (1997), *Education: culture, economy and society*, Oxford University Press, Oxford.

Reid, D.J. and Johnston, M. (1999), 'Improving Teaching in Higher Education: student and teacher perspectives', *Educational Studies*, vol. 25, no. 3, pp. 270-281.

Robison, R. and Goodman, D. (eds) (1996), *The New rich in Asia: mobile phones, McDonald's and middle-class revolution*, Routledge, London/New York.

Ronowicz and Yallop (eds) (1999), *English: One Langauage, Different Cultures*, Cassell, London/New York.

Rosen, S. (1984), 'New Directions in Secondary Education', in Hayhoe, R. (ed), *Contemporary Chinese Education*, Croon Helm, London, pp. 65-92.

Rosen, S. (1991), 'Political Education and Student Response: some background factors behind the 1989 student demonstrations', in Epstein, I. (ed), *Chinese Education: problems, policies and prospects*, Garland Publishing, Connecticut.

Ross, H. (1991), 'The "Crisis" in Chinese Secondary Schooling', in Epstein, I. (ed), *Chinese Education: problems, policies and prospects*, Garland Publishing, Connecticut.

Sang Bing (1998), 'The Study of Traditional Chinese Learning and Western Learning in the Later Qing and Republic of China Period', *Social Sciences in China*, Winter, pp. 86-97.

Scott, Peter (1995), *The Meanings of Mass Higher Education*, Society for Research into Higher Education, Milton Keynes.

Seybolt, P.J. (1973), *Revolutionary Education in China: documents and commentary*, International Arts and Sciences Press, New York.

Sharpe, K. and Qiuhong Ning (1998), 'The Training of Secondary Modern Languages Teachers in England and China: a comparative analysis', *Compare*, vol. 28, no. 1, pp. 58-73.

Shen Fuwei (1996), *Cultural Flow between China and Outside World throughout History*, Foreign Languages Press, Beijing.

Shotnes, Stephen (1987), *Overseas students - destination UK?*, UK Council for Overseas Student Affairs.

Smith, Larry E. (ed.) (1987), *Discourse Across Cultures: strategies in world Englishes*, Prentice Hall, New York/London.

Smith, Mark (1998), *Social Science in Question*, The Open University, Milton Keynes.

Spence, J. (1996), *God's Chinese Son*, Harper Collins.

State Education Commission of China (1992-1997), *Educational Statistics Yearbook of China*, SEC, Beijing.

State Education Commission of China (1994), *The Graduate Education in China*, Department of Foreign Affairs, SEC, Beijing.

State Education Commission of China (1995), *Education law of the People's Republic*, SEC, Beijing.

State Education Commission of China (1996), *Basic Education in China*, SEC, Beijing.

State Education Commission of China (1996), *5-year Plan for Education and Development towards Year 2010*, SEC, Beijing.

State Education Commission of China (1996), *Introduction to Education in China*, SEC, Beijing.

State Education Commission of China (1996), *Regular and Higher Education in China*, SEC, Beijing.

Su, Songxing (1995), 'Vocational and Technical Education: promoting change and influencing young people's ideas about employment in China', *Prospects*, vol. 25, no. 3.

Tang, Catherine (1996), 'Collaborative Learning: the latent dimension in Chinese students' learning', Watkins and Biggs (eds) *The Chinese Learner: cultural, psychological and contextual influences*, CERC and ACER, Hong Kong/Australia.

Tennant, Mark (1994), *Psychology and Adult Learning*, Routledge, London.

Thomas, R.M. (1983), 'The Two Chinas: a prologue', in Thomas, R.M. and Postlethwaite, T.N. (eds), *Schooling in East Asia: forces of change*, Pergamon Press, Oxford, pp. 87-103.

Thorens, J. P. (1998), 'Globalization, Academic Freedom and University Autonomy', *Prospects*, vol. 28, no. 3.

Triandis, Harry (1998), 'Collectivism vs. Individualism: a reconceptualisation of the basic concept in cross-cultural social psychology', in Verma, G. K. and Bagley, C. (eds), *Cross-cultural Studies of Personality, Attitudes and Cognition*, Macmillan Press, London/Basingstoke.

Tsui Kai-yuen (1998), 'Economic Reform and Attainment in Basic Education in China', *China Quarterly*, pp. 104-127.

Valdes, Joyce Merrill (ed.) (1986), *Culture Bound: bridging the cultural gap in language teaching*, Cambridge University Press, Cambridge.

Van der Molen, Henk, J. (1996), 'Creation, transfer and application of knowledge through the Higher education system', in *Goals and Purposes of Higher Education in the 21st Century*, Jessica Kingsley Publishers, London.

Volet, Simone and Renshaw, Peter (1996), 'Chinese Students at an Australian University: adaptability and continuity', Watkins and Biggs (eds) *The Chinese Learner: cultural, psychological and contextual influences*, CERC and ACER, Hong Kong/Australia.

Wang Chenzhi (2000), 'The Revival of Private Education in Reforming China', http://Irs.ed.uiuc.edu/students/cwang2/pepaper.html.

Weiner, R. et al (1997), *Living in China: a guide to teaching and studying in China including Taiwan and Hong Kong*, China Books and Periodicals, Beijing.

Winnie, Y.W. and Lai, A.Y. (1991), 'Curriculum Dissemination in the People's Republic of China', in Morris, P. and Sweeting, A. (eds), *Education and Development in East Asia*, Garland Publishing, Connecticut, pp. 82-105.

Winter, Sam (1996), 'Peer Tutoring and Learning Outcomes', Watkins and Biggs (eds) *The Chinese Learner: cultural, psychological and contextual influences*, CERC and ACER, Hong Kong/Australia.

Wong, Jan (1996), *Red China Blues*, Bantam, London.

Woo, Henry K.H. (1993), *The Making of a New Chinese Mind: intellectuality and the future of China*, China Foundation, Hong Kong, pp. 1-23.

World Bank (1997), *China 2020*, World Bank, Washington.

World Bank (1997), *China: Higher Education Reform*, World Bank, Washington.

Wu, D.Y.H. (1992), 'Early Childhood Education in China', in Feeney, S. (ed), *Early Childhood Education in Asia and the Pacific*, Garland Publishing, Connecticut.

Xu Guo-zhang (1987), "Code and Transmission in Cross-cultural Discourse: a study of some samples from Chinese and English", Smith (ed) *Discourse Across Cultures: strategies in world englishes*, Prentice Hall, New York/London, pp. 66-72.

Yan, Z. (1998), 'Brain Drain from Chinese Universities in the 1990's', *Journal of Contemporary China*, vol. 7, no. 17, pp. 103-123.

Yeung, A.S., Chui, H. and Lau, I. (1999), 'Hierarchical and Multidimensional Academic Self-Concept of Commercial Students', *Contemporary Educational Psychology*, vol. 24, pp. 376-389.

Zhang, Meisuo (2000), 'Cohesive Features in the Expository Writing of Undergraduates in Two Chinese Universities', *A Journal of Language Teaching and Research in Southeast Asia (RELC)*, Singapore, vol.31, no.1, pp. 61-95.

Zhao Yong and Campbell, Keith P. (1995), 'English in China', *World Englishes*, Blackwell Publishers, vol. 14, no. 3, pp. 377-390.

Zhaowu, H. (1998), *An Intellectual History of China*, Foreign Languages Press, Beijing.

Zhixin Su, Jilin Su et al (1994), 'Teaching and Learning Science in American and Chinese High Schools: a comparative study', *Comparative Education*, vol. 30, no. 3, pp. 258-262.

Zhou Yan (1998), 'Brain Drain from Chinese Universities in the 1990's', *Journal of Contemporary China*, vol. 7, no. 17, pp. 103-123.

Zhu, M. (1999), 'The Views and Involvement of Chinese Parents in Their Children's Education', *Prospects*, vol. 29, no. 2.

Zou Ji (1992), 'The Assignment of Jobs to College Graduates', in Timothy King and Zhang Jiping (eds), *Case Studies of Chinese Economic Reform*, Economic Development Institute of the World Bank, Washington.

Index